World
Super*bikes*
The first 15 years

Neil Hodgson leads the charge of the heavy brigade – Assen 2002.

World
*Super*bikes
The first 15 years

Text **Julian Ryder**
Photographs **Kel Edge**
Foreword **Paolo Flammini**

World Superbikes – The first ten years was published in November 1997
This new edition, with the subtitle *The first fifteen years,* was published in November 2002

British Library Cataloguing in Publication Data:
A catalogue record for this book is
available from the British Library

ISBN 1 85960 897 3

Library of Congress control no. 2002107504

Haynes North America, Inc.
861 Lawrence Drive, Newbury Park,
California 91320, USA

Published by Haynes Publishing, Sparkford,
Yeovil, Somerset, BA22 7JJ.

Tel: 01963 442030 Fax: 01963 440001
Int. tel: +44 1963 442030 Int. fax: +44 1963 440001
E-mail: sales@haynes-manuals.co.uk
Website: www.haynes.co.uk

Printed and bound in Great Britain by
J.H. Haynes & Co. Ltd., Sparkford

Contents

Foreword

by Paolo Flammini,
President, Superbike International

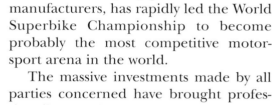

The World Superbike Championship is now 15 years old.

Speaking above all as a motorcycle racing fan rather than as an organiser, I feel absolutely certain that it is difficult to find a motorsport series that has provided us with more exciting races and passionate duels than the World Superbike Championship, right from its very first edition.

The human battle between so many riders of incredible courage and skill, and the technological confrontation

between the major Japanese and Italian manufacturers, has rapidly led the World Superbike Championship to become probably the most competitive motorsport arena in the world.

The massive investments made by all parties concerned have brought professionalism and performance excellence but, unlike in other sporting disciplines, they have not cancelled out its fundamental elements: love of the sport and the sense of friendship.

Seeing riders battling 'no holds barred' for the entire race and then congratulating each other on the podium sums up the real meaning of the sport and makes us all happy to be a part of this world. Just like the riders, the same can be said of their fans, who are ready to cheer on their rivals, should they so deserve it.

With so much material available and with the passion and competence of Kel Edge and Julian Ryder behind it (by the way, we miss Julian's TV commentary!), this book represents a full-scale immersion into the excitement that the World Superbike Championship has provided us with over the years and a fantastic opportunity to relive many of its greatest moments. I sincerely hope you enjoy reading it as much as I have, and as for us — well, we're preparing for the next 15 years!

See you on the track.

In the beginning...

A race track in California in the early 1970s. A young racer called Steve McLaughlin is wondering what to do. Like most of his contemporaries he races a Yamaha two-stroke, but as his father is a Honda and Ducati dealer his sponsorship has dried up. The Big Bore Production class, started by the AFM club to get away from the Yamaha-dominated pure-race-bike classes, is about to go out and McLaughlin notices that everyone in the pit lane has stopped to watch the Honda CB750s, Ducati V-twins and Guzzi Le Mans do battle with the Norton Gang on their hot Commandos. The seeds of a big idea are sown.

In a surprisingly short space of time Big Bore Production would grow into a worldwide racing class called Superbike. It would attract factory teams from all of

The first national-level Superbike race in the USA, Daytona 1976. Reg Pridmore leads eventual winner Steve McLaughlin. Both are on R90S BMWs.

Eddie Lawson poses with the road-going replica of his 1981 Kawasaki Superbike.

Japan's big four manufacturers, completely turn around the commercial fortunes of the ailing Ducati factory, make stars of its leading men, like the charismatic Californian Fred Merkel, and turn Carl Fogarty into not just Britain's best-known bike racer since Barry Sheene, but a genuine household name.

As with most things, what America does today the rest of the world does tomorrow. And so it was with Superbikes. The American tradition was to race bikes based on road-going (or 'production') machinery, even the American Motorcycle Association's Grand National Championship, the majority of which was raced on dirt ovals rather than tarmac. Harley-Davidson's and Indian's factory teams duelled through the 1920s and '30s in the top division, Class A, but gradually Class C for non-factory bikes (first introduced specifically for amateur riders in 1933) took over as the most popular formula.

This is why Indian built 50 special 648cc Scouts in 1948 just to stay competitive; they even won Daytona with one in 1954, a year after the factory had ceased production. This is why Harley-Davidson stayed a power in the land for so long with their antiquated side-valve motors. This is why Triumph won the Daytona 200 with a Tiger 100, why various homologation specials were built by Norton and Matchless to try and get their Manx and G50 racers into American competition, and why in the heyday of the British industry the Norton Commando was the privateer's weapon of choice. It was quite natural for American riders to race the new generation of bikes coming out of Europe and Japan in the late '60s and early '70s.

The word 'Superbike' had been coined to describe that quantum jump in road-going technology, the Honda CB750, when it was unveiled at the Tokyo Show of 1968. By the early '70s, that taste-free decade's tendency to stick the word 'super' on the front of everything had become a habit, and anyway it was better than Formula 750 or Formula 1. McLaughlin remembers that the first race he saw actually billed as a Superbike event was at Laguna Seca in 1973, promoted by Gavin Trippe and Bruce Cox, who would go on to invent and promote the Transatlantic Trophy. Many Australasian racers were visiting the States at this time and McLaughlin recalls spending a lot of time with Warren Willing, who told him about an Australian class called Superbike, full of Kawasaki 750s, that stopped in 1971. They talked a lot and gradually McLaughlin formed the basic outlines of the new class's regulations. As the rider's representative on the AMA (American Motorcyclist Association) for eight years, he was well placed to put his ideas into practice, and together with tuner Jerry Branch he drafted the first set of Superbike rules for the AMA.

The trouble was that the word 'Superbike' meant different things in different countries. In the USA the class started out as Production Superbike, becoming simply Superbike in 1976 when it became an American Championship class. The first AMA Championship Superbike race was run at Daytona as a support class to the main event. McLaughlin, already well on the way to earning his 'Motormouth' nickname, won the race on a BMW R90S in a photo-finish with his team-mate, expatriate Englishman Reg Pridmore, with American journalist Cook Neilson third on his legendary Ducati 750SS, the 'California Hot Rod'. Neilson won the race in 1977, but the Japanese bikes would soon take over.

Superbikes in the Transatlantic Trophy at a damp Donington Park: Paul Iddon's Suzuki GSX-R750 leads Dale Quarterly's Yamaha FZ750 and Ron Haslam's Honda VF750.

Steve McLaughlin (left) is reunited with his mechanic and his 1976 Daytona-winning Superbike at the 1996 meeting.

In the UK the Superbike label was attached to a championship that allowed the works two-stroke triples from Suzuki and Kawasaki to compete, but excluded the overbored 350cc TZ Yamahas that had a habit of winning everything they were allowed to enter – including the Daytona 200. Two nations divided by a common language.

British fans got their first look at real Superbikes in the Transatlantic Trophy events of the mid and late 1970s. A team of Americans would visit Britain for a series of six-match races on three different circuits over the Easter weekend and pull in enormous crowds. The top Grand Prix men – Barry Sheene, Kenny Roberts – would be at the front on GP two-strokes, but there in mid-field was the American

Wes Cooley on a big, high-barred Yoshimura Suzuki Superbike based on the road-going GS1000S. It wasn't competitive with the two-strokes, but it was faster than any production-based bike had a right to be, and it sure looked good. McLaughlin also won at Daytona on one of them.

It's important to realise that there had been other World Championship formulae loosely based around the idea of a big-bike class to run separately from the established Grands Prix. The first shot at this was Formula 750, which ran as a World Championship from 1977 to '79. Although intended as a series based on production machinery as proposed by the ACU (Auto Cycle Union, the governing body of the sport in the UK), which saw it as a way of getting the British Triumph/BSA triples into World Championship racing, it turned into a Yamaha TZ750 series when Yamaha made more than the required homologation limit of 200 bikes. Neither Suzuki nor Kawasaki contested the full series as factory teams – indeed, in the first year only two of the 47 points-scorers weren't on TZ750s! The series provided good racing, albeit in some strange places, but it never had the confidence of the public or of the sport's international governing body, the FIM. Strangely, it did do one thing that the non-GP series had always been intended to do: give privateers a chance. In two of its three years, the F750 title went to a privateer, not a factory Yamaha rider.

The second attempt was also inspired by Britain. As compensation for the Isle of Man TT losing its status as a Grand Prix, and therefore ceasing to be a World Championship event, three new races were run at the 1977 TT meeting with a World Championship on offer for the winner of each. The top class, Formula 1, went on to expand well beyond the parochial boundaries of Mona's Isle, while F2 and F3 faded quietly away – at least as World Championships. More properly known as TT Formula 1, the F1 regulations allowed four-strokes from 500 to 1,000cc and two-strokes up to 500cc. Bikes had to retain the main engine castings of the homologation street bike, but the choice of chassis, suspension and fuelling system, among other major considerations, was left to the constructor. F2 was for four-strokes of up to 600cc and two-strokes of up to 350cc; and F3 400 and 250cc respectively. You can detect here without too much trouble the origins of the Supersport classes.

Leaving aside the quaint idea that someone can call themselves a World Champion after just one race, TT F1 was a qualified success. The one-race championship didn't last long, but F1 did confine itself mainly to the closed-road circuits shunned by the Grand Prix establishment, or the less popular and less safe venues about which they were equally cool; places like the street circuit of Vila Real in Portugal and the round-the-industrial-estate track at Kouvala on Finland's border with Russia, as well as the traditional strongholds of the roads in Ireland and the Isle of Man, with only the occasional foray to venues like Speedweek at Assen, which also hosted the Dutch Grand Prix. The series was a home-from-home for British riders, notably the great Joey Dunlop, who won the title five times in a row from 1982 to '86.

TT F1 regulations spread, first to the Endurance World Championship, then on to national championships in most important racing centres including the USA and Japan. Because of the nature of the technical regulations, important championships were dominated by factory bikes. Honda's ultimate F1 bike, the RVF750, was a technical masterpiece; a four-stroke GP bike as far removed from the street bike on which it was allegedly based as a Formula 1 car is from a Touring Car. The Honda dominated the World Championship, but important and innovative bikes such as the Yamaha Genesis and the hub-centre-steered Elf were only able to race and be developed under the comparatively free F1 rules. But by then the Superbike writing was on the wall.

Steve McLaughlin had retired from racing in 1980 and left the bike scene completely for the TV industry in Los Angeles. But when Superbike became the class for the Daytona 200, track-owner Jim France got in touch. France is a key figure in the genesis of Superbike as well as being the man who invented Battle of the Twins and an ex-racer who used to compete under a pseudonym. France's problem was that half of his entry came from Europe – and Europe was blissfully ignorant of all things Superbike. Worse still, by tradition Daytona does not pay start money.

The solution, says McLaughlin, was to put him on a plane to Europe, where he organised a series of package deals that kept up the standard of entry for the Daytona 200 and introduced European racers to Superbikes. It wasn't an easy job and ironically McLaughlin got most help from Mike Trimby, General Secretary of IRTA (the International Racing Teams' Association) and no friend either of 'Motormouth' or Superbikes. It was an important step towards allaying Europe's traditionally patronising attitude towards racing based on production machinery; the Grand Prix classes were all for prototype machinery designed from first principles with the sole purpose of racing. Anything else was regarded as inferior – not real racing – but on the world stage, and certainly in terms of numbers of competitors, it was Grand Prix racing

It was a step towards allaying Europe's patronising attitude

that was in the minority. In 1960 the 500 GP championship was run over just six races, and all of them took place in Northern Europe apart from a race at Monza. As recently as 1980 there were just eight races, none of them outside Europe.

In 1985 McLaughlin based himself in Paris, linking up with an old friend, French journalist Philippe Debarle. They detected more than a little antipathy towards TT F1, which was seen in the wider world as something only of interest to the British, a contrivance to compensate them for the Isle of Man's loss of status. 'It became obvious,' says McLaughlin, 'that there should be a World Championship, or at least that people should think there would be a World Championship.' That way everyone would be working to the same set of rules, not inventing them as they went along to suit local conditions. There were plenty of people in the FIM's corridors of power who agreed, notably Luigi Brenni, the highly popular (at least with the riders) President of the Road Racing Commission, and men of influence on the Technical Commission like Mitsuo Itoh of Suzuki, with whom McLaughlin had raced, and Michihiko Aika of Honda. The American FIM representative, Ed Youngblood, worked long and hard on the idea of a Superbike World Championship, but crucial aid in getting the proposals through the labyrinthine committee politics of the FIM came from an unexpected quarter, the ACU. Its patrician President, Vernon Cooper, renegade Honda dealer and TT aficionado Bill Smith, and Donington Clerk of the Course Colin Armes, all helped to convince the Japanese, who strangely enough were worried about the TT's future viability – then took care of a lot of the detail work in the regs. None of

Honda jumped from VFR technology to the RC30 for the first World Superbike Championship.

Steve McLaughlin in typically flamboyant mood.

these men could by any stretch of the imagination be called natural allies of McLaughlin, yet they played an important part in getting Superbike off the launch pad.

In 1986 UK fans had seen triple American Superbike Champion Fred Merkel and a young Kevin Schwantz duel their way through the Transatlantic Trophy run for the first time under Superbike regs; the following year Schwantz again did battle with a Honda rider – this time Wayne Rainey. In 1987, after much political wrangling, Superbike finally deposed F1 as the blue riband of the American championships in readiness for the first Superbike World Championship the following year.

Ironically, the Formula 1 World Championship was just starting to gain credibility outside the closed-road ghettos. In '87 the tiny Italian Bimota factory took the title with their YB4EI; this was based on Yamaha's FZ motor but with their own chassis and fuel injection, and ridden by ex-500 Grand Prix star Virginio Ferrari, who would later go on to Superbike prominence as Ducati's team manager. F1 would continue as a World Championship for two more years and give the wider world advance notice of Carl Fogarty's talent, but from now on the four-stroke spotlight was firmly fixed on Superbike. At least non-Americans now knew what a Superbike was.

British fans had been amazed at how stock Merkel and Rainey's Hondas looked – at least until you got close to them. And that was just the idea. Superbike is a production-based silhouette class intended to enable the fan to relate the bikes on the track to the bikes in the showrooms. 'Race on Sunday, sell on Monday', as one Honda engineer put it, echoing sentiments first expressed in sportscar racing, Superbike's closest relative on four wheels. The fundamental differences between Superbike and F1 are that in

Superbike the racer has to keep the frame and fuel system of the road bike on which it is based. The silhouette of the road bike is also preserved by the regulations' insistence that the shape of the original fuel tank, seat and fairing be retained.

However, things are very different inside the motor, where the tuners are given free rein, and in the suspension department, where the original equipment, as well as the swinging arm, can be replaced provided it is of the same type as the original equipment (ie telescopic, leading-link, etc). Crucially, the motor can be overbored up to the class limit; in fact, the only thing about the motor's internals that can't be touched is the stroke. The requirements for retaining the standard carburettors are particularly rigorous: the size, type and number of detachable jets and manufacturer's part numbers have to be listed on the homologation documents along with dimensioned drawings of the inlet tracts. For the first season, the Japanese manufacturers homologated all their 600 and 750cc four-cylinder bikes plus Honda's unlikely Transalp and Africa Twin, Bimota their YB4 and Ducati their new 851 V-twin.

The idea of Superbike as affordable racing that wouldn't be dominated by the factories' teams was yet again outflanked by the Japanese factories, which did what Yamaha had done to F750 and manufactured their way around the regulations. Honda drew on their experiences with the RVF750 and built a barely disguised racer with lights on called the RC30. In the UK this retailed for an astonishing £8,499 on its launch in March 1988, and £1,000 more by October thanks to the strength of the yen; a Honda VFR750 would have cost you £4,249. Yamaha set a trend that would later be taken up by Kawasaki, by bringing out a homologation special model alongside the pure street-bike version of their 750. The big flat-slide carbs (as opposed to the emissions-legislation-orientated constant-velocity types on the mass-produced model), close-ratio gearboxes and single seats made the R-models – as in FZ750R as opposed to plain old FZ750 – highly unsuitable for street use, but a good starting point for a racer. The Japanese factories did, however, stay away from any direct works team involvement with the new championship, preferring to leave any commitments to local importers.

Ducati's 851 had seen the light of day for the first time at the Bol d'Or 24-hour race at the end of 1987, and was the first of a generation of liquid-cooled fuel-injected twins that would rebuild the factory's fortunes on and off the track over the following years.

Building completely new bikes may seem a rather extreme, not to say expensive, reaction to the regulations, but the class had a long and honourable history of bending the rules. Some ten years after the 'California Hot Rod', Cook Neilson related how he used to dream of getting the AMA Superbike teams round a table and in turn own up to one way in which they'd each deceived the scrutineers. He'd start off by admitting that he got the 'California Hot Rod' through the noise test by fitting a rev counter geared to read way above the speed at which the engine was turning. A caption in *Cycle* magazine read: 'Slow hand, quick needle'. With a four-cylinder motor, the best way to get under the noise limit was to close up the electrodes on one cylinder's spark plug; this shorted it out and prevented that cylinder from firing and therefore making any noise.

On the chassis front it was often difficult to equate the positioning of engine mounting lugs with those on the relevant street bike. An Antipodean, who'd better remain nameless, once remarked to the author how strange it was that you could get the cylinder head off a standard Kawasaki Z1000 with the motor in the frame, but you couldn't do the same with a certain Superbike racer – the implication being that the team had shortened the frame's down-tubes to raise the motor and increase the ground clearance.

By the start of the first World Superbike Championship that sort of crude cheating would have been impossible and unnecessary, simply because the technology of top-of-the-range street bikes had moved on so far that they had almost become racers themselves.

McLaughlin's regulations set an upper limit for four-cylinder motors of 750cc, and 1000cc for twin-cylinder bikes. The twins also got a lower minimum weight limit, 140kg as opposed to 165, a double whammy that would cause some controversy in years to come. However, the fact that the regulations remained unchanged for seven years shows just how well-thought-out they were. Of course no one thought that the small manufacturers of V-twin motorcycles, as opposed to the big four Japanese manufacturers of four-cylinder bikes, would be able to take advantage of these generous allowances; the idea was to compensate for the antiquated designs of the Ducati 900SS, BMW Boxer, Moto Guzzi Le Mans and any Harley-Davidson you care to mention. The small factories were also given a much lower production limit for homologation; Honda and the rest of the Japanese had to make 1,000 units to qualify for Superbike, Ducati and the rest of the minnows just 200 bikes.

But even Honda had their doubts about being able to sell 1,000 RC30s. Aika-san, who'd supported McLaughlin at the FIM and championed the Superbike cause within the company, announced with some trepidation that the order book would be opened. They received 5,000 orders on the first day. Production was hastily doubled, the first

It was so well planned, the rules were not changed for seven years

1,000 bikes being earmarked for Japan and other prospective purchasers going into a ballot. At least there was no doubt about Honda producing the required number of bikes for homologation. When it came to Ducati McLaughlin had his doubts and said so. Loudly.

Ducati's brilliant designer Massimo Bordi had produced a new fuel-injected four-valve-head motor for Ducati's new owners Cagiva. He got permission to build the 200 homologation machines, but with the warning that his job was on the line if they didn't sell. McLaughlin's view that Northern Italy – especially Bologna – was run by the communists was shaped by experiences in the family's Ducati dealership. 'Capitalist-running-dog Americans got engines that self-destructed the first time they were started,' he says, with only a trace of exaggeration, 'and then they took eight months to supply spares.' He announced that he and Debarle would be arriving one morning to inspect production of the new bike. An unplanned bout of partying at Virginio Ferrari's meant that they had to make a few excuses, and eventually turned up at 6.30pm to find the whole of the sales department formed up outside the factory. Bordi hadn't let them see the bike yet. With exquisite manners Bordi then proceeded to torture his visitors with an extended tour of the factory: he showed them crankcases, he showed them pistons, he showed them everything but what they had come to see. The fact that Debarle was in plaster and on crutches only added to the torture. Eventually the visitors – not the sales department – were ushered through a locked door and the sheets were theatrically removed from two bikes. There were the prototype Ducati 851s with white-painted frames and the word 'Superbike' on the fairing. Debarle broke into tears and there was much Latin arm-waving and hugging. The World Superbike Championship really was going to happen.

chapter one

1988
Out of
the blocks

It wasn't just a matter of getting the rules right. McLaughlin also had to get the practicalities sorted. His organisation had secured from the FIM the rights to run and promote the championship when he got a call from the New Zealand-based media conglomerate Global Sports & Promotions, part of the Madison Corporation; one of their directors was in

Fred Merkel and the Honda RC30, the combination that would dominate World Superbike for its first two years.

Los Angeles and would like to talk to him. They met, they talked, the Kiwi flew home. The next call said come to Auckland – 'the first of about 14 trips to Sheep City.'

The New Zealanders wanted the championship and bought a controlling share in McLaughlin's operation, which was transferred to a company set up for the purpose called Sports Marketing. It was this company that organised TV coverage for the nascent championship and came up with a travel fund for riders,

thanks in large part to the behind-the-scenes efforts of Keith Jones, MD of Sports Marketing and Global Sports & Promotions and the perfect detail-obsessed workaholic counterpart to McLaughlin's flair and enthusiasm. McLaughlin owned 35 per cent of Sports Marketing, but he no longer held the purse-strings. He was, however, the very public face of the new championship.

At one point McLaughlin had 19 circuits bidding to hold a round of the new championship, but that came down to nine for the start of the season. Some countries were much more difficult than others. Getting Hungary on board took a lot of work, as the sponsoring government department had lost a packet on a TT F1 race the year before. McLaughlin hung around for days in Budapest calling the ministry twice a day. Finally he got to meet the main man, who turned out to be a bit of a drinker. A bottle and a half of whisky later, McLaughlin was told that there were some Finnish (!) friends who might help out with some sponsorship.

Sure enough, McLaughlin later met up with two Finns in one of Hollywood's most expensive hotels. They were stereotypical hard-drinking, silent Finns, until McLaughlin told them that he could get them into the back lot of one of the big movie companies. Suddenly they were like kids in a sweet shop. The sponsorship duly arrived and the Hungarian race was in the calendar.

There were dates in Europe, Japan, Australia and New Zealand – and not a closed-road circuit among them. The only serious loss was Assen, which had been going to switch its Speedweek F1 race to Superbike, but, says McLaughlin, under the influence of his enemies switched back. This gave F1 enough dates to continue calling itself a World Championship, not that this was seen as a

To describe Fred as merely Californian is to be guilty of the wildest understatement.

The lettering on the back of Merkel's helmet says 'If you want blood you've got it'.

great problem for Superbike. Grands Prix, on the other hand, still had Gardner, Lawson, Rainey, Schwantz, Mamola and Sarron – a veritable battle of the titans – and that was just the 500s. In the 250s there was an epic struggle between Garriga and Pons, with support from Mang, Cadalora and a whole host of others, plus a brash new American kid called John Kocinski. Superbike would have a hard time taking spectators and sponsors away from that lot.

The main weapon in the sponsorship war is television, and Sports Marketing broke new ground in contracting a part of the giant CBS organisation to provide

coverage. Superbike would be shown at some odd times and on some minor stations, but it would be shown. This was before the satellite revolution in Europe and at a time when the Grands Prix got no regular coverage in important markets like the UK. Looking back, the original TV coverage seems flimsy, but at the time it was a major breakthrough for the sport of motorcycle racing. The travel fund of $25,000 per meeting attracted a classy hard core of riders who would contest the whole championship. Thus the product they were selling looked good, but despite all their efforts Sports Marketing did not secure the major sponsor that would defray their considerable expenditure and guarantee the future of the series.

For the promoters the challenge was to find that elusive backer, but on 3 April 1988 at the UK's Donington Park attention focused for the first time on the riders and the racing. Just before the first race, McLaughlin was called to the International Jury's room: 'That's it,' he thought, 'it ain't going to happen – something's gone horribly wrong.' Instead he found himself on the receiving end of a couple of generous speeches from people he wouldn't have thought of as his friends.

There were a couple of hiccups, though. First there was a skirmish on the grid when the Clerk of the Course would not let mechanics help riders push-start the bikes for the warm-up lap. Lucchinelli shrugged and leaned the Ducati – 'You need at least six Italians to start that thing' – against the pit wall. Other riders made more vociferous protests until McLaughlin negotiated a truce by pointing out to officials the cost of the TV cameras aimed at them. More significantly, the $100,000 guarantee that Sports Marketing was supposed to have

Davide Tardozzi and the factory Bimota – fast but fallible.

paid to the FIM before the first race had not arrived. It was, says McLaughlin, the first inkling he had that something was wrong.

But his efforts had brought together an interesting cast of characters and an intriguing mix of machinery. The Japanese factories stuck to their promise not to field works teams, and the smaller Italian manufacturers saw a chance to grab the limelight. Bimota didn't even consider defending their TT F1 title, sacked their rider Virginio Ferrari and sent out a two-man team of ex-GP crasher Stephane Mertens of Belgium and Italian Davide Tardozzi, whom many saw as the pre-season favourite. Bimota's YB4EI was within the letter, if not the spirit, of the technical laws; its beautifully crafted aluminium chassis made at Bimota's Rimini factory housed a heavily tuned and fuel-injected Yamaha FZ750 motor. Because of the size of the company, the homologation limit was 200 units. Bimota say that they made them and the majority went to 'Japanese collectors', but McLaughlin is still of the opinion that Giuseppe Morri, Bimota's boss, played a very clever game and never made anywhere near the required number of bikes.

That's it, he thought, something has gone horribly wrong

Most people thought that the factory flouting the rules most flagrantly was Ducati. They fielded the 1981 500cc GP World Champion Marco Lucchinelli. It is an open secret that the first Ducati 851 that raced at the Bol d'Or in '87 was illegal under the prevailing TT F1 regulations in that it was well over the 750cc limit despite being billed as a 750. The Superbike paddock suspected that there were not many more than the two new 851s at Donington in existence, let alone the 200 required. McLaughlin is adamant that on a visit to Bologna he

Marco Luccinelli and the new Ducati 851 brought a certain Latin something to Superbike.

personally counted 207 851s in production. True, it was after the first homologation date, but it was before the second cut-off date, so again there is no doubt that Ducati were operating within the spirit if not the absolute letter of the law.

The Japanese factories were represented by comparatively low-profile operations. Embarrassingly, the aluminium-framed homologation special Yamaha, the FZ750R, was almost absent and the quick Yamahas were standard steel-framed FZs. The quickest of them was piloted by a tiny Italian, Fabrizio Pirovano, an ex-motocrosser with just a couple of seasons of road racing under his belt. Kawasaki and Suzuki were not really in the frame; their GPX and GSX-R 750 sportsters were not readily adaptable to the race track. The American Yoshimura Suzuki team of Doug Polen and Scott Gray, in the UK for the Eurolantic (née Transatlantic) Challenge that was wrapped around the first World Superbike meeting, did not enter at Donington. Even F1 ace and technical wizard Anders Andersson of Sweden was

LEFT:
(Top) Kawasaki's first winner: Adrien Morillas.
(Bottom) Suzuki's first winner: Gary Goodfellow.

having problems making the 1988 Slingshot CV carbs work on his GSX-R. The Americans used non-standard carbs, as allowed by their domestic rules, along with 1mm oversize bores, a freer set of rules that McLaughlin had favoured for the new World Championship.

It was clear that the main Japanese challenger would be the purpose-built Honda RC30 and that the top rider would be the expatriate American Fred Merkel. 'Flyin' Fred' had been American champion three times in succession for Honda before being sacked by Honda America for undisclosed reasons. The rumour mill was of course alive with stories of sex and drugs and rock 'n' roll, or more prosaically failing to follow team orders and allow team-mate Rainey to win, but all parties maintain a diplomatic silence to this day. Very few American rac-

Terry Rymer showed his promise with a rostrum finish in Portugal on a very well-used RC30.

ers have been able to cope with Europe's strange habits, strange food and strange languages, but Merkel removed himself to Italy, where he restarted his career in Italy's new Superbike Championship with help from local sponsor Oscar Rumi.

Charisma is a very over-used word and you only really understand what it is when you meet someone who has it, someone who walks into a crowded room and is instantly the centre of everyone's attention. Merkel has it in spades. In Italy he would send the crowds wild with daredevil riding, then, having won, march out on to the track and brandish an enormous Stars & Stripes at them, ignoring the hail of boos, whistles and more solid protests aimed at him. To describe him

merely as Californian is to be guilty of the wildest understatement. He looked every inch the surfer with his long blond curls and bandannas. His riding style was wild and he affected enormous knee-sliders that covered most of his shins, which spent most of the time on or just above the tarmac as Fred slid the Honda in a manner that Europeans had yet to come to terms with. Fred was fast, Fred was glamorous, Fred was a star, and like all Californians seemed to know instinctively what to say when a microphone was pointed at him. And he was keen to remind any commentator he could corner that it was he, Flyin' Fred Merkel, who had started the fashion for the standing-on-the-pegs flag-waving air-punching slow-down-lap celebration, not Kevin Schwantz. He was just what Superbike needed.

The struggle for the title was a season-long war between the speed of the Bimotas and the consistency of Merkel and the Honda, with the occasional significant interruption. The honour of winning the first ever World Superbike race went to Davide Tardozzi, but for the only time in the Championship's history the results of the two races held each day were combined to give an overall winner. Lucchinelli won the second leg and, when Tardozzi crashed while lying 2nd, took the overall victory as well. He wasn't that sympathetic to his fellow countryman: 'Tardozzi eez a square 'ed,' he announced to a puzzled group of journalists, before adding, 'First he fall on that side,' while theatrically striking the left side of his face, followed by a whack on the right side and 'then he fall on that side!'

The two-race formula turned out to be a stroke of genius. If a rider crashed or

Fabrizio Pirovano and the steel-framed Yamaha were surprisingly competitive.

The Osterreichring, before its 1996 revamp, was the most spectacular circuit on the calendar.

had a mechanical problem in the first race, he had a chance to redeem his day in the second. And the Superbike guys didn't have to share the prize money, which was the responsibility of the organising circuit, with too many support class racers. The paying public got value for money, too – although in some places the undercard was a little short on quality. Steve McLaughlin says that with TV in mind there was also the possibility of showing a race on either side of an F1 car GP.

The first unexpected win came in the second race at Hungary when, in front of a massive crowd, Frenchman Adrien Morillas gave Kawasaki their first World Superbike win on a steel-framed GPX750 prepared by endurance legends Godier-Genoud; he then survived an amazingly petty protest from Bimota about the shape of his bike's seat. The first double came next time out at the superfast Hockenheimring, where Tardozzi took both wins as Merkel's Honda blew up trying to keep up.

Unexpectedly, Suzuki took a win in Japan, although it was more down to the tactical nous of Gary Goodfellow than the bike. On a drying track the expatriate New Zealander riding under a Canadian licence did what bike racers very rarely do; he pitted to change wheels. The slick

tyre he put on the back of the GSX-R enabled him to hold off Merkel and win. The second race saw a little bit of history, although no one knew it at the time. The race was stopped and restarted after an oil spill bought down a bunch of riders, including the leader, Marco Lucchinelli. At the second time of asking the winner was a young Australian by the name of Michael Doohan on a Yamaha. He'd been a promising hotshot in domestic 250cc production racing and, in what has become the usual Aussie racer production line method, had been picked up by the Yamaha importer's Superbike team. It was the exact route travelled by Wayne Gardner and Kevin Magee, who'd also had to prove themselves in Japan and on

four-strokes before graduating to 500 GPs. The Australian press was already predicting a stellar future for Doohan, although not even the most enthusiastic Ocker could have realised just how good he'd be. To slightly less acclaim, a quiet young Kiwi called Aaron Slight scored points in both races on a Bimota.

The speed of Tardozzi's Bimota kept him at the head of the championship table from Hockenheim onwards, with one interruption from Pirovano, so when the Superbike paddock decamped to the Antipodes for the last two rounds in Australia and New Zealand the Italian was odds-on for the title, especially when Ducati decided not to make the trip. Ostensibly the reason was lack of budget,

Stephane Mertens, Bimota's other rider.

but as they'd been able to go to Japan this didn't ring quite true, especially as Lucchinelli was still in with a chance of the title. The conspiracy theorists had an explanation. They reckoned that the Australian scrutineers, used to policing the ultra-strict regulations for the Castrol 6 Hours, the world's most important box-stock production race, would throw Ducati out. It was common knowledge that since the Austrian round the factory 851 was in fact an 888 thanks to a 94mm bore. This was confirmed by the capacity of the Lucky Replica launched later in the year at the Cologne Show – 888cc. But in Japan the Duke's motor was allegedly measured at 998cc; as the rules forbid altering the motor's stroke, this meant a bore of 99.5mm, and the scrutineers would obviously have measured the stroke to calculate the capacity. But, said the men who'd worked on eight-valve Ducatis, you can't bore the standard barrels out to 99.5mm – you'd be through

the metal and into the water jacket.

And there was more. Ducati claimed that Lucky's bike weighed 152kg, but Stefano Carrachi's semi-works NCR 851, with its carbon-fibre bodywork and titanium fasteners, tipped the scales at 166kg. This, said the specialists, meant weight must have been lost from the motor, and that meant magnesium castings, so the original material had been changed, again contrary to the regulations. This surreptitious development work would probably have got past the scrutineers in most countries, but the ultra-sharp Aussie scrutineers would have spotted it a mile off.

Ducati must have regretted their decision when Tardozzi crashed in qualifying at Oran Park and could only manage 10th and 11th in the races. Merkel took a 3rd and 4th to close to within 2½ points of Tardozzi and level with Pirovano. The final round at Manfeild Park was wet, stretching already taut nerves to breaking point. The coolest man was Fred Merkel, who won the first race from Pirovano, until then reckoned the rain-master, with Tardozzi 5th.

The track was drying for the second race, the worst of all circumstances. Merkel and Pirovano both went out on wets, while Tardozzi contrived to crash on the warm-up lap. Much arm-waving followed as Bimota people tried to get Mertens off his bike, while Tardozzi stood helplessly by the grid in tears. Mertens, who already knew that Bimota didn't want him next year, was having none of it. The track dried rapidly, and to add insult to Bimota's injury the Belgian, who'd gambled on slicks, cleared off for the win as Merkel wobbled round in 5th. Pirovano lost touch and in a last desperate throw of the dice tried to do a Goodfellow and pitted for slicks. It was too late. Fred Merkel was the first World Superbike Champion.

The question was, would there be another one?

chapter two

1989
Survival

It was unanimous. The first year of the new championship had been a success. Superbike had taken over from TT F1 as the premier four-stroke championship thanks to getting the right mix of men and machines on to the right circuits. TV coverage had been good compared to anything that had gone before, and the big Japanese factories were now starting to take an interest in supporting the series.

Unfortunately, the single big series sponsor hadn't materialised, but talks with Japan's largest advertising agency, Dentsu, looked promising – not least because all four major manufacturers were clients.

But McLaughlin and Jones didn't get the chance to try for the big prize. The bosses at Madison had seen the best part of a million pounds sterling spent on Superbikes with no sign yet of a return. They decided that enough was enough and pulled the plug, leaving the World Superbike Championship without an organiser and without TV coverage. Just six days before the first round of the year, Sports Marketing ceased trading. The FIM's Management Council was informed at a meeting on Good Friday, three days before the first race. There was a very strong possibility that the World Superbike Championship would not happen.

Of immediate concern to the riders was the promised travel fund for the top 25 riders of last year. Any rider who'd planned his season around the Superbike Championship had just lost a major chunk of his guaranteed income and was faced with the prospect of telling his sponsors that all the TV coverage they'd been promised wouldn't be happening. The FIM guaranteed payments for the first round only, and Joe Zegwaard, President of the FIM Road Racing Commission, was deputed to try and sort out the mess.

Not that you'd have known that the championship was in crisis from the quantity and quality lined up for the first round. Champion Merkel returned to defend his crown, but with more backing from Honda head office than he'd enjoyed the previous year. His RC30 came from HRC, the Honda Racing Corporation, and was fielded by the Italian Rumi team with some useful sponsorship from an underwear manufacturer. The only help Fred had received the previous year had been an engine for the Austrian round supplied not by HRC but by Honda R&D (these distinctions are important when you're dealing with something as big as the Honda Motor Company). That motor had been slower than the ones his team built, as was the motor from the same source supplied to Virginio Ferrari,

They pulled the plug, leaving WSB without an organiser or TV coverage

but this time Flyin' Fred could expect the best kit available.

There was one big imponderable in his campaign, however – his tyres. The Rumi team of Merkel and a young Italian called Piergiorgio Bontempi had an exclusive deal to use Pirellis. The Italian tyre company was always a big player in the supersport classes that use treaded road tyres, but had never provided slicks for a front-runner at World Championship level. Over in the 500 GPs, Pierfrancesco Chili was also using Pirellis, but both he and Fred were on their own trying to develop their equipment while the Michelin and Dunlop factories had years of experience and feedback from all their teams. Looked at optimistically, Fred had Pirelli's undivided

LEFT: *The riding style and celebrations were as vivid as the colour scheme: Merkel in action.*

Giancarlo Falappa gets a good talking to from his team.

attention and must therefore have a magic tyre. The alternative view was that he would be struggling with lack of experience and an underdeveloped product. The analogy with Kenny Roberts's arrival on the GP scene ten years previously as Goodyear's only runner seemed a good one. When Kenny won his titles everyone assumed that his tyres were very special. Only later did the truth emerge – they were usually awful. Fred, said the paddock sages, would have similar problems.

Peter Ingley, the vastly experienced tyre engineer brought in by Pirelli to run their operation, says the truth was as usual somewhere in the middle. 'There was one track – Canada – where we were at a definite disadvantage and one where we were at a definite advantage.'

Falappa's riding style was, er, unconventional.

Crucially, neither Dunlop nor Michelin were yet taking World Superbike seriously and, says Ingley, 'By the time Michelin hit the panic button we were on a roll.'

Ingley also claims to have introduced the true qualifying tyre to bike racing this year. Some racers need to set pole position as part of their psychological war with the opposition – Merkel is one of them – while some racers simply want to be on the front row. 'I built Merkel a true one-lap qualifier and used the tactic I'd observed Senna using in F1, setting pole at the last moment, leaving no time for anyone to beat it.' Merkel took pole four times in the season, as did Ducati's Raymond Roche, but Fred also started from 2nd – usually behind local heroes in Australia or the States – four times compared to Raymond's twice.

There was more than one HRC-supplied RC30 on the grid. Stephane Mertens left Bimota to run his own team with ace tuner Jean d'Hollander, another Belgian, fettling his motors. But the lanky Belgian missed the first race of the season after a dreadful crash at Brands Hatch on Good Friday during the Eurolantic Challenge when he tangled with Joey Dunlop at Paddock Hill Bend. Courageously, he returned for round two in Hungary, but couldn't race with the front men and dropped more vital points. Dunlop came off worse and, much to the displeasure of Irish fans who raked over Mertens's reputation as a crasher, missed the Isle of Man TT.

At Ducati, Marco Lucchinelli gave up full-time riding and instead managed the

RIGHT: *Merkel and team size up the opposition – from pole position.*

team of ex-500 GP star and 1981 World Endurance Champion Raymond Roche with virtually unknown Baldassarre Monti as back-up. The Frenchman, now 32 years old, was a notorious hardcase – even by the standards of his tough home town of Toulon – and also a rider of proven world class. His major problem would be the lack of reliability that had also plagued Lucchinelli the previous year. Not only was the 851 a new bike, but the use of electronic fuel injection was also new to motorcycle racing applications and gave rise to many of the mechanical failures. Bimota suffered as well, giving rise to all sorts of unlikely rumours, such as the Air Traffic Control radar at East Midlands Airport 2 miles up the road from Donington interfering with the electronics. Which didn't explain why the motors also stuttered on tracks miles

Doug Polen's first World Superbike win, in the rain in Japan.

from airports. However, when the Ducati kept going it was very, very fast. Fast enough for Roche to post double wins at the two fastest tracks in the calendar, Hockenheim and Brainerd. The shape of things to come.

Bimota moved Tardozzi to a privateer team and signed ex-GP privateer Fabio Biliotti, plus a total unknown, an ex-motocrosser with the looks of an angry bull terrier – Giancarlo Falappa. It was an inspired signing. Biliotti would fail totally to come to terms with a big four-stroke, while Falappa's wild riding style would endear him to fans everywhere, if not his competitors. Bimota's bikes were as beautifully crafted as ever and right on the four-cylinder bikes' minimum weight limit of 165kg thanks to lavish use of carbon-fibre, but the new generation of Japanese machinery negated any advantage that the hand-built aluminium chassis used to give.

Both Yamaha and Kawasaki had new

bikes in the showrooms, the OW01 and ZXR750R, homologated for Superbike racing with aluminium chassis, close-ratio gearboxes and – vitally – flat-slide carbs. Fabrizio Pirovano got an OW01 and sponsorship from the Italian importer, Anders Andersson deserted Suzuki for the first time in his career and turned up with a beautifully prepared Yamaha with very trick Ohlins suspension, and young English hope Terry Rymer would do most of the championship on the UK importer's Loctite-sponsored bike. Terry's season would be interrupted by domestic commitments

Robbie Phillis had a very special Kawasaki for the last two rounds: the taped-up rear light shows it was built for the Suzuka 8 Hour endurance race.

and hampered by Dunlops that didn't seem able to last a World Championship-length race, but here at last was a genuine championship hope for British fans to get behind.

Kawasaki didn't have any full-time challengers, but the French endurance squad of Patrick Igoa and Christophe Bouheben put in some useful rides at the beginning of the season, as did the Kawasaki Australia duo of Rob Phillis and

Aaron Slight at the end. Their main problem was that the ZXR homologation bike was much more of a roadster than a racer, certainly compared to the Yamaha and especially the Honda, and needed considerable development and a lot of weight to be shed before it would be a competitive Superbike racer. Suzuki's French endurance team dabbled but soon realised that their GSX-Rs were still less competitive than the year before. They didn't even contest their home round at Circuit Paul Ricard. Suzuki got a win, though, and again it was in Japan and in the wet where Doug Polen coped best with monsoon conditions.

But once again the championship would be fought out between a hard core of championship regulars – Merkel, Mertens, Pirovano and Roche – with the local heroes confusing things in Japan, Australia and New Zealand.

Despite all the political activity going on behind the scenes, the championship ran smoothly. Joe Zegwaard turned up at every race and took a lot of flak for a situation that was not of his making. His hostile reception was not helped by the fact that he'd been one of the main enemies of McLaughlin, and therefore Superbike, in the FIM's internal politicking.

The big surprise of the opening round at Donington Park was Giancarlo Falappa on the Bimota. In race one he ran with a fraught bunch including Roger Burnett (on a third HRC-supplied Honda RC30), eventual winner Pirovano, Rymer and Merkel at the front before tangling with a backmarker and dropping right down the order, but not before he thoroughly outraged most of the opposition. 'Who's the wanker on the Bimota?' asked Burnett after the race. 'He doesn't know what he's doing – he's got fuel blowing on his tyre and he doesn't know why it's sliding!' Falappa then won race two and looked almost composed, not bad for his

Flyin' Fred and flyin' Kiwi.

37

Daryl Beattie appeared in World Supers for the first time on an RC30.

first meeting outside Italy. Photographs of him in among other riders show all the bunch bar one leaning off the bike to the inside of the corner in the usual fashion, but Falappa is sitting almost upright pushing the bike down into the corner motocross-style. Giancarlo smoothed his style out a little without compromising his aggression and won two more races. He also became a star. The contrast between the on-track psycho and the off-track teddy-bear was wonderful. Asked if he was married to his girlfriend Paula, he searched his English vocabulary and replied, 'We are for life … she is my life.' Only an Italian could get away with a line like that.

The other new star was Terry Rymer, a gangling 22-year-old South Londoner who'd performed wonders in '88 on a very standard RC30. As one of the UK Yamaha importer's riders, his priority was really the domestic championship, so as well as missing two World rounds he had very little time for testing, and it showed. That and Dunlop's season-long problems conspired to hold him back, but at least he won a race right at the end of the season and redeemed his year. Ducati's new boy Baldassarre Monti also shone, but the factory didn't have a bike for him at the start of the year and didn't send him to Australia or New Zealand.

Superbike's first excursion to its spiritual homeland, North America, was a success – at least with the fans. Rounds three and four were at Mosport in Canada and Brainerd in the USA, and attracted 30,000 and 20,000 spectators respectively. But the barrier-lined Mosport track was obviously dangerous by the standards to which the European riders were accustomed. It is in a beautiful part of the world, but the armco barriers and concrete walls that line it caused the regular riders to warn that they would expect some heavy modifications if they were to return the following year. The North American races also saw the return to top-level competition of the American ex-500 GP star Mike Baldwin on a private Bimota. With Biliotti yet to score a point, the paddock wondered if he was being lined up as a replacement, and when the Italian quit before the Austrian round the wondering was over. Baldwin couldn't get to Europe for Austria, but made it for France and the rest of Bimota's season. With no travel money available and the championship gone, Bimota did not go to the final two rounds.

Unbelievably, the championship went down to the wire again. Roche had won most races but had also had his Ducati break down far too often. This time Merkel had led since the second round with only one break when Mertens got his nose in front after Hockenheim, but when they went to the final two rounds in Australia and New Zealand Flyin' Fred led by just 2 points. It would be another test of nerve, but the regulars would be outshone in the final two rounds by the locals. The Yamaha Australia team fielded Mike Dowson, already a winner this year, and their new hope Peter Goddard, who had won his first international race in Japan the previous week, on full factory machines. Kawasaki flew in a full factory bike from Japan for Rob Phillis who, with team-mate Aaron Slight, was preparing for a full-time assault on the championship in 1990. A promising young man called Daryl Beattie, the Australian 250 champ, was given an RC30. Dowson and Goddard split the wins and legend has it that the latter's win in the first race on a track that started wet and dried came about because the

team manager simply decided to put one of his riders out on slicks and the other on wets! Well behind the locals, Mertens scored 8th and 4th places compared to Merkel's 11th and 5th to go top of the table by just 3 points.

And so to new Zealand for the final showdown. Qualifying hardly separated them: Merkel got the pole position he needed for his self-confidence, but Mertens was also on the front row. The race was wet and Terry Rymer got the holeshot and pulled away from a pack of five riders that included Merkel. Mertens started badly but easily forced his way up to 6th when the season was decided by a freak accident. On lap 22 Mertens was approaching Higgins Bend when his

Terry Rymer scored his debut win in New Zealand and was quite pleased about it.

Merkel's crew signal to him that Mertens is out and he is World Champion again.

The broken brake disc that shattered Stephane Mertens' dream of being World Superbike Champion.

front wheel appeared to lock up and he crashed heavily, lucky to escape unscathed; the bike meanwhile cleared the gravel trap and went through a row of trees before smashing into a low wall and bursting into flames. 'For two laps before I felt a vibration when I braked,' said Stephane, 'and I nearly lost the bike at the hairpin. I was braking for the bend just before the back straight and the next thing I know I was on the ground. We think the front disc broke up and locked the wheel.'

The Belgian bravely climbed on to his spare bike for the second race and won it by a country mile, but Merkel, who had stormed through to 3rd in race one despite knowing Mertens was out, took 3rd again and retained his championship – Pirelli's first at World level – by the meagre margin of 7 points.

chapter three

1990
The red menace

Joe Zegwaard may have looked like a punchbag through most of 1989, but from the US GP at Laguna Seca on 16 April onwards he was in regular contact with Dentsu's representatives, trying to seal the deal that Sports Marketing had been negotiating for the Japanese to take over the series. Zegwaard says that he was strung along for nearly the whole season without getting a firm answer from Japan. What he didn't know was that Dentsu was embroiled in negotiating the biggest TV deal ever for the rights to the Barcelona Olympics, so a little old Superbike championship was way down their list of priorities. Of course Zegwaard couldn't let the teams know

He could be mean, he could be moody, but in 1990 Raymond Roche was magnificent.

Diesel Jeans turned out to be a popular series sponsor …

about these negotiations, which meant that he was still the target for frustration within the paddock. His mood wasn't helped when McLaughlin made the occasional appearance and was treated like a visiting deity.

In the face of continued procrastination from Japan – or Zegwaard's inability to close the deal, depending on who you talk to – the FIM had to make a decision. Right from the first meeting after the crash of Sports Marketing there had been an offer on the table from the Flammini Group to take over the championship. There was also an offer from McLaughlin in partnership with an un-named Japanese backer, but Zegwaard made it quite clear within the FIM that this offer would be accepted over his

dead body. After one last plea to his Dentsu contact failed to elicit a decision, Zegwaard felt that he had to recommend acceptance of the Flammini Group's offer.

This Italian concern, fronted by ex-Formula 3000 car racer Maurizio Flammini, already ran Italian national races plus several Grands Prix. They quickly put in place a deal with Dentsu for the TV rights and secured a high-profile series sponsor, Diesel Jeans.

McLaughlin meanwhile fetched up in Germany where he started another Superbike series, the Pro-Superbike Championship. Ironically, he had a lot of help from a TV producer he had once thrown out of the Hockenheim paddock for filming a news item with too many

Practising for dealing with officialdom.

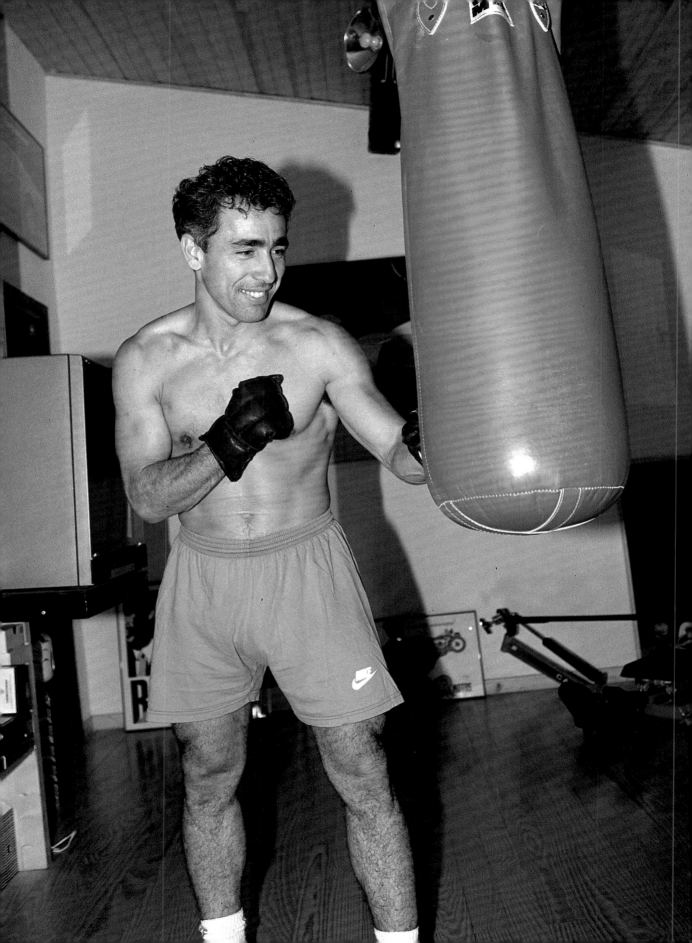

cameras. 'That's not a news item, that's a programme – get the **** out of here; you're dealing with CBS! They've got more damn lawyers than there are people in Munich!' Pro-Superbike was a great success thanks in no small part to TV coverage financed by the large subscription that teams had to pay to join the series.

McLaughlin took the separation from his creation philosophically – outwardly at least. There was one time when he got upset, though. An American magazine printed a feature on the most important men in the development of Superbike; they named France as the most important, with McLaughlin only 4th behind Kawasaki team boss Rob Muzzy. That one obviously rankled.

Flammini built well on the foundations laid over the first two years of World Superbike, and the championship got its first fully fledged Japanese works team in the shape of Rob Phillis and the Shin-Etsu Kawasaki. Basically, the Team Kawasaki Australia operation, which had helped Rob to 6th overall in 1988 from just four rounds and seen him finish no lower than 6th in three events in '89, moved to Germany for the season. Although in reality he is a dedicated family man, outwardly Phillis is a very abrasive character, and very much a party animal – with the emphasis on animal. He was already 33 years old with six Australian Superbike Championships under his belt, and here at last was the chance of a crack at a world title that he had longed for. He had the tools for the job: a works ZXR with fully kitted motor plus an array of trick suspension, six-piston brakes and lightweight parts that put it bang on the minimum weight limit for four-cylinder bikes. At last Kawasaki had a competitive runner with a realistic shot at the championship, but Phillis had a bad crash at Hockenheim, ironically bringing

No team orders at Ducati! Falappa leans on Roche.

45

Roche had an altercation with a lady marshal after a practice crash at Brainerd, he later apologised and gave her one of his crash helmets, but it didn't save him from a fine.

down fellow countryman Mal Campbell in the process, and didn't manage to win a race until the penultimate round in Australia, but then promptly backed it up with a win in New Zealand.

There were few changes elsewhere to either men or machines with the significant exception of Bimota's withdrawal from the championship, which gave Ducati the chance to sign up Giancarlo Falappa as Roche's team-mate. Monti moved to Rumi as Merkel's understudy. Apart from Phillis, the only other full-time newcomer of note was experienced 500 GP man Rob McElnea alongside

Terry Rymer in the Loctite Yamaha squad, but once again the team would not do a full season as they struggled to cope with domestic commitments alongside the World Championship.

The tyre situation got more interesting as Michelin favoured Phillis, Roche, Mertens and Pirovano with their A-grade tyres, Merkel stuck with Pirelli, and the British Loctite Yamaha squad were the only top-flight runners on Dunlop. Michelin were obviously taking the Superbikes seriously now, and their A-grade men ended up as the top four in the championship.

Raymond Roche's Ducati didn't look very different from the previous year's model, but one significant new characteristic had been built in over the winter: reliability. He had won more races than anyone else the previous season but had ended up 3rd in the championship, so Raymond made his wishes very clear before the start of the 1990 season, and when Raymond makes something clear you have very little option but to listen. In '89 he had carried an officious Canadian security guard on the bonnet of his hire car for most of the pit lane, and this year he had an altercation with a female marshal in the USA after he'd crashed in qualifying. He apologised to her after the meeting and presented her with one of his crash helmets. This didn't save him from a 1,000 Swiss francs fine imposed by the FIM jury, so Raymond wrote 'I am not Roche-Child' (as in Rothschild) on another of his crash helmets. Interviewing him after a bad race was not a job journalists looked forward to. After his team-mate Falappa beat him with a wild last-lap overtake at Donington, Raymond gave three one-word answers to the circuit's commentator before the journalist gave up and ran away.

Fabrizio Pirovano enjoyed Malaysia.

A rostrum full of happy Aussies at home. From left: Peter Goddard, Robbie Phillis and Mal Campbell.

The Ducati's reliability problems were all down to trivial factors, mainly electrical. Roche reckoned that they were trying to run a road bike system on a racer and was determined that he was not going to suffer another six breakdowns as he had in '89. His efforts weren't wasted. The Ducati only failed to get him to the finish twice – in Germany, when he blew the motor, and in the last race of the year, when the oil filter fell off – but as he'd secured the title with two cautious rides at the previous round it didn't matter.

The low point of the year was the serious injuries suffered by Giancarlo Falappa in qualifying for the Austrian round on his return from breaking a wrist in Canada. Ducati team manager Marco Lucchinelli did not want him to ride, but Giancarlo was chasing pole-setter Mertens's blistering time with just a few minutes of final qualifying left when he went down in the very fast left-hand kink at the top of the circuit, hit the 200-metre board and, in the words of a shocked Rob McElnea, 'Lay there in a big **** heap', with his legs bent up under his back. He'd broken both femurs, shattered his left shoulderblade with accompanying muscle damage, and rebroken his left wrist. Davide Tardozzi had been first on the scene and may have saved Falappa from strangulation by his helmet strap. Like all other witnesses to the accident, Tardozzi was very shaken; he was still muttering 'Stupido, stupido!' to himself in the paddock as Falappa was helicoptered to hospital and out of the 1990 World Superbike Championship.

His team-mate Roche's view was that it was simply a matter of experience. 'The problem with a young rider like Falappa is he crashes because he says "I want to be in front", but thinks "I want to be in front immediately".' Reminded of his own wild youth, Raymond would say, 'I am an old man now, I don't want to crash.' His views on the rest of the opposition are also

Giancarlo Falappa just before his near-fatal crash in Austria.

enlightening. Merkel and Phillis are 'good riders', as is Mertens who is also 'very aggressive'. McElnea is 'very fast' and so is Pirovano, but only for 10 laps. The rest of the grid wasn't very fond of Fabrizio either; the little Italian was the usual culprit when the racing became a contact sport. Stephane Mertens's team felt aggrieved enough after a coming together in Australia, which caused their rider to crash, to put in an official protest. But Roche reserved the description 'completely crazy' for Baldassarre Monti.

Roche embodied some of the schizophrenia of the Superbike World Championship itself. He was in the veteran class with a distinguished 500 Grand Prix career behind him. He was good enough to be 3rd in the World Championship in 1985 but he never won a GP, and that always rankled. He

LEFT: *Hot lap. Roche and Mertens in action.*

Rymer saved the best to last again, winning in New Zealand.

approached racing in Superbike as a job, and his heart was obviously still with the 500s, but he was realistic: 'It's better to have a good bike in Superbike than a slow one in GPs.' Neither was he very impressed with the disjointed calendar or the lack of adjustability on his bike: 'With Superbikes, after tyres, suspension, that's it.'

Nevertheless, Roche was obviously more motivated than he'd been in 1989. His win at the Hungaroring and getting pole at Sugo, both circuits to which the Ducati was unsuited, were, for him, the highlights of the year. 'When I drive the first laps at Sugo I say "Ooooh I cannot win", but we work a very long time and we try to set.' It was the same in Hungary, where some more hard work on suspension settings, gearing and tyres gave Raymond the chance to win.

Against that there were cases when the motorcycle simply worked from the beginning. 'In Spain I have only seven laps practice and pole position.' The main problem was the difficulty of changing the 888 Ducati's internal gear ratios. Because the bike didn't have a quick-change cluster gearbox, the team would change the whole engine, not just the gears, choosing from one of three engine/gearbox combinations taken to each meeting. Roche also preferred to use taller gearing, because a bigger rear sprocket would have an effect on the rear suspension, and so condemned himself to slow starts. But it worked and Raymond would admit that the bike was the best out there, although he was worried about Kawasaki's new ZXR750R.

'Now I think Ducati has a small advantage because the engine is very fast but the frame is very difficult to drive. If they don't do something with the bike then they will be ruined when the Japanese make their changes.' The problems were all due to the engine, which was very long and therefore dictated a long wheelbase and heavy, slow steering, but there was very little chance of Ducati changing their hallmark V-twin motor.

As it turned out, Raymond really did not need to worry – well, not about Ducati's ability to win, anyway.

The Ducati team celebrates the company's first Superbike World Championship.

chapter four

1991 Revolution

After the traumas of its first two years, the Superbike World Championship could be forgiven for a modicum of self-satisfaction, especially as the Grand Prix 500s were embroiled in a political dog-fight between the IRTA, the FIM, Bernie Ecclestone's organisation, and Spanish TV giant Dorna, which threatened to split the sport apart. But what happened in 1991 threw into stark relief the inherent problems of the Superbike class.

What happened was Doug Polen and the Fast by Ferracci 888 Ducati.

The Texan's domination was utter and total – he wrapped the title up with five races to spare, and up to then had only been beaten once in a straight fight when he had no machinery problems. Polen had a works Ducati 888 but he didn't ride for the factory team; instead the veteran

Doug and Dianne Polen – note her name on the sleeve of his leathers.

His style could sometimes look awkward, but in 1991 it was overwhelmingly effective.

Giancarlo Falappa made a welcome return, but he was not yet back to his fighting weight.

Italian-American tuner Eraldo Ferracci prepared his bikes to great effect, Dunlop produced a steady flow of new tyres that Polen seemed to be able to assess and use instantly, and – last but not least – he rode brilliantly. From the 12 rounds and 24 races (excluding the Canadian round that was boycotted by all the regular riders on safety grounds), Polen was on pole an astounding ten times, and wasn't lower than pole position on the grid until the 11th round when Rob Phillis went faster at Magny-Cours. Doug set the fastest lap of the day nine times and won 17 races, including no fewer than six double wins. No one, not even Carl Fogarty, has managed to better those marks for a season's racing.

It was also the first example of a phenomenon that would crop up regularly in the future, that of a nominally private Ducati often being quicker than the factory bikes. Ferracci's rider Jamie James had gone well in the USA the previous year and showed well in the North American rounds of the World Championship, and for his 1991 campaign he linked up with two Italian ex-works mechanics, Giorgio Nepoti and Rino Carrachi, whose tuning firm Scuderia NCR (literally Team Nepoti Carrachi Racing) had built the factory's

racers since the mid-'70s in their Bologna workshop a stone's throw from Ducati's factory. Their endurance racers, based on the original 900SS, were works of art, but the bike of theirs that everyone remembers is the one on which Mike Hailwood made his legendary comeback to the Isle of Man TT in 1978, which was prepared by Steve Wynne of the British company Sports Motorcycles. This event was as significant for the fortunes of the factory as Paul Smart's Imola 200 win in 1972 on the first ever racing Ducati V-twin, for more than any other company Ducati's commercial fortunes were always inextricably linked with their racing success. Incidentally, there was another British rider on an NCR-built, Sports Motorcycles-prepared Ducati: one George Fogarty, who happened to have a

Hockenheim: Pirovano hits the deck, Falappa takes to the grass, Mertens carries on regardless. Shortly after this, Fabrizio hit a marshal.

young son named Carl. The firm's World Superbike Championship successes would push sales of their road bikes to undreamed-of levels.

Polen's domination was underlined by the performances of the other factory Ducatis, which, now down on or very near the class's 140kg minimum weight limit for twins, won every race that Polen didn't until ex-GP star Kevin Magee popped up on a factory Yamaha in Australia. They also set the fastest laps that Polen missed out on (although Aaron Slight shared that honour at the Australian round on a Kawasaki). Raymond Roche got the only other double win that anyone managed in 1991, but the man who beat Polen in a straight fight was Stephane Mertens, who'd abandoned his Honda RC30 for a factory Ducati and Pirelli tyres.

This was the year when Superbike racing became like most other forms of road racing, in that any rider, no matter how gifted, had to have a factory bike to win. And not just any factory bike, but the right factory bike. The statistics show that you needed a Ducati, despite Robbie Phillis's heroic efforts to keep on terms with the very promising ZXR750R. The Aussie, now 35 years old, managed to beat the other Ducatis fairly regularly, especially towards the end of the year as the bike got more trick bits, but he rarely bothered Polen.

It could have been worse – he could have been on a works Honda or Yamaha. Even Fred Merkel struggled; he only got on the rostrum once all year, as it became clear that the RC30 was now very long in the tooth. Against all expectations, Carl Fogarty ended up as top Honda rider after a season of consistent top-ten finishes and no crashes; his one DNF was

Blast-off at Donington. The front row is Polen (53), Roche (1), Monti (8), Rymer (7) and Merkel (27); the second row is Phillis (4), Pirovano (2), McElnea (19).

the result of a broken gear linkage. This did not fit with Foggy's (undeserved) reputation as a crasher and machine-breaker, and the fact that he was riding for the Honda Britain team on relatively standard machinery and had real problems with front suspension set-up made his season all the more praiseworthy. The career of his team-mate and friend James Whitham was nearly ended by the front-end problems he suffered. The highlight of Fabrizio Pirovano's Yamaha year was punching a German marshal about twice his size when he attempted to dissuade the diminutive Italian from restarting after a crash. On the racetrack he managed only one 2nd place and three 3rds.

There was one new machine on the grid, Bimota's hub-centre-steered Tesi with Ducati V-twin power, but it didn't make much of an impression. The Zimbabwean Russell Wood was its regular pilot, although the British privateer Steve Manley was in the saddle at round one and scored a World Championship point for 15th in the bike's first World Championship race.

Polen's flying start to the season was aided and abetted by Dunlop, who took the Superbikes very seriously right from the start of the year. Michelin, who shod the works Ducatis of Roche and Falappa, again took too long to fully commit the resources needed to fight for the title. Pirelli's new tie-up with Stephane Mertens bore fruit with a win in the second race of the first round, but it was significant that the Belgian crashed in the first race trying to keep up with Polen. Equally significantly, Roche hurt himself in a qualifying crash trying to match the Texan's time, and would do so again at round three. The pattern was set that early. The other factory Ducati rider, Giancarlo Falappa, was still recovering from his Austrian crash the previous season, and was not a realistic candidate for

Stephane Mertens enjoyed his first year on a Ducati.

victory. Most teams wouldn't have given a man in his condition a factory bike, but the Ducati team likes to think of itself as a family and this was a way of helping a much-loved family member get better.

With hindsight it is now possible to say that Kevin Magee's races in Japan and Australia were among the most significant events of the Superbike World Championship so far. Here was a man who had won a 500 Grand Prix appearing in the new championship, the first GP winner to do so after Lucchinelli. He was obviously fully recovered from the serious head injuries that had curtailed his career, and was anxious to prove a point or two. In Japan he got on the rostrum just once with 3rd in the second race, so those Superbike regulars couldn't be that shabby, could they? In Australia he won one race, as we now expected the locals to do, but lost the second to Polen. Another landmark: the first win for a foreigner in an Australian round of World Superbike, and more proof of just how quick Doug Polen was.

Polen's domination brought the issue of the Superbike formula to a head. Right at the birth of the class, the regulations had been skewed to encourage smaller manufacturers – and back then Ducati were a very small manufacturer – to go racing. How can you complain, said the Italians, when we try harder and build a good bike; if V-twins have such an advantage you should build one too. The Japanese camp didn't quite see it like that. To them the double whammy of the capacity advantage and the 25kg minimum weight difference was simply unfair, and it wasn't just a matter of top speed. Well, they would say that, wouldn't they, but it was most definitely a fact that you needed a works Ducati to win. Even a

Here was a man who had won a 500 GP appearing in the new championship

good private 888 couldn't get near the carbon-fibre-bedecked Fast by Ferracci or Lucchinelli bikes. The Ducati's lighter weight allowed its riders to brake later for corners and give their tyres an easier time than the four-cylinder guys, while the extra capacity and the nature of the big twin motor launched the bike out of low and medium speed corners on a wave of mid-range power and torque as if it had been fired from a gun. This was the route to works bike domination that had led to a crisis of sorts in the 500 GP class, and while there was no doubt that Ducati were doing nothing against the letter of the law, there was grounds for worrying about the future viability of the class.

Some years later Steve McLaughlin had an interesting insight into the minimum weight differential. He says unequivocally that it was a sop to Ducati to get them to commit to Superbike. However, the way he wrote the first set of rules the differential was 25 pounds, and somewhere along the way to the FIM's headquarters in Switzerland pounds got turned into kilograms without being divided by any conversion factor. What was meant to be a token gesture was turned into a major advantage for the V-twins.

There were also the perennial worries about some of the venues and the gappy, disjointed calendar. The first of these problems came to a head at Mosport Park in Canada where improvements for which the regular riders and teams had asked had not been done. The track had always been dangerous and over the previous two years improvements had been requested and carried out. But this time, in a display of unanimity unusual for motorcycle racers, the event was boycotted, which is why the names Pascal Picotte and Tom Kipp appear on the roll

The reasons why the regular championship contenders didn't enter for Mosport were terribly obvious – and very close to the track.

of World Superbike race winners. Along with the cancellation for the third time running of the Brazilian round, this avoidable situation appeared to be totally ignored by Joe Zegwaard and the FIM, which was now doing its best to pretend that Superbike didn't exist.

But the vast majority of the paddock was preoccupied with what to do about Polen and Ducati if the combination returned for 1992. Doug Polen and his wife Dianne appeared to lead a blameless life: they donated money to their local police force to help them buy mountain bikes for chasing drug dealers (honest), and they were both always more than happy to talk to the media. In fact, the problem wasn't getting Doug to talk, but to stop him. Behind this squeaky-clean facade there was a very astute business-man as well as a calculating racer. He'd always raced in classes that paid the best, and had banked a large amount of Suzuki contingency money for winning one-make series races on that company's GSX-R750 and 1100s. He'd then gone to Japan to race Yoshimura Suzukis, effec-tively works bikes, and won both the TT F1 and F3 (400cc) titles, the first time anyone had won both – and a foreigner as well! There was also the small matter of a World Superbike Championship race win. And all this after he'd missed almost a whole season in the late '80s when a gory accident at an American championship race tangled his foot with the rear chain and sprocket and he lost all the toes from it.

Not only couldn't they cope with him on the track, but he also wasn't the usual Superbike rider off it. After the bucca-neering Merkel and the tough-as-nails Roche, what do you make of a guy who races with his name on one sleeve of his leathers and his wife Dianne's name on the other?

Robbie Phillis and the Kawasaki threatened Ducati domination late in the season.

chapter five

1992
Déjà vu

This was the year when Superbike marked time. The personnel were much the same as the previous year, as was the machinery. And the result was the same, too, although Doug Polen had to work a lot harder to retain his title than he did to win it.

The most noticeable absentee wasn't a rider, but a team manager. Marco Lucchinelli had been caught in possession of a substantial quantity of cocaine in 1991 and was now behind bars, so the Ducati teamsters had to be reshuffled. Doug Polen was now part of the official factory team alongside the almost completely recovered Giancarlo Falappa, with another ex-500 GP World Champion, Franco Uncini, as team manager. Raymond Roche ran his own bike on Michelins and a shoestring budget, while Mertens and the Spanish rider Daniel Amatrian got full factory bikes. Davide Tardozzi also got factory equipment, but he was usually acting as test pilot for development parts.

As usual, Ducati built a small number of 888 Corsa replicas of the previous year's works bike for sale to privateers, but unusually they were only 7kg heavier than the new works bikes and very competitive. Both the factory bikes and the Corsas retained the 1991 frame and bodywork – it was obvious that the 888 was approaching the end of its development life. The question was, could the Japanese factories take advantage?

Honda certainly couldn't. The RC30 was now well past it, but team Rumi sol-

LEFT: *Doug Polen, who led an apparently blameless life.*

RIGHT: *Number one again.*

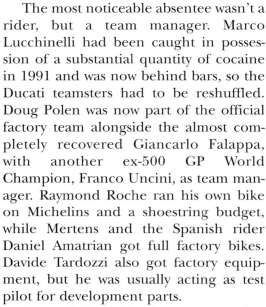

diered on with Baldassarre Monti on what was essentially Fred Merkel's bike from the previous season. Merkel himself surfaced in the new factory Yamaha team alongside Pirovano run by BYRD, the racing arm of Belgarda, the Italian importer. However, a testing crash shattered his heel and put him on the sidelines for most of the year.

Suzuki had a new bike, the GSX-R750WN, cooled by water rather than oil, but it was handicapped by the Slingshot carburettors fitted to the road-going homologation version. The French rider Hervé Moineau, four times World Endurance Champion, put in some solid rides on it, but never looked like getting on the rostrum.

Once again the Japanese challenge was left to Kawasaki, and again the only man who regularly got in among the ruling Ducatis was the indomitable Rob Phillis, although Pirovano underlined his rain-master reputation with a double at a very wet Monza. But it was Phillis's team-mate Aaron Slight who won the opening race in Spain on the newly and appropriately named Moving Kawasaki.

Four rounds into the year, Phillis was leading the championship thanks to wins at Spa and Jarama and solid points-scoring finishes everywhere else. Unfortunately, this splendid form rather undermined his argument that the Ducatis had an unfair advantage. Later in the season, when he was again holding forth in his caravan on the injustices of the regulations, his wife Carol (a saint if ever there was one) casually remarked, 'You didn't say that when you were leading the championship …' Ouch.

Phillis's motivation wasn't helped when news leaked out at the last European race of the season that his services would not be required on the works team next year, but he still finished 3rd in the championship and prevented a

The style was still strange, and he was still quick as well.

Polen leads the plunge down to Eau Rouge at Spa, followed by Pirovano and Russell.

Ducati clean sweep of the top three places. As usual, Phillis fought to the end – the adjective 'gritty' could have been coined just for him – but this was the end of his full-time World Superbike career. His role in establishing the credibility of the series should not be underestimated, but you can't help feeling that if the World Championship had come about when he was in his 20s instead of his mid-30s, history, and the record books outside of Australia where he will always be a hero, could have been a little different.

One works Ducati rider didn't do himself justice – Stephane Mertens. For the first time in the history of the championship he didn't score a race win and ended a lowly 7th. The lanky Belgian had

Polen wasn't riding for Ferraci in 1992 but the Italian-American still tuned his bike.

been 2nd, 3rd and 4th in the championship in the previous three years, but now it appeared that his challenge was over. He was always a fearsome competitor on the fast tracks, but his introverted nature meant that this very likeable racer never stamped his personality on the championship.

Doug Polen didn't score a victory until the first race of round three, but he made up for lost time with a double and went joint top of the points table. This wasn't going to be easy. Other riders, notably his team-mate Falappa, used Dunlop-shod Ducatis to their full potential; Roche stayed injury free, benefited from Michelin's increased interest in the championship, and his bike was the quick-

est thing out there. This was another case of the non-factory-tuned Ducati being quickest thanks to the attentions of tuner Rolando Simoneti, whereas the factory squad wasn't allowed to interfere with their motors.

Polen didn't just have trouble in the World Championship – his campaign back home in the States was dogged by a new star, an intense, lanky young man called Scott Russell who'd beaten Polen at Daytona and would eventually beat him in the American Championship. Russell, who'd been lured away from the American Yoshimura Suzuki team by Kawasaki team owner Rob Muzzy, returned home after just four rounds of the World Championship, but the paddock had seen enough to know that here was a new star.

Russell was on the rostrum twice at Donington Park in the UK, the second round of the season, but not too many people noticed because another relative youngster, Carl Fogarty, announced to the world outside of British closed-road racing that he would be a force to be reckoned with. Desperately short of money and considering giving up the Ducati 888 Corsa that his family was helping to finance, Fogarty fell while leading the first race, then won the second going away. Here was proof that a privateer could still win a World Superbike Championship race on an over-the-counter bike.

It was the first act in a year of miracles for Fogarty that would see him set an Isle of Man TT lap record that still stands, and win the World Endurance Championship with Terry Rymer. He got on a Superbike rostrum once more, at Assen, a circuit he had dominated in TT F1 competition and would come to dominate in Superbike, but his record of six mechanical failures shows how difficult and expensive it was to keep a private Ducati on the track. Nevertheless, that win at Donington was

Scott Russell only did four rounds but he made a big impression.

the turning point in the career of the racer who would go on to beat most of Doug Polen's records.

Donington was an emotional moment for Fogarty, his family and British bike fans in general. But for the Superbike paddock the most emotional moment of the year was Giancarlo Falappa's double win in Austria at the Zeltweg track where he had been so badly injured in 1990. They were also his first wins since the accident, and the Italian would be an ever more formidable opponent through the second half of the season, as not just his race fitness but also his confidence returned. Amazingly, he still had all his old aggression, but it was now tempered with precision and tactical awareness. His fans were glad to see that the trademark standing wheelie was still in his slow-down-lap repertoire, though.

Doug Polen's slow start to the season was mainly down to a lack of winter testing. He didn't sit on the bike until Daytona in March, by which time the Kawasaki teams had done a good deal of testing. Although his Ducati was basically the 1991 bike with new suspension, it still took a lot of time to get dialled in; the double win in Hockenheim was the turn-around point for his season and came about when Doug reverted to his 1991 settings. Not long before he'd won his first race of the year, an American Championship round, he had made massive changes in one hit – '16 clicks on that, 24 clicks on that' – and they worked. It was the first time all year that the bike had been anywhere near right, and in typically nerveless style he then hunted down early-season leaders Roche and Phillis to retain his championship at the

RIGHT: *Rob Phillis got a new team-mate for 1992, Aaron Slight.*

INSET: *Falappa looked even more threatening than usual on the Austrian rostrum in the sponsor's products.*

74

Kevin Magee turned up late in the season to give Yamaha a win in Australia.

last round in New Zealand.

He went there with a 26-point lead over the Frenchman, quite enough to cruise round and let Roche win. But he didn't – he won the first race with Roche back in 3rd and equalled Fred Merkel's achievement of retaining the championship. He also scotched any ideas that his first title had been won purely because he had a superior machine or that he was purely a mercenary riding for the money and not prepared to step close to the edge. He could go back to the States for a year safe in the knowledge that the marks he had set would take a long time to be surpassed.

As for the championship, it hadn't really progressed. The riders' elected representatives, Polen and Phillis, weren't at all happy with some of the tracks on which they had to race, notably Monza, where a concrete wall just 20 feet from the edge of a 150mph corner was a disaster waiting to happen. Surprisingly, Spa-Francorchamps didn't come in for too much criticism, although it had long since been abandoned by the GPs as too dangerous. This stagnation in the championship – no new bikes, no new riders, no new sponsors – didn't matter too much because the GPs were in the throes of their Bernie Ecclestone/Dorna/IRTA revolution and all the critical analysis was focused on the 500 class. But Superbike's easy ride with the fans and media was coming to an end – it had to shape up quick or go the way of F750.

RIGHT: *Carl Fogarty impressed everyone on his private Ducati.*

INSET: *Fogarty's debut World Superbike win came on home ground at Donington – Roche and Russell shared the victory lap.*

chapter six

1993
The big time

There were a lot of changes on the track for the sixth year of the World Superbike Championship, but by far the most important change happened off the track. The teams had been starting to worry about where the championship was going in terms of its promotion and sponsorship. Most worrying of all, TV coverage had been patchy, but Dentsu's three-year contract was now over and the Flammini Group took the brave step of guaranteeing coverage of every round. Up to now, a race only got on air if a local TV station decided to cover it and provide a so-called world feed for stations in other countries. This meant that there were gaps in the coverage, a major disadvantage if you're trying to sell coverage of the whole title race. Can you imagine not being able to watch a couple of rounds of the car F1 championship because, say, Hungarian TV didn't have the budget to cover the race? Flammini now took the decision to put in their own crews if they couldn't contract a local station to be host broadcaster. The championship could now guarantee consistent coverage and the improvement was instant and impressive.

Bravely, Flammini now pledged TV coverage of every WSB round

Of course these things don't happen overnight; they were the result of a lot of work over the preceding months and years, which helped to explain the seeming stagnation over the previous two seasons. British fans benefited from a last-minute deal with Sky TV to show the Superbikes after the UK-only satellite channel had lost the GPs to the pan-European station Eurosport. At the time it seemed like a piece of useful opportunism for all concerned, but by the end of the season Carl Fogarty was being hailed as Britain's first nationally known motorcycle racer since Barry Sheene.

Fogarty – 'Foggy' to every British biker – replaced Raymond Roche in the factory Ducati squad while Roche himself moved up to become a very laid-back team manager. The Italian factory restricted itself to supplying just two teams, Roche's official squad and the Grottini team, managed by another recently retired racer, Davide Tardozzi. They were the only recipients of the works 926cc motors; Ducati had learned last year that trying to keep half a dozen factory riders' bikes reliable was more than they could do.

Scott Russell's determination and the Muzzy Kawasaki's reliability were just enough to fight off Foggy and the Ducati.

Ducati's twins were fast but they were also fragile, and needed the regular replacement of such trifling components as the crankcases. In a token gesture to the Japanese teams, the minimum weight limit for twin-cylinder bikes was raised by 5kg to 145kg, reducing the differential to 20kg. Nobody noticed any difference.

Tardozzi kept Stephane Mertens and, in what was seen as a politically significant coup, signed up the Spaniard Juan Garriga, who had been in 500 GPs for three years after a sparkling career in the 250s. Here was a man coming to Superbike who was good enough to get on the rostrum in 500 GPs, so he would provide an interesting yardstick. It wasn't as strange a choice as it first seemed; Garriga wasn't just a two-stroke rider, but also had a good Ducati CV, having ridden NCR endurance racers and been one of the riders for the first 851 Ducati's debut at the Bol d'Or alongside Virginio Ferrari and Marco Lucchinelli.

Once again it looked as if the main opposition to the Red Bullets would come from Kawasaki. The old ad hoc arrangement of the Australian team running out

LEFT: *It was this close all year.*

BELOW: *There was a conspicuous lack of mutual congratulations on the slow-down laps and rostrums.*

of Kawasaki Germany's premises, where the riders lived in caravans, changed. The Muzzy squad was now the official factory team, owned by the mustachioed American but still managed at the tracks by the abrasive Aussie Peter Doyle, who'd run Phillis and Slight. Scott Russell replaced Rob Phillis as the team's number one rider, with Slight again playing the role of loyal number two, a part with which he would have more and more difficulty as the year wore on.

Honda still didn't have their RC30 replacement ready, but the Rumi team soldiered on with the American Tripp Nobles as rider. More significantly, Ducati decided not to launch their new bike until Honda did, so the only new bike on the grid was the YZF750 Yamaha, which would again be ridden by Pirovano and Merkel. Terry Rymer also rode a Yamaha in a private team with a Portuguese rider and the backing of that country's Pepsi importer.

All the behind-the-scenes progress was fine, but the championship had lost its top three riders from last year: Polen went back to the States to ride for Fast by Ferracci, Roche was now Ducati's team manager, and Phillis was also back on domestic duty. The infrastructure was getting better, but what would the show be like? There was no need to worry. Fans at the trackside and at home in front of their TVs were treated to the first year of an epic confrontation that would dominate Superbike for two seasons – Carl Fogarty and Ducati versus Scott Russell and Kawasaki – a script with plenty of sub-plots: the little Italian factory versus the might of Japanese industry, the taciturn Brit versus the flashy American, Lancashire versus Georgia, you name it.

Not that it looked that way at the start of the season. Foggy fell on the very first

The last privateer victory in World Superbike: Andi Meklau at home in Austria.

lap of the first race at Brands Hatch (the Irish round!), putting himself out of the second race as well, and destroying his wet-weather confidence for years. His team-mate Falappa belied his wildman reputation with two beautifully controlled wins in appalling conditions and promptly backed them up with a win in the dry at Hockenheim. The German round also saw Juan Garriga's only visit to the Superbike rostrum with a 2nd behind Russell in the second race, but he only lasted two more meetings before his obvious disenchantment with racing led to his replacement in the Grottini team by Mauro Lucchiari, a young Italian rider held in high regard by the factory.

First it was Russell refusing to shake Fogarty's hand ...

Fogarty didn't post a win until the third round in Spain, where he then made up for lost time with a double win and went on to dominate the middle of the season with doubles in Sweden, Indonesia and Holland. But to the increasingly exasperated Foggy it seemed as if every time he won, Russell was second. Russell was also exasperated by what he saw as the Ducati rider's machinery advantage, and even though he was racking up the points he was unhappy that he wasn't winning. As it became clear that the championship was between the two of them, a small amount of personal needle crept into the proceedings. First it was Russell refusing to shake Fogarty's hand on the rostrum, then it was Fogarty making disparaging gestures at the American, all grist to the tabloids' mill.

The Austrian round provided a couple of landmarks. On a rapidly drying track at Zeltweg, local man Andreas Meklau used his local knowledge to fit slick tyres

The last Yamaha victory in World Superbike for four years: Fabrizio Pirovano in Portugal.

Big crowds weren't confined to the UK. This is Hockenheim.

and romp home an easy winner, the last time a privateer would win a World Superbike race. Just to show that it wasn't a fluke, he also notched 3rd place in the second race. This was also the last appearance on a World Championship rostrum for Fred Merkel, who had split with the works Yamaha team. He brought a private Ducati home in 2nd place in the second race in conditions bad enough for the race to be shortened.

Fogarty only actually led the championship for the 3 hours between the two Japanese races at the end of August. He won the first race in front of two local Kawasaki riders with Russell back in 8th on a motorcycle that was plainly well down on power compared to the Japanese Kawasaki riders' bikes. A strange way to go about winning a World Championship. Harsh words were exchanged behind locked garage doors, and new motors were fitted to the Muzzy bikes. In the second race Fogarty and Russell duelled at the front until Carl crashed heavily while lapping a tail-ender; Scott then led home a Kawasaki clean-sweep of the first four places and retook the lead of the championship. Even Fogarty's now expected Assen double next time out didn't dislodge the American, who finished second both times.

So, with a slim 7-point lead, Russell went to Monza where the first race was wet. The two Muzzy Kawasaki riders led, and when Aaron Slight slid past his team-mate on the front straight everyone expected that he'd be signalled to let Russell through for those vital extra points. But it didn't happen, and when Foggy then fought back to beat Russell for 4th place in the second race, they went to Donington just 9 points apart instead of 12.

Several significant events took place at the British round, where a large crowd expected Fogarty to put the pressure on the American, who was rapidly assuming the status of folk devil for Carl's fans. When Russell committed the classic Donington Park mistake of trying too hard on cold tyres going down the fast and treacherous Craner Curves in qualifying, it looked as if the fans were going to get their wish. Such was the ferocity of the crash that Russell had to be carried up the steps of his motorhome when he got out of the medical centre. A journalist asked if he could get anything for him, and received the laconic reply 'Yeah, the race put back to Monday.'

On race day Russell put in one of the gutsiest performances the championship has ever seen, beating Fogarty in the first race, then drawing Fogarty into a crash – ironically on Craner Curves – early in the second race. All this on a motorcycle that the Muzzy crew had to alter significantly even to let Scott sit on it, so badly beaten up was he. Aaron Slight and Russell then fought for the lead until the Muzzy crew signalled Slight, who was leading, to let his team-mate through. The New Zealander was not amused and gesticulated angrily next time round.

It would have been an easier decision to accept if he'd had to drop back at Monza, but now that both riders knew that Fogarty was on the floor it was almost impossible. With those extra 3 points Russell went into the last two rounds with a lead of 32 points. Was it worth depriving Slight of what would have been only his third World Superbike win for 3 points? Kawasaki people said that it was very easy to see a scenario in which

Rob Muzzy and crew conspire on pit wall.

Fogarty might win the title by three points, so of course it was. Which didn't explain the lack of a signal at Monza.

So Donington turned into Scott Russell's first double win; it was now the American's championship to lose rather than Fogarty's to win.

What had been a triumphant season for the championship degenerated into near farce over the last two races – scheduled for the Estoril circuit in Portugal, and Mexico – and undid a lot of the good work that had gone before. The Portuguese track had been brought up to

Falappa's T-shirt says it all – he's really a big pussycat.

the required length by adding two new bends at the far side of the circuit. Unfortunately, the new section consisted of two bends so tight that they made the walking-pace Governor's Bridge hairpin on the Isle of Man TT look like Hockenheim's super-fast Ostcurve. The result was inevitable – dominoes on the first lap. And then there was the small matter of the lack of run-off on some corners, notably turn two. Theoretically the championship was still up for grabs, and when the starter held them on the line for an age before the first race, Scott Russell's clutch cooked itself and he pitted after a handful of laps. Unfortunately for Fogarty, he crashed before his pit crew could signal him the news. The removal of the two top men let Fabrizio Pirovano in for his only win of the season and what would be the Yamaha YZF750's only win until the end of 1997.

Fogarty duly won the second race from Russell, and duly made his feelings known with a series of explicit hand gestures aimed at his rival. Foggy's 11 wins made him by far the most successful rider of the year. Russell by contrast had only won five races, and that was the source of Foggy's frustration; he had trouble getting his head round the fact that although he had won more than twice as many races as his rival, he wasn't champion. 'I just can't believe Russell's luck,' was the mantra repeated to any journalist who enquired. Maybe the truth of the matter lies in another statistic: Fogarty crashed four times and Scott Russell just once, and that was when he was torpedoed by Giancarlo Falappa in Spain.

Russell meanwhile, who had backed up his wins with many more lower rostrum finishes than Fogarty, further infuriated the Englishman by being so laid-back that he was almost horizontal, and implying that you had to use your brains to be a champion.

They think there's a round left; there isn't. Russell, Fogarty and Pirovano on the rostrum for the second race in Portugal.

The championship should have gone down to the wire in Mexico, but a bizarre set of circumstances saw the race cancelled. The Circuito Hermano Rodrigues is part of a giant complex that hosts a diverse range of events as well as motorsports. The Superbike race was tangled up with preparations for a Michael Jackson concert, and there were typically convoluted Latin American political rivalries involved. The riders knew that they had a problem when stray dogs and footballs were seen on the track during qualifying, but the last straw was when Scott Russell, flat out on the long straight, saw a pick-up truck cross the track in front of him.

It would be easy to blame the Flammini Group for scheduling a race at a track that wasn't ready for World Championship racing, but there had twice been post-season internationals at the track as shake-down events. Indeed, the first of these events at the end of 1990 had been the first time that Doug Polen had sat on a Ducati. He had won both the non-championship races and set himself up for his first World Championship campaign. No, scheduling a race in Mexico was a perfectly valid and well-planned attempt to broaden the horizons of the championship. Unfortunately it backfired and left the championship and its organisers looking less than professional at the end of what was otherwise Superbike's most competitive and highest-profile year yet.

chapter seven

1994
Star wars

You know when a race series has really achieved global significance: Honda enters a factory team. Having made the RC30 for the first year of World Superbike, the planet's biggest motorcycle manufacturer finally launched its replacement, the RC45, for 1994 and sent a full works team with Castrol sponsorship to do battle for the title. Now when Honda enters – as their advertising slogan used to say – Honda wins, so the new set-up was the most lavish in the paddock. The factory's official team ran out of the Louth, Lincolnshire, workshops of Honda UK alongside the GP motocross team with Neil Tuxworth as manager, although it's a mistake to think that he had a massive amount of influence on the choice of riders. Japan recruited Doug Polen to lead their comeback – and why not? He was the most successful rider in the championship's history, and the men at Honda head office had seen his All-Japan TT F1 and F3 championship wins on unfancied Suzukis at close quarters, and had noted the fact that he had defeated Honda's supposedly superior machinery on the way. Polen, meanwhile, had filled his year off from World Superbike productively, winning the American Superbike Championship on a Ferracci Ducati.

The RC45 didn't look too different from the old RC30 – an aluminium-framed V4 with single-side swinging arm – but as is usual with Honda, every component was new and improved. The only obviously new feature was fuel injection, a major escalation of the technological war between the Japanese factories. As the Ducati 851/888 was the only other World Superbike contender to have electronic fuel injection, the natural assumption was that the RC45 would be not only competitive, but probably also the bike to beat. Polen's team-mate was Aaron Slight, happy to leave his long-time employers at Kawasaki but destined, so everyone thought, to another season as his team's second rider.

Ducati had held over their 888 replacement for a year in order to meet Honda's fire with fire. The result was the 916, a bike so beautiful that it instantly became an object of desire featured not only in the motorcycle press but also in car and style magazines all over the world. It looked very different from its

There was always a British fan with a flag for Carl at every track.

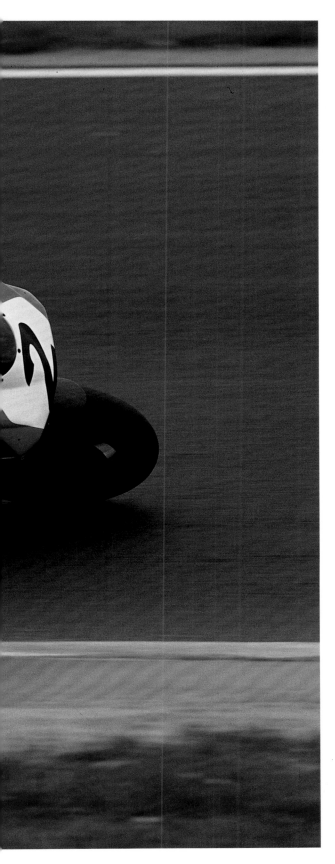

predecessors, but wasn't that different. The modifications were all aimed at making the bike more of a racer; any concessions to the comfort of customers who bought a Ducati 916 for road riding were forgotten. The engine had its stroke lengthened by 2mm, a vital step as Superbike regulations prohibit any alteration to a homologated engine's stroke, and it was canted forward in the frame to get more weight on the front wheel. This allowed the all-new chassis to feature a shorter wheelbase, variable geometry was built into the steering head, and a single-sided swinging arm was used. But it was the shark-nosed looks of the thing that set the pulse racing as only a machine conceived and produced by Italians can. The factory's only problem would be building enough of them to meet demand.

The minimum weight differential between the fours and twins had been shrunk by 5kg in 1993 by raising the twins' minimum limit to 145kg, still leaving a gap of 20kg. For 1994 the gap was reduced by a further 5kg, this time by reducing the fours' minimum weight to 160kg. Ducati's response was to overbore the 916 factory race bikes by 2mm for a capacity of 955cc, echoing the way they'd increased the capacity of the first 851 to 888cc, then to 919 and finally 926cc. As already mentioned, this was all within the letter of the law, which imposed a limit of 1,000cc on twins, but arguably not within the spirit of the rules. The only comfort for the opposition was that Ducati's hard-pressed race shop could only make and maintain a very limited number of 955cc racers. The factory's priority was the works team of Fogarty and Falappa,

It was the shark-nosed look of the 916 that set the pulse racing

Fogarty and the new Ducati 916 were winners right from the start.

Honda's new works team featured Superbike's most successful rider, Doug Polen (left) ...

now under the management of Virginio Ferrari, who brought with him a much more professional-looking set-up than Roche's down-home team, complete with giant transporters, hospitality unit, and all the other requirements of the modern paddock. Only Honda's encampment was bigger. Davide Tardozzi replaced Stephane Mertens with Fabrizio Pirovano, who'd finally given up on Yamaha. There was one other works 916 run by Moto Cinelli, Ducati's UK importer for competition bikes, for fans' favourite James Whitham.

Kawasaki stuck with Scott Russell as their number one and replaced Slight with Terry Rymer, happy to get back on a works bike after a frustrating year as a privateer. Belgarda Yamaha fielded an all-

Italian line-up of young chargers Massimo Meregalli and Mauro Lucchiari, the latter poached from Ducati, although the relationship would only last three races before Lucchiari returned to Ducati and the experienced Paolo Casoli replaced him.

One extra factory 955 Ducati would make an occasional appearance in the hands of Troy Corser. The 22-year-old Australian was already champion of his own country and would concentrate on winning the American Superbike title for the Fast by Ferracci team, but he still found time for three European races plus the Australian round. Corser was the first of a new phenomenon in Superbike, an up-and-coming racer using the series rather than GPs to hone his skills and

... and Aaron Slight (below), poached from Muzzy Kawasaki

It was the Fogarty versus Russell battle of 1993 all over again: here they lead Yasutomo Nagai at Sugo's hairpin.

raise his profile, even though the 500s might be his ultimate objective. He qualified on the front row in his first race at Donington and got on the rostrum as well. Clearly he would be a force to be reckoned with when he joined the World Superbikes full time in 1995.

Down among the privateers, it was immediately clear that the Ducati was still the bike to have, even in Corsa trim. Two rising stars, Jose Kuhn of France and Michael Paquay of Belgium, tried to make

their mark with RC45s and had dreadful seasons. Only Simon Crafar, one of those New Zealanders who races anything anywhere, could do anything with one. He took the Team Rumi RC45 to top privateer slot and 5th in the championship without the benefit of significant factory help, just beating Andreas Meklau's Ducati despite the fact that the Austrian made the rostrum twice and Crafar could finish no higher than 5th all year.

Much of the season was confused by events that followed fuel tests from the first round at Donington Park. Fogarty, Russell and Slight left the UK neck-and-neck with 35, 34 and 33 points respec-

tively, and went to Hockenheim where Russell took control after Foggy broke his wrist in qualifying and Slight crashed in the second race. That incident was explained away as pilot error, but was in fact that rarest of things, a factory Honda engine blowing up. Rule one of working for Honda is that the company's products do not break, so Aaron had to take the blame. Polen appeared to have come to terms with the RC45 with a 3rd in the second race, and Rymer got on the rostrum in the first race despite an elbow full of stitches. It was to be Rymer's last top-three finish in World Superbikes, while Polen would only get on the rostrum

twice more in the season (two 3rds in Austria) as he struggled to adjust to the new Honda and the change to Michelin tyres after spending most of his career on Dunlops.

Then the FIM announced that the fuel test from Donington showed that Aaron Slight and Andi Meklau's fuel samples had tested over the allowed limit of dienes. Both used Elf racing fuel and the French company immediately said that it was their mistake, not cheating by the teams. However, the riders had all their points from the Donington meeting docked. Honda were not amused; Neil Tuxworth had to stop some very angry

This is Assen. Foggy fans were everywhere.

Japanese team members from packing up and going home, while head office engaged some very expensive lawyers. The test results only came through after the third round at Misano, by which time the top three were well spread out with Russell on 110 points, Slight second on 79 and the still not fully fit Foggy third on 46.

But after the next round in Spain, when Slight had all of his Donington points for two 2nd places taken away, Scott Russell had 112 points, Foggy was second with 88, and Slight suddenly still had only 79. The telescoping together was exaggerated by Foggy taking a double win and Russell amazingly crashing twice, the start of a temporary slump in

the American's form that continued to the next round in Austria, where Foggy scored another double and went back to the top of the championship. Russell also crashed heavily twice in testing between the Spanish and Austrian rounds, once in Europe and once in Japan, while team-mate Rymer was growing disenchanted with the penny-pinching attitude of the Muzzy team. Would you believe they bought wheels second-hand – from the works Kawasaki endurance team?

Honda had the lawyers wound up by now and successfully appealed to the FIM's International Disciplinary Court on a variety of technicalities, not least that Slight was being punished for using illegal fuel in two races despite having only been tested after one. Slight had all his 34 points returned and went back on top of the championship, where he stayed up to round nine at Mugello. However, between rounds eight and nine a counter-appeal by Virginio Ferrari on behalf of Ducati and, bizarrely, Oriol Bulto on behalf of the FIM's own Technical Commission, finally ended the affair and saw what most people thought was justice done. Slight had his 17 points for 2nd place in the race after which he had been tested taken away again, but was allowed to keep his points from the other race. The result was that Fogarty left round eight at Assen 2nd in the championship, and arrived for round nine at Mugello leading.

The legal wrangling all but overshadowed a near tragedy at Albacete. In untimed practice, Giancarlo Falappa highsided the factory Ducati out of a slow corner and was rushed to hospital with severe head injuries. The prognosis was not good; local doctors warned us to expect the worst, but he was flown back to Italy where he teetered on the brink before making a miraculous recovery. Giancarlo never raced a motorcycle again, but he is alive and in good health. Some people who saw him a year or so after the accident were upset by his appearance – he was limping and had lost a lot of weight. Part of the problem was that non-life-threatening injuries had been ignored in the battle to save his life, and he needed a series of operations to get back unrestricted movement. We lost a great racer, the first true star to emerge solely in Superbike, but we still have that charming teddy-bear of a man, and for that we should be grateful. His factory ride was taken over by Mauro Lucchiari.

With both the Honda and Ducati teams struggling to get their new bikes to handle – Ducati with rear suspension problems, Honda with chronic understeer and a front end that wouldn't track over bumps – Kawasaki should have been able to capitalise, and at the start of the season it looked as if they would. Russell

led the championship even after his double-DNF in Austria, but didn't win again until Japan. Unfortunately, the bike the factory gave him for Sugo was repossessed after race day and he had to soldier on with his Muzzy bike, which was starting to suffer from lack of development as the year wore on and the opposition got their act together. Just when Russell looked like he was wresting the initiative back from Fogarty and Slight, he suffered a mechanical failure in the second race at Mugello as he was looking set for a double win. What looked like a championship lead turned to 3rd place as Foggy won.

British fans flocked to Donington for the rearranged European round only to see Russell again win twice in the wet as Carl struggled with a bad tyre choice in the first race and too many Ducatis in front of him in the second. Those British fans now bit their nails for four weeks (that calendar again) until the final round in Australia, where either Slight, Russell or Fogarty would win the title.

When the regulars got to Phillip Island they found that a new star had

Aaron Slight bears the scars of a close encounter with his own front disc brake.

*A Honda mechanic removes a drum of the offend-
ing Elf race fuel after the results of the Donington
tests became known.*

joined them. A chunky teenaged ex-
motocross champion called Anthony
Gobert had won the Australian
Superbike Championship for Honda and
would obviously be a hot property, but
Rob Muzzy got there first, putting him on
Terry Rymer's bike. Amazingly, young
Gobert promptly put the Kawasaki on
pole – and he'd never even sat on a
ZXR750 before. He did the decent thing
in the first race, letting his team-mate
Scott Russell through on the line for 2nd
place behind a charging Carl Fogarty,
then won the second race. The
Englishman could afford to take it easy in
race two and shadowed Russell until the
American's rear Dunlop disintegrated
and he waved Fogarty through to 2nd
place and his first World Superbike title.
British fans, starved of success in a championship that mattered to the world at
large, elevated Foggy to the status of
demigod. His stunning wild-card rides in
the 1992 and '93 British GPs on a private

*Russell blasts off the line for the final showdown
at Phillip Island. Corser is nearest the camera
with newboy Gobert and Fogarty (obscured) in the
background.*

Gobert's happy to win his first World Superbike race, Fogarty's happy to be World Champ, Corser's just happy.

Yamaha, then the factory Cagiva, convinced his fans that Superbike was just as good as the GPs. Attendances at the British GP went into a steep decline, while the Superbikes would get two UK races, both of which would pull in more punters than the GP. For the first time since the days of Barry Sheene, Britain had a bike racer who was recognised outside the narrow confines of the specialist press.

The UK was the most extreme example of the new popularity of the championship, but for the first time its final acts were played out on the world stage, and with just the right amount of personal acrimony between the top contenders, something that had been eliminated from GPs by the dead hand of major

sponsors. The barely disguised mutual dislike of Fogarty and Russell from 1993 matured into a more healthy respect for each other; most of the tabloid-delighting quotes they came out with this season were deliberately contrived to keep interest in the championship at boiling point. In truth, it didn't need much help; an Englishman, an American and a New Zealander on three different makes of bike swapped the points lead all season and went to the last race all mathematically capable of winning the title. The quality of the racing (and the lap times) showed that a top Superbike rider would be competitive in the GPs given the right machinery.

The big question over the close season was what would Honda do? The biggest motorcycle company in the world does not take kindly to losing – and their new flagship had failed to win a race in its debut season.

chapter eight

1995 Outlook Foggy

This was supposed to be the most competitive Superbike season ever, with more factory bikes and more riders capable of winning than ever before. The Ducati was still the best all-round bike, but the opposition was catching up. Honda would surely be contenders after a winter's intensive development, Yamaha was fielding a full factory team for the first time, and there were two new high-profile Ducati teams plus a semi-works Kawasaki squad. But it wasn't just the machinery, it was the quality of new riders that really impressed. Both Anthony Gobert and Troy Corser came to World Superbike for full seasons, Gobert continuing the relationship with Muzzy Kawasaki from the final race of last season, Corser on a factory Ducati in Austrian businessman Alfred Inzinger's new Promotor team with Andreas Meklau as his team-mate. It was a very high-profile operation with Davide Tardozzi as manager and probably the best hospitality unit in the paddock, all funded by Inzinger's Power Horse energy drink company.

A third young gun arrived from America to ride one of the factory Yamahas, Colin Edwards II. This 21-year-

The Foggy/Ducati/Michelin combination was devastating in 1995.

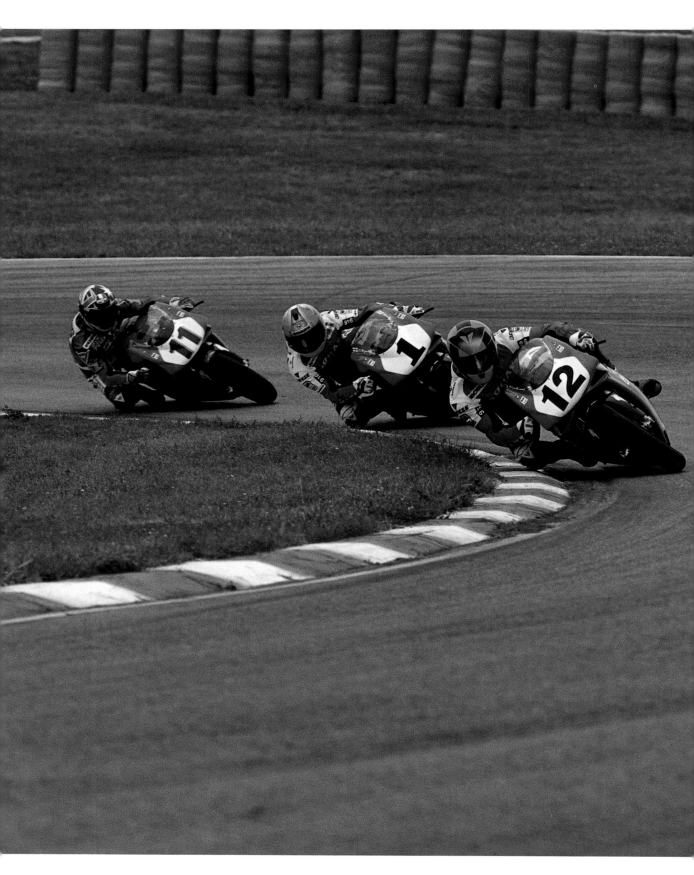

old Texan had been a demon 250cc racer before switching to the American Superbike Championship in 1994, and was now being sent out on the World Championship trail. Unusually, his contract was with Yamaha in Japan, not the Belgarda team itself. Rumour had it that he was on a long-term contract that would see him through Superbike and on to a 500 GP bike in three years. After the flood of talent from the USA that started with Kenny Roberts in the late '70s and brought us Freddie Spencer, Wayne Rainey, Eddie Lawson, Kevin Schwantz and Randy Mamola in GPs, and Merkel and Russell in Superbikes, the well **Edwards was seen as the only US rider worth having** appeared to have run dry. Apart from converted dirt-track ace Mike Hale, who was contracted to Honda, Edwards was seen by the paymasters in Japan as the only American youngster worth having, and Yamaha signed him up long term.

Edwards's team-mate came direct from head office: Yasutomo Nagai. Very much a Yamaha man throughout his career and now 29 years old, Nagai had been sufficiently highly thought of to partner Eddie Lawson in the Suzuka 8 Hour race and to be sent to Europe for the first time at the end of 1994 to help Yamaha win their first Bol d'Or with the Sarron brothers. His reward for that high-profile win and his work developing the YZF750 was the chance to go for a world title. All that the Superbike paddock knew of him was that he fitted the old stereotype of the win-or-crash kamikaze when they'd seen him at Sugo the year before. He set pole and got on the rostrum in the first race, then went from 2nd to 5th on the last corner of the

This is Misano, Lucchiari leads Fogarty and Corser.

second race attempting the impossible for a win. His win in the Bol, a 24-hour race, contradicted that image, and so would his riding when he got to Europe full time.

The Yamaha team still ran out of Belgarda's Italian workshops, but with Christian Sarron as team co-ordinator and ex-GP mechanics Davide Brivio and Fiorenzo Fanalli looking after the bikes. It was an impressive set-up, and the CVs of the men in charge made excellent reading. Fanalli had worked with Lawson at Yamaha and had then been chief mechanic for Cagiva's GP team, while Brivio was similarly experienced with top Yamaha teams.

Virginio Ferrari kept Lucchiari as Foggy's team-mate and recruited ex-racer turned suspension guru Anders Andersson from Ohlins to work full time for the Ducati team. As well as the Promotor squad, there was another significant Ducati outfit in the shape of the

Troy Corser's challenge was blunted by frequent machinery problems.

Gattolone team and their rider Pier-Francesco Chili, a 250 and 500 GP winner as well as an ex-European 125 champion. Ostensibly this was not a works team, but by the middle of the season he was admitting to getting some help from Bologna – again the phenomenon surfaced of a private 916 (or rather 955 Corsa) being quicker than the works bike. Ferrari's and Inzinger's teams received sealed engines from the factory, whereas the Gattolone team's tuner could work on their motors. Chili quickly became a favourite with the fans thanks to his habit of making a bad start then charging through the pack. When he got to the front he usually either crashed or won. He did both at Monza where the victory of an Italian rider on an Italian bike at an Italian race produced one of the more emotional celebrations seen at a Superbike round.

The other new privateer outfit was the British Revé Kawasaki team. This was set up by businessman Ben Atkins for his friend John Reynolds, with David Jefferies as second rider and machinery

equal to that of long-time Superbike contender Piergiorgio Bontempi, who rode for the Italian importer. World Championship motorcycle racing also returned to the USA with the first American World Superbike round for four years; in the absence of an American GP it was the most significant road-racing event of the year in North America.

On the technical front, carbon-fibre disc brakes were banned as a gesture to reducing costs (replacing Ducati 916 crankcases at regular intervals cost a damn sight more) and the minimum weight limit for both twins and fours was raised by 2kg to compensate. None of the bikes altered significantly, but there was a major hiatus in tyre supply. A massive earthquake devastated the industrial city of Kobe where Dunlop made their race tyres; the damage was comprehensive and would mean that the Yamaha and Kawasaki factory teams would suffer severe problems for the first half of the season. On the political front, the increasingly fractious relationship between the Flammini Group and the Grands Prix establishment resulted in a slanging match at the start of the season when it was announced that a 600cc four-stroke championship called Thunderbikes would run as a support class at GPs with a view to becoming a full World Championship. As Flammini was running the Open Supersport Championship alongside Superbikes, the Italians regarded this as an intrusion on their territory. The fact that Flammini had run the 250cc European Championship at Superbike meetings, and the movers and shakers in GPs had previously regarded anything with a four-stroke motor as an oil-spewing device of the devil, was conveniently forgotten. The inevitable compromise was that Thunderbikes excluded the new 748cc Ducati while Open Supersport allowed them. In the event, Thunderbikes would only last one year, while Flammini would

Aussie parentage but totally Texan: Yamaha's Colin Edwards.

go on to develop the Supersport class as a natural accompaniment to Superbikes.

There was yet another shock before the start of the season: Honda and Doug Polen parted company. The announcement was made only a week before the first race, leaving the Castrol Honda team no time to recruit a second rider. Polen had been half-way through a two-year contract and the strange timing of the split was thought to be down to some high-level arguments as to who signed the cheque that paid Doug off. He was always a very astute businessman and would not have taken kindly to the brush-off, but this being Honda the press release said that the parting was amicable and any investigation was met with a discreet silence.

The result was the mighty Honda works team fielding just one bike and giving Polen's to Simon Crafar, who ran it in his Rumi team's colours. Aaron Slight had to carry the whole burden of development and try to make the still recalcitrant RC45 competitive on his own. Given the situation in which he found himself, his achievements this season were remarkable. They included the RC45's first pole position at Monza for round four, then its first win in round five in Alabacete, where Aaron craftily conserved his tyres and fought off a late challenge from Fogarty. He also demonstrated that the Honda was probably the quickest bike on the track, but putting the power on the tarmac, especially on bumpy tracks like Misano and Laguna Seca, was still a major problem. Slight had a nightmare at Misano where he could only manage 16th and 13th places.

Honda's problems were nothing next to Muzzy Kawasaki's. Their new bikes managed to be around a second a lap slower than last year's, and their best finish in the first two rounds was Gobert's 6th at Misano. Worryingly, Anthony was crashing regularly in qualifying as he struggled with the unfamiliar task of setting up a Superbike. Russell's form was strangely subdued, and when he arrived at Donington, limping as a result of what he said was a mountain-bike accident, things looked even worse. Unbelievably, they deteriorated even further on race day, and on his best circuit too. In the first race he led early on but ended up 6th, then retired ignominiously in the second when a hastily fitted carburettor component worked loose. Only after the race did the truth emerge. Russell was limping as a result of broken toes sustained while testing the 500cc GP Suzuki

Dramatis personae: on the left Fogarty, Slight, Reynolds and Meklau; on the right Russell, Corser, Lucchiari and Bontempi.

at Brno in the Czech Republic. Kevin Schwantz's decision to retire mid-season had thrown both GP and Superbike paddocks into a frenzy of speculation. Every top Superbike man was linked at one time or another with the ride, but it was Russell who got the job. Gobert and Corser were the other men in the frame.

The disarray of the non-Ducati teams led to a unique event, a rule change in mid-season. Ducatis won every race at the first three rounds and, just after Scott Russell's defection to the Grands Prix became common knowledge, the FIM announced another revision of the minimum weight limits. That for the twins was revised upwards by 8kg and downwards for the 750cc fours by 2kg to reduce the difference to just 5kg. According to Carl Fogarty's chief mechanic and friend, Anthony 'Slick' Bass, even the factory 916s weren't on the minimum weight limit, but they still had to have 7 or 8 kilos of lead bolted on to meet the new limit. In practice, the new limits made very little difference to Ducati's domination; essentially this was a political move, a gesture to those who thought that a championship run by an Italian company and dominated by Italian motorbikes might be in danger of losing the sympathy and support of the Japanese factories. Carl Fogarty, blunt as ever, wasn't impressed, and voiced the opinion that people were forgetting that Ducati had the best riders – meaning himself, Frankie Chili and Troy Corser.

Back on the racetrack, Corser was suffering from machinery problems that would effectively prevent him from making a challenge for the title. Two crashes at Monza didn't help either. Promotor team manager Davide Tardozzi knew that once Troy got his debut win, more would follow quickly. He was right. Corser's first World Superbike win came in the second

James Whitham added to the fun both on and off the track.

Meklau hits the deck, Polen and Edwards take to the grass.

race in Austria, his team's home round, and he added three more victories and four pole positions in the season. His countryman Gobert had to wait longer, until Laguna Seca, for his first win of the year, but he again won the final race of the year at home in Phillip Island.

Laguna Seca also saw the return to World Championship competition of Freddie Spencer, who got a 7th place in the first race, but the revelation of the meeting was Mike Hale, who scored a 3rd and 4th on a Honda America RC45, as did his better-known team-mate Miguel DuHamel. Hale's performance was impressive enough to get him a Promotor Ducati for the last two meetings as a try-out for a full-time ride in 1996. The American round was also the only really bad meeting Fogarty had all year; he could not get to grips with the circuit and only finished 5th and 7th, but even that wasn't enough to deprive him

of the championship lead that he'd held since the opening day of the season.

The next venue was Brands Hatch for the European round, giving the UK two championship rounds, a privilege normally reserved for Italy and 'San Marino'. Despite all Fogarty's successes, he had never won a race at the Kent circuit at any level of competition, and this extra home round put pressure on him, coming as it did right after the setback of Laguna Seca. Foggy fever now had the UK firmly in its grip, and 45,000 fans turned up at Brands, the largest ever crowd for a World Superbike race. They were rewarded with a weekend of total domination – pole and two wins in an atmosphere that any British fan too young to remember the heyday of Barry Sheene had never experienced.

Home fans were further cheered by what they thought was a brace of 4th places from John Reynolds, but a protest

Gobert made a big impression in his first full-time season.

converted his second race result to 3rd when Yasutomo Nagai was deemed to have made a pass under a yellow flag and was penalised by 1 second. Reynolds thus achieved the dubious distinction of finishing in the top three at his home race but not getting to stand on the rostrum. Yamaha were not amused – they thought that it was a home-town decision and said Nagai would get his revenge at Sugo. He nearly did, for Fogarty, who could have won the title at the Japanese round, crashed out of the first race in what was almost a carbon-copy of his 1994 high-side. Nagai tried an impossible move at the last corner of the first race and ended up 3rd. In the second race he blocked Fogarty more than once on the first lap before the Englishman forced his way past and, visibly annoyed, pulled away for a remarkable win given the cracked bones in his wrist and ankle.

Fogarty had two weeks to recover

Bontempi, Reynolds, Edwards, Corser and Nagai in typically close company.

before he went to Assen, where he was now a racing certainty to take the title thanks to an astonishing lead of 128 points over Corser and 154 over Slight. It was like a third British round, there were so many Foggy fans in the crowd and so many Union Jacks on display. He duly retained his title by winning the first race from surprise package Simon Crafar. The extent of his lingering Sugo injuries were demonstrated on the slowdown lap when he asked a fan to tie a flag around his neck as his wrist wasn't strong enough to support a makeshift flagpole. Entertainingly, the fan misheard and leapt on the back of the Ducati for the pillion ride of a lifetime. Fogarty duly extended his unbeaten Assen run in the second race, with John Reynolds actually getting to stand on the rostrum in 3rd place.

Tragically, the celebrations were overshadowed by a second-race crash that would lead to the death of Yasutomo Nagai. Superbike's first fatality was the result of an innocuous crash on oil left by a blown engine. Any racer would expect

to walk away from such a crash several times a season, but as Yasu was about to get to his feet after a gentle slide on to Assen's grass his bike dug in, flipped in the air and came down on him. He suffered massive head and chest injuries. His breathing was maintained artificially until his parents and girlfriend could get to Holland from Japan, when the decision was taken to switch off his life-support machine. It was a reminder of just how dangerous motorcycle racing can be, even on one of the safest circuits in the world. Yamaha pulled their team out of the rest of the season as a mark of respect, although there was one other poignant gesture when Yamaha's 125 GP rider Yoshiaki Katoh wore Nagai's spider's web crash helmet design for the rest

Yasutomo Nagai became the first fatality in World Superbike at Assen, one of the championship's safest circuits. It was a tragic reminder that despite all the advances of recent years this is a very dangerous sport.

of the season.

The remaining two rounds were about Slight's and Corser's battle for 2nd place, which was won by the Australian who also emphasised his class by becoming the only man to qualify on the front row of the grid for every race of the year. Off track, the annual game of musical saddles was more spirited than usual. Fogarty, having turned what was supposed to be the closest Superbike season ever into a cakewalk, decided that he needed a new challenge. So he signed to ride for Honda in 1996.

chapter nine

1996
The Troy boy

Superbike's increasing significance was underlined by the arrival of a works Suzuki team for 1996, making a full set of the big four Japanese manufacturers plus Ducati. Even more significantly, one of the most talented riders of recent years – an

Team manager Davide Tardozzi was a vital element of Troy Corser's campaign.

ex-GP World Champion no less – arrived. John Kocinski had taken a year off racing in 1995 when it became obvious that no 500 GP team, or more likely their sponsors, was willing to risk taking on the troubled genius. How could a man who had won the 250 title and four 500cc GPs on two different makes of bike not be a hot property? His reputation said he caused teams to implode and was difficult if not impossible to deal with. There were also rumours of strange behaviour, a cleanliness fetish and other personal problems. None of which alters the fact that he is a genius of a racer. Kocinski had very important fans in the shape of Maurizio Flammini and the Castiglioni brothers, bosses of the Cagiva Group which owned Ducati, so his path to the works Ducati team as Fogarty's replacement was a smooth one. His team-mate was Fogarty's friend and fellow-Lancastrian Neil Hodgson who was signed first on the strength of his impressive performances as a 500 GP privateer. He first realised who his team-mate would be when he saw John in the restaurant across the road from Ducati's headquarters one lunchtime.

Still, the 22-year-old managed to give every impression of enjoying his new status as a works rider, and would engagingly confide how he couldn't believe he was being chauffeured to circuits in the Cagiva

company helicopter: 'Me, just a lad from Burnley. And they're paying me well!' He was also loyal to his team-mate in public, although in private he would wonder why the American would 'let himself down with some of the things he says.' Kocinski said all the right things in public, professing himself happy to be in Superbikes and ready to enjoy his racing again. It wouldn't last.

Suzuki's first factory team in Superbike was run by the English Harris Performance operation, with Lester Harris as manager and John Reynolds and Australian Superbike Champion Kirk McCarthy as riders. The new GSX-R750 turned out to have power and good top-end speed but was afflicted by a strange high-speed instability that took most of the season to iron out. Along the way both riders, the even-tempered Englishman and the tough little Aussie, became very disenchanted.

He was smooth, he was stylish, Corser was the class act of '96.

Reynolds still won't talk about the year, while McCarthy now lays sarcastically heavy emphasis on the Great in Great Britain when the Suzuki team's home country comes up in conversation. The other bikes stayed much the same although the minimum weights for fours and twins were now equalised at 162kg which meant the Ducatis had to add 7kg. The Thunderbike series run at GPs didn't manage a second season, so Flammini reacted by running a Supersport round outside Europe for the first time as part of the gradual move towards the objective of a second World Championship series.

The Promotor team again fielded Troy Corser, most pundits' pre-season tip for the title, alongside American Mike Hale who'd impressed at Laguna last year, then

LEFT: *The champ had a spectacular line in celebration wheelies.*

backed that up with impressive guest rides in the last two rounds. Frankie Chili again had what was alleged to be a private bike but he obviously had the key to the factory's back door.

Over at Honda Fogarty had to come to terms with the RC45, a bike that was still all but impossible to set-up for bumpy tracks, a task complicated by wet winter testing and the fact that the first round was at Misano where the Castrol Honda team had had a nightmare in 1995. Foggy promptly made it even more difficult by crashing heavily in qualifying although he scored useful points in both races. Much attention was focused on how the relationship with his team-mate Aaron Slight would develop. Fogarty had not been

RIGHT: *John Kocinski won first time out on the works Ducati.*

BELOW: *By mid-season Kocinksi wasn't talking to team manager Virginio Ferrari. Engine man Ivo Bertoni and mechanic Mike Watt consult in Sugo.*

Fogarty stalks Corser and Chili at Monza.

charitable about Slight in the past, he always seemed to need one competitor to focus his efforts on, but they did a good job of hiding whatever mutual dislike was left.

Fogarty's early season was dire. He had the worst weekend of his career at Donington where he simply couldn't get the bike to work and felt he let his home fans down badly. Then his friend and mechanic Anthony 'Slick' Bass was sacked from the Honda team on the Monday after racing. Surely things couldn't get worse? They did.

His team-mate Aaron Slight won the first race at Hockenheim with Carl a distant fifth. New mechanic Nick Goodison and Carl decided on a radical move, jacking the back end of the bike up to throw more weight onto the front wheel. It

Enigmatic? Difficult? Contradictory? Probably. A brilliant rider? Definitely.

worked and Carl won his first race on an RC45. It was also the first time the bike had won both races at a round. Carl's spectacular double at Assen was the first time one rider won both races on an RC45. It was also the point at which Carl announced he was going back to Ducati in 1997. Carl reckoned he had proved his point, that he could win on a four-cylinder bike, and obviously wasn't finding the British-based Honda team as homely as he thought he would.

Aaron Slight made a conscious attempt to change his image as the nice guy – and we all know that nice guys come second – by dyeing his hair different colours for every round, and when he ran out of colour options he went in for outrageous Mohicans and a variety of sculptured goatee beards. He was still a nice guy, and he still racked up the points with a hatful of

podium placings but he still only won once.

The Honda was obviously an improved bike compared to the previous year but still had major problems on bumpy tracks. You wouldn't have known it at Sugo, though. The local Honda men gave the regulars the same sort of lesson they used to get in Australia in the early days of the Championship. Yet another talented youngster, Yuichi Takeda, won the first race and Takuma Aoki romped away with the second race and into the Repsol Honda Grand Prix team. It obviously was possible to get the RC45 to both go fast and handle on tight tracks.

Yamaha and Kawasaki were again reduced to the role of bit-part players. Muzzy Kawasaki backed up the precocious Anthony Gobert with Simon Crafar, at last getting the works bike his talent and dedication deserved but the bike was still obviously not on a par with the opposition. The season started with Gobert giving an astonishing display of machine control as he slid his way around Misano to beat John Kocinksi in race two, only to have the victory taken away for a technical infringement. A carburettor part had been modified, which is illegal. The team said it was part of the inlet tract not the carb and the modification was therefore legitimate but the FIM didn't agree. Gobert didn't win again until Laguna Seca when an electrical fault made Kocinski's Ducati run rich and run out of fuel on the last lap. After he broke his collarbone in qualifying for Indonesia in August he didn't appear again until the final round in Australia at the end of October, prompting dissatisfied mutterings from his team and fuelling rumours

Clearly it was possible to get the RC45 to excel on tight tracks

Chili celebrates his win at Monza.

123

Kocinksi tries in vain to bumpstart his Ducati after it ran out of petrol on the last lap of race 2 at Laguna.

of a move to 500 GPs which would be proved correct.

Yamaha draughted in Wataru Yoshikawa alongside Colin Edwards to replace the late, lamented Nagai and slimmed the team's structure down. Christian

Neil Hodgson scored his debut rostrum at Laguna Seca, and was much relieved.

Sarron was no longer in charge, leaving Davide Brivio to front the team. Along with Dunlop tyres being back to normal operating level, this helped the team to threaten the top men everywhere, score a lot of points – Yoshikawa even set a new lap record at Laguna Seca – but never quite manage to win. Edwards was as personable as ever and smiled for the cameras but in private he was getting very frustrated with seconds and thirds.

Over at Ducati Virginio Ferrari was getting more than frustrated with his star rider's behaviour, and by Sugo he and Kocinksi weren't communicating at all but were complaining about each other to anyone who'd listen.

Thankfully for Ducati, the Promotor team were in better shape and Troy Corser was riding superbly. Not that you could always tell from his smooth, unhurried almost classical style. When he

Suzuki's first season was dogged by a high-speed stability problem, John Reynolds did not have a good year.

was a youngster his dad had worried about it, saying he looked like he was out for a Sunday ride not a race. His mum pointed out that as he was winning it didn't matter, did it? You don't argue with Carol Corser, so Troy's style stayed unchanged – you need a stopwatch to see if he's really trying.

At Donington Park he really was trying, his pole-position time was under the absolute lap record set by Kevin Schwantz on a 500 Suzuki – a landmark achievement for a bike based on the 916 you can buy in the shops. It was one of Troy's good weekends when everything worked for him and he set pole, won both races and set the fastest laps. He did it at Donington and he also doubled at the Czech Republic and Spain. It might have been more but for a worrying recurrence of the engine problems that had dogged him the previous season at three consecutive races: Brands, Sentul and

Sugo. As Kocinski's bike was conspicuously reliable, Alfred Inzinger, Corser's team owner, started to believe in conspiracy theories.

Troy did have two bits of luck, though. He crashed twice at Hockenheim, both times at the fast and fearsome Ostkurve and both times he walked away.

All of which meant that Corser never pulled away at the top of the championship until the last couple of rounds. In Albacete everyone except Troy suffered from tyre problems while the Australian stormed away to a convincing double and took a 26-point lead to the last round at home in Australia.

Four men went to Phillip Island with a mathematical chance of the title – Corser, Slight, Fogarty and Kocinski – although it

Fogarty took the Honda's first double win at Assen. Here he leads Chili on the run from the chicane to the flag.

would have taken an act of God for anyone except Troy to win. The title was settled in the first race, the act of God happened in the second, too late for the others. Aaron Slight didn't care about the sums and lived up to his haircut by charging after Corser and the returning Gobert, who'd dyed his own unruly mop of hair red for the occasion. Aaron's hope was alive until lap 13 when he lost the front end and slid out at the splendidly named Siberia corner. To the joy of the home crowd Corser cruised round to third place and the title. At the start of the second race the flock of seagulls that inhabit Phillip Island failed to get out of the way on the first corner and Corser, who'd made the holeshot, had his fairing smashed and his clutch lever broken. The remains splattered all over Colin

Edwards who continued to a blood and feather smeared third. Troy pitted for repairs then rejoined to pull wheelies for the fans until the flag went out and he treated them to enormous standing wheelies. Gobert celebrated his first double win by taking his clothes off on the rostrum.

At 24 years old Troy was Superbike's youngest World Champion and the first Australian to take the crown. As befits one of the young lions, he looked on the Superbike title as another step on the career ladder towards his objective of a 500 GP title. The plan was that the whole Promotor team would move into the GPs with works Yamahas and Luca Cadalora as lead rider alongside Troy. It was also an open secret that Anthony Gobert would go to GPs in 1997. It was to the World Superbike Championship that GP team managers looked first when they needed a new rider. On the one hand this proved the status of Superbikes and the worth of

Troy Corser and ecologically unsatisfactory mascot.

the title, but on the other it meant that good young riders were likely to move on. Success as ever was a double-edged sword. There were obviously going to be a lot of changes in the Superbike paddock in 1997. What no-one knew at the end of 1996 was that the GPs would give back just as much as they got and that the riders who left Superbike were going to suffer very mixed fortunes. There were already rumours about the financial status of Alfred Inzinger's Power Horse company which would drastically affect Troy Corser's competitiveness in GPs and eventually lead to his return to the World Superbike Championship.

Foggy wasn't always comfortable on the Honda …

chapter ten

1997
Happiness is a warm Honda

Troy Corser and Anthony Gobert left for the supposedly greener fields of the 500 Grands Prix, and in exchange Superbike got Scott Russell back. It is a mystery quite why the Lucky Strike Suzuki GP team wanted to get rid of the rider who had kept their team credible in the

John Kocinksi and the Honda evolved into the best combination on the track.

absence of their chosen number one and had got an increasingly uncompetitive bike on the rostrum twice in his first full year. It resulted in a man reckoned to be a potential GP winner being welcomed back to Superbike, not just by his new Yamaha team but by the fans. Russell had always had their respect, now they actually liked him too. The American is a complex man who has coped with a great deal of pain in

his personal life, of which being estranged from the mother of his daughter is only the latest example. He now comes across as a more sympathetic person whose brave and undervalued performances in 500 GPs proved to anyone who ever doubted it that a good Superbike rider could also be a good 500 rider.

If Russell was the good American, John Kocinski swiftly became the baddie in the black hat. He couldn't get away from Ducati quickly enough and finally got his wish, a Honda ride. Fogarty happily returned to the laid-back family atmosphere of the Ducati team: no more two hour debriefing meetings after qualifying to decide on suspension settings.

If Kawasaki had leapt forward, Suzuki was the reverse

There were big changes at Suzuki and Kawasaki. Both John Reynolds and Kirk McCarthy went back to their own domestic championships with sighs of relief to be replaced at Suzuki by James Whitham and Mike Hale. Since Whitham left the Championship he'd been diagnosed with, and cured of, cancer of the lymphatic system and made a successful comeback in the British Championship. As cheerful as ever, he was now even more philosophical about racing. 'I'm looking forward to going back to hospital with something nice and simple – like a broken leg.'

Kawasaki parted company with Rob Muzzy's organisation and replaced it with the German set-up headed by Harald Eckl who had been running a 125cc GP team with Marlboro sponsorship. The approach came from Kawasaki Germany, but Eckl took his time to make his mind up. He had no experience of four-strokes having been a 250 GP rider himself, but he saw the opportunity as a good one for himself and his staff. Simon Crafar kept his ride

Foggy shadows Kocinski, the story of the year.

Wet wet wet. Aaron Slight leads James Whitham and Fogarty at Misano.

and Japan sent over the relatively unknown Akira Yanagawa. He'd been the fastest Kawasaki qualifier at Sugo in 1996 but had never been a Japanese Championship contender so his CV didn't prepare anyone for the impact he would make. The pace of the green bikes was just as surprising. The team had very few new parts at pre-season testing but when it came to the first race the factory had magicked up an astonishing amount of new power.

All the other factory-supported riders kept their seats: Chili with his semi-detached Gattolone Ducati team, Slight at Honda, Edwards at Yamaha and Hodgson at Ducati. On the technical front, the most significant move was Honda quietly homologating a new fuel-injection system with two injectors per cylinder which added mid-range flexibility to the outright top speed the RC45 already had.

The new season opened where the old one had finished, on the glorious curves of Australia's Phillip Island circuit, and revealed several new truths that would set the pattern for the season. The most striking new aspect of the grid was that the Kawasakis had found not just extra speed but a new star in Akira Yanagawa. The Japanese rider started the weekend as a nervous newcomer but by the end of qualifying his grin was so wide that, to quote the editor of *Australian MotorCycle News*, 'I thought the bottom of his face was going to fall off.' He qualified second, scored a solid fourth in the first very wet race and then ran with the front group until getting nudged off line by a backmarker and running out of road in race two.

If Kawasaki had leapt forward over the winter, the reverse was true of Suzuki. Not only were their bikes slower than the previous year, the works team was soundly beaten by the local importer's team as well. 'I could have kicked my hat round faster,' said Whitham. Team manager Lester Harris was realistic: 'It was a disaster.' Honda had a good day. Kocinksi won the first race in the wet and Slight the second in the dry, out-dragging Edwards to the line. The American came out of the last corner in the lead with his front wheel in the air and the rear tyre spinning – he couldn't have done any more but he still got beaten. Two things about Honda were now evident: Kocinksi was going to win if it rained, and the team was rapidly curing the old problem of how to get all that power to the ground.

When it rained at Misano, Kocinski won one race and came second in the other. Fogarty led out of the last corner at Monza but found himself beaten to the line by both Hondas. The days when the Ducati 916 was the power king appeared to be over.

Fogarty and Slight seemed to have swapped characters over the winter. The Briton – for whom winning was all, and

If looks could kill. Foggy gives Kocinski the laser treatment at Assen.

second meant first loser – only won one of the first six races. Slight won three races in the first four rounds, more than he had ever managed in a season, and also fell off twice. Slight's tactics now matched the ever more ferocious haircuts as he tried to shake off the tag as Superbike's Randy

Slight turned himself into a win or crash racer – this time he's won at Donington.

Mamola – the best guy never to win the title. But the king of the rostrum-or-straw-bales school of racing was still Ducati veteran Pierfrancesco Chili, now firmly established as everyone's favourite. He ruined his chances of the title by crashing in the very first race hard enough to put him out of the second. He then won race one of round two and broke down in race two. In the UK at Donington, where the only more popular Italian is the jockey Frankie Dettori, he fell in race one then overtook Slight on the final bend of race two to finish second. You could hear the cheer in Bologna.

There was the odd scrap of comfort for Suzuki and Yamaha. Jamie Whitham used the Suzuki's undoubted power at Hockenheim and Monza, the two fastest tracks on the calendar, to get two third places although the GSX-R was still conspicuously unhappy over the slower, bumpy circuits like Laguna Seca and Brands Hatch. Scott Russell followed up Edwards's Aussie rostrum finish with a fighting third at Hockenheim and a second at Brands Hatch. The German race was a little gem: Scott got away with the leaders, vital on the long straights of Hockenheim, then gleefully outbraked, blocked and otherwise harried the faster bikes, finally putting himself in the right place on the right-hander into the stadium section on the last lap. In the second race, Whitham did much the same but it was a race that should have been won by Neil Hodgson. He had a 2-second lead at one point but was mugged by Fogarty, his team-mate, on that same right-hander with enough force to rattle him into running wide on the next left and losing any chance of a rostrum. Fogarty was celebrating on the slowdown lap when James came alongside him and a wonderful pantomime of jabbing fingers followed until Foggy realised his friend would be on the

Superbike welcomed Scott Russell back with open arms – he appeared to be enjoying himself too.

Frankie Chili was the pole king, with four in a row in the middle of the season, from Italy to Austria.

rostrum with him.

Having ridden the best race of his Superbike career, Hodgson then broke a kneecap in a training accident. It was symptomatic of the way his luck had run over the past couple of years and ruined what was a vital season for the youngster just as it looked as if everything was coming together.

Monza also saw the last of Colin Edwards in Superbike. He was hit by fellow Yamaha man Jean-Philippe Ruggia in untimed practice with enough force to break the American's wrist. After trying to come back at Laguna Seca, Edwards decided to have everything fixed at once. As well as the wrist he would have a collarbone replated and both sets of cruciate knee ligaments repaired so not surprisingly he didn't reappear and was replaced by

British young gun Chris Walker for the next four meetings and Noriyuki Haga for the last two rounds. Edwards left Superbike with some prophetic words: 'The Championship is Fogarty's to lose.'

Kocinksi, meanwhile, was making a stealthy start to the season. The atrocious weather at the first two rounds undoubtedly helped him and he scored two wins and a second in the wet, but in the dry he only managed seventh in the second race at Australia and then tenth and fifth at Donington. Things changed at the fast tracks, he was second in Hockenheim's first race but claims he was bumped by Fogarty on the first lap of the second race and could only manage fourteenth.

Kocinski was also living up to his reputation for being difficult. Aaron Slight and he didn't exchange any information and Slight said publicly that he wouldn't accept team orders. The American also decided that he wouldn't talk to certain journalists and avoided the cameras of some photographers. He even got the Honda team's PR man to fire off a three-page letter of complaint to one American magazine. No matter what question he was asked he would answer by telling you how happy he was to be on a Honda – so often that it became a paddock and press room joke. Journalists would go up to each other and ask in mock seriousness: 'Did you know Kocinski was happy to be on a Honda?' It was also noticeable how close he was to Japanese members of the Castrol Honda team. The rumour mill said that Kocinski's objective was to get a ride in 500 GPs with Honda and that he had to win the Superbike title first, although it seemed more likely that Honda would want to see the number-one plate on track in Superbike in 1998, the 50th anniversary of the founding of the Honda Motor Company.

One thing was certain. The two men who looked likely to contest the title now heartily disliked each other. Carl Fogarty likes to have a hate figure with which to whet his will to win. First it was Scott Russell, then Aaron Slight, who Foggy

At the A1-Ring Akira Yanagawa became the first Japanese rider to win a round of the Championship outside Japan.

Fogarty on his way to winning the first race in Austria in front of Yanagawa, Chili, Slight, Crafar and Kocinski.

Akira Yanagawa's dog Mew makes friends with John Kocinski on the Austrian rostrum.

enjoyed sniping at, but that was all kindergarten stuff compared to the intense dislike he and Kocinski developed for each other. Before the Brands Hatch round, Kocinski used one of the tabloids to refer to the Ducati team as 'the Mafia', a phrase he'd also used about his old employers in Kenny Roberts's Yamaha GP team. Foggy retaliated in another tabloid by calling Kocinski 'a freak of nature'. This was not the slapstick of Foggy and Russell playing to the gallery: it was genuine hostility.

Carl Fogarty's very untypical start to the season – in which he seemed to be happy with points rather than wins – gave way to a crisis of confidence after Kocinski's double win at home in the USA. At both Brands Hatch and the A1-Ring he crashed soon after Kocinski had come past him. In the UK he took Simon Crafar down with him, in Austria he punted Kocinski into a sand-trap but the American was able to rejoin and finish third. That incident plus Chili crashing and taking down the luckless Crafar ('if he had a duck it'd sink' – Steve Parrish) gave Yanagawa a clear run to the flag and his debut win. He broke new

James Whitham gave it a hundred per cent, as usual, on the recalcitrant Suzuki.

ground by taking his pet miniature terrier Mew to the rostrum and announcing that the hound liked the taste of champagne so he must win more races.

The next round was at Assen where Fogarty hadn't been beaten since 1992, surely a vital test for his mental toughness. In the first race Kocinski was nothing short of awesome. He made an appalling start then swept through the field overtaking every other works bike as if it wasn't there and ghosting past Fogarty on the penultimate lap. Fogarty fans were relieved to see that at least he coped with the sight of Kocinski in front of him. In the second race Kocinksi made another dreadful start but could only carve through to third this time as Chili shepherded Foggy home. Assen was a one-all draw but Kocinski got another boost when it was announced that Niall Mackenzie was likely to lose his third-place from Brands Hatch following a fuel

test. As Kocinksi had finished one place behind the Scot, that meant an extra three points if the FIM confirmed the finding.

All of which made the Spanish round crucial. Fogarty had done the double there twice for Ducati and said he had to win both races to stand a chance of the title with only the Far Eastern rounds left. Kocinski took pole as he had done at Assen, his first of the season, with Foggy second, but ominously for the British rider the next Ducati rider was Frankie Chili back in seventh and over a second slower. The writing was on the wall.

Albacete is a difficult place to pass except, according to Kocinski, if you're on a Honda. He delivered this gem to a TV reporter, but for once there was a ghost of a smile and a hint of irony. He had been notably nicer with the press since Brands Hatch when, according to one American insider, John had been told by the men from head office to lighten up; but this was different, the guy was positively relaxed and enjoying himself. He enjoyed the first race even more when Fogarty crashed out of a safe second place. That, said Carl, was what you got for riding a bike over its limits, before adding that the title was now

Noriyuki Haga won at Sugo and saved Yamaha's face.

gone. While the Honda team had not just kept Kocinski happy but developed the RC45 into the best bike out there, the Ducati team appeared to have stood still. Chili was the first Ducati home in fifth. In the second race a wayward Gregorio Lavilla punted Foggy into the sandpit on the second corner, Carl got back on the track dead last and was up to ninth when he again lost the front end. The first Ducati? Chili again, this time in seventh.

Kocinski, now with a 55-point lead, lost no time rubbing salt into his old team's wounds. 'The next race is in Japan, I think Ducati'll feel far from home.' He was right. No Ducati rider made the rostrum, and Foggy fell again. Kocinski's third place in the second race was enough. He became the first rider to win a GP and a Superbike World Championship. He was obviously very happy to be on a Honda. However, two very risky manoeuvres in Indonesia lost him a lot of the Brownie points he had gained with Honda over the season. It looked like the leopard had not changed his spots after all.

chapter eleven

1998
Lionheart roars again

Reigning Champ Kocinski did not return to defend his crown; he departed for GPs without a backward glance. He left behind him a motorcycle that was now probably the best package out there. Aaron Slight continued with

Carl Fogarty got the 1998 Ducati behaving more like his old '95 machine and started enjoying life again.

Castrol Honda but at last had a team-mate he could get on with in Colin Edwards. The young American had abandoned the allegedly uncompetitive Yamaha without a win to his name, but no one doubted that he was a winner.

There was also the small matter of 1998 being the 50th anniversary of the Honda Motor Company. That's the sort of landmark the Big H takes very seriously.

Pre-season, the smart money was on Aaron and the RC45, not just because of the V4's improvement but because of what was happening at Ducati. As Carl Fogarty had found on his return to the Bologna team in 1997, the 996 Ducati was very different from the 955 he'd left behind in '95, and the bike still wasn't to his liking when the season got under way. There was also a lot of politics to contend with. Ducati had contracted three riders – Foggy, Frankie Chili, and Troy Corser, returning to Superbike after an abortive year in GPs. They solved this embarrassment of riches by running two works teams. Virginio Ferrari's flagship Ducati Corse team took Chili and Corser, while Foggy was happy to be the only rider in the Ducati Performance team managed by Davide Tardozzi – who'd taken Corser to his title.

Ducati's assurances that all three factory riders would be treated equally were soon being doubted, not least by Tardozzi, who complained that the flow of testing information went one way only.

By mid-season Ducati's new American owners had decided that there would be only one works team in 1999, and that it would have only two riders, which cranked inter-team tension up another notch. The fact that Ferrari and Tardozzi could hardly be described as best friends added fuel to the fire, but it wasn't until Assen that the general public became aware of the friction.

Suzuki continued with the carburetted version of their GSX-R750, despite having a fuel-injected model in the shops, but at least their fortunes improved over the season. And they didn't suffer the sort of humiliation at the hands of importer teams that had so embarrassed them at Phillip Island in 1997 when Troy Bayliss and Peter Goddard outperformed the works team by a distance. Goddard replaced Mike Hale in the World Superbike team, bringing with him a wealth of experience, not least in bike development. The fact that he'd won the Australian Superbike Championship and the World Endurance

Fogarty was in the single-rider Ducati Performance team but had Davide Tardozzi as his manager.

Championship on GSX-Rs didn't hurt either. James Whitham, who'd scored Suzuki's only rostrums the previous year, retained his place. For the first half of the season Goddard outperformed his team-mate, but Whitham came on strong in the second half. The highlight was his race-long pursuit of Fogarty at Brands Hatch in front of 82,000 people, which ended with James setting a new lap record on his way to third place, Suzuki's only rostrum of the year.

The four-cylinder bike everyone thought would do the business was the Kawasaki. Akira Yanagawa was many people's tip for a hatful of race wins and a shot at the title, and surely Neil Hodgson would at last live up to his potential on a bike he immediately seemed at home on. But the Green challenge never materialised. After all the team's 1998-spec motors blew up in their final pre-season tests, Yanagawa struggled in Round 1 at Phillip Island, where he'd been a contender in '97. It took the team half a season to regain their momentum. Akira was competitive in Round 7 at Kyalami, setting the fastest lap of the second race.

Then came Laguna Seca. Yanagawa and Doug Chandler – still fast, still wearing green – trailed a runaway Troy Corser, with the American closing fast on the Japanese. Going into the Corkscrew something happened on Doug's bike – probably a clip-on broke – and he fell under braking. The bike slid straight on and scooped up Akira as he arrived at the apex. It was a horrible-looking crash, a cartwheeling blur of dust, men, and machines, with Yanagawa doing a sickening impersonation of a rag doll before ending up crumpled and motionless on the far side of the track. His team-mate Neil Hodgson was one of the first to stop and stood waving on the track, trying to get the authorities to put the red flag out. The race was restarted, but an equally horrible start-line pile-up that badly injured Bontempi and – crucially – Slight meant another red flag, and the result was taken from the lap before the Chandler/Yanagawa crash. With cruel irony, that gave the lower two rostrum places to the Kawasaki riders (the first Green rostrums of the year) while they were both on their way to hospital.

The four-cylinder team that wasn't supposed to do well was Yamaha, yet they confounded all expectations thanks to the arrival of a new star – no, make that superstar – Noriyuki Haga. Nori-chan (he prefers the informal mode of address usually used for children rather than the customary Haga-san) had saved much corporate face in the penultimate round of 1997 by winning. It wasn't just Yamaha's only win in Superbike, it was the factory's only win in any World Championship road-racing class, including all three GP formulae and World Endurance. Frankly, no one expected anything more this season, but Noriyuki astonished the world by leaving the first round level on points with Fogarty at the top of the table, with a third place and a win.

Between the first two Superbike rounds he took time out to debut on a 500 as a wild-card entry in the Japanese GP. With apparent ease he ran with the top men and ended up third – and it should have been second, but for the vastly experienced Tady Okada mugging him at the chicane last time round. Jaws dropped in both Superbike and GP paddocks. When Haga went to Donington (for the first time, don't forget), won both races and stormed to the top of the table, chins hit the floor Tom and Jerry style.

The flip-side to the instant deification of Haga was the descent into personal hell for Scott Russell. He'd put a price on his return to the team – a switch to Michelin tyres. Uniquely, the team let him change to the French rubber, but Haga stayed with Dunlop. The sight of the new boy comprehensively outperforming him on the tyres he'd rejected cannot have been comfortable for the ex-champ. There followed a succession of mystery retirements and lacklustre races. The nadir came at Laguna Seca, where

Scott led the second race after the most blatant of jump-starts only to crash half-way round the first lap. He arrived back at the Yamaha pit grinning sheepishly where he was pointedly ignored by his crew. The sight of a great champion in decline wasn't made any more palatable by the fact that he'd started the year winning a record fifth Daytona 200.

The major innovation for 1998 was SuperPole, an idea lifted from the Suzuka 8 Hours and some American four-wheeled racing in an attempt to spice-up qualifying for the TV cameras. In SuperPole, the top 16 from regular qualifying go forward to do one flying lap that decides their grid position; one mistake, and that fastest time in regular qualifying mutates into the fourth row of the grid. Not surprisingly, the riders were unanimous in disliking the system intensely. Even Troy Corser, by far the best qualifier of the year, said on every

Gregorio Lavilla demonstrated that he was far and away the Championship's best privateer. Here he's on his way to third place at home in Spain.

Honda's new boy Colin Edwards prepares to experience another newcomer – SuperPole.

possible occasion how much he disliked the concept.

The trouble with SuperPole is that it's fine until the weather refuses to co-operate, as at Donington, Albacete, and Assen. British wild card James Haydon became the first man to crash in SuperPole when he fell on his out-lap at Donington. He'd been kept waiting for over 30 seconds in near-freezing conditions and his tyre had cooled off so much – probably by 30° – that he knew he was in trouble as soon as he left the pit lane. The riders' insistence that SuperPole might endanger their safety seemed to have some basis in truth, but it was the farce at Albacete that was really embarrassing. Rain halfway through SuperPole saw the top 16 split into two groups, with the result that the top eight were slower than the second eight. Try explaining that to TV viewers or newspaper readers.

And that's the nub of the matter. SuperPole was designed for TV, yet there's nothing visually exciting about one bike going round a track on its own no matter how fast it's doing it. SuperPole can seem exciting when the hour-long process is edited down to a five-minute highlights package, but live it's right up there with watching paint dry. Thankfully the wet-weather rules were changed after Albacete, to a system almost identical to that used by Formula 1 – that is, a 50-minute final session for the fastest 16 from regular qualifying, which, like dry SuperPole, discounts all that has gone before. It was used twice and both times provided brilliant entertainment in totally different ways. Let's face it, if the F1 cars use this system it must be TV-friendly; Bernie's boys don't arrive at their procedures by chance.

Over the 15-year history of the Championship, the two perennial complaints have been the disjointed calendar and the quality of the supporting races. This season started out with two races a month from March through to October, with one race in both April and September. It was the best-planned schedule yet, but the collapse of the Tiger Economies of the Pacific Basin saw the opening round in Indonesia and the final round in Malaysia cancelled. The result was a month of waiting between the penultimate round at Assen and the finale in Sugo. Not ideal, but on this occasion unavoidable. To no one's surprise, the Brazilian round was also cancelled, but this cloud had a silver lining: Superbike became the first World Championship motorsport to return to South Africa after the fall of apartheid and the election of Nelson Mandela.

The Supersport World Series that supported the Superbikes was supposed to receive full World Championship status, and even though it didn't get that promotion the class went a long way towards answering criticisms of the support classes. Works teams from Ducati, Suzuki, Honda, and Yamaha gave the class real strength in depth, and the fans full value for money. Tragically, the class lost its finest exponent when Michael Paquay died at Monza after a qualifying accident. The Belgian had been European Supersport Champion in 1993 on a Honda, and again in '95 on a Ducati, and was leading the Castrol Honda team as they prepared for the World Championship due in 1999. As well as being a superb rider – the best yet produced by the class – he was also a thoroughly decent person.

Noriyuki Haga's impact on the Championship was immediate and impressive, but two big crashes in qualifying for Round 3 at Monza slowed him down. He had to be carried to his bike, but managed to race and scored enough points to keep the Championship lead. But Monza was really noticeable for the maiden victory of Colin Edwards. It had been a while coming, and when he backed it up in Race 2 to score a double we were treated to the unusual sight of a works Honda blowing up. In all his years in World Superbike Aaron Slight had

Corser and Haga added considerable entertainment value – although Troy was unamused by this attack at Laguna Seca. Nori always liked to put on a show for the fans.

never scored a double win, something that really bugged him. The sight of his new team-mate heading for the double caused Aaron to over-rev the RC45 for longer than the prescribed ten seconds riders are allowed to use in emergencies. The result was a very big bang.

Happily Aaron didn't have to wait long to score his own double, and the fact that it came at Misano made it doubly sweet. The Italian track has historically been Ducati country – the only non-Ducati wins in the previous six rounds held there were from Scott Russell in 1994 and John Kocinksi in his championship year. But most team personnel remembered 1995 when the Castrol Honda team suffered its most humiliating weekend as Aaron struggled to 16th and 13th places. Aaron's double was proof positive that the RC45 was now the best all-round package on the grid. Revenge, the Italian saying goes, is a dish best eaten cold.

Everyone had a month to calm down before the Sugo showdown

Frankie Chili also got his first ever double at the new Kyalami venue in South Africa, and to the amazement of many it was in the dry! This was the race where Gregorio Lavilla backed up his wet-weather third place at home in Spain with a dry-race third place and proved he was a cut above the rest of the privateers. The fact that he was also Spanish was politically useful.

Well into the season four men had pulled away from the field. The usual suspects Slight, Fogarty, and Corser were there, but – surprisingly – so was Frankie Chili. Three of them had had bad meetings – Fogarty in the wet in Germany, Chili at home in Misano, and Slight at Laguna Seca, where the injury he picked up threatened to put him out of Brands Hatch as well – while Corser plugged away, and although he didn't win a lot he

always seemed to be on the rostrum. Not that his achievements should be underestimated; after all, he hardly sat on a bike all through 1997. He did win two races, but more often faded in mid-race only to push hard at the end, giving rise to serious doubts about his level of fitness.

Fit or not, Troy led the championship

going into the penultimate round in Holland, but only by the slim margin of 1½ points from Slight, with Foggy 17½ points further back and Franki Chili still in touch another 13 in arrears. The scene was set for the Battle of Assen.

The first shock came in Race 1 after the three Ducati men broke away from Slight. First Troy drifted off the pace of the other two. Chili was faster on the back of the circuit but Foggy seemed to be able to retake first at will at the chicane. Clearly it was going to come down

The three men who went to Sugo with a chance of the 1998 title: Foggy, Aaron Slight, and Troy Corser.

to the last lap or even the last corner. Sure enough, Chili shadowed Carl into the last lap and took him on the sweeping turns behind the paddock. Carl shaped to pass at the chicane but made a slight mistake and couldn't get through. Afterwards, Foggy did a passable imitation of Mick Doohan moaning about acting as a tow-truck for riders who couldn't get round on their own. It was merely a warm-up for what was to come.

Race 2 was a replay of Race 1, and again it looked as if Chili was waiting to mug Foggy on the last lap. Carl got it

slightly sideways on the curves at the back of the paddock, which forced Chili to back off, but he did get past on the ultra-fast left on the run to the chicane and arrived at the corner slightly in front but on the outside. It looked as if Foggy was going to get back past on the brakes when Chili lost the front end and fell. At no point did the two Ducatis touch, but while Foggy was celebrating in the pit lane an incensed Frankie arrived and tried to attack Carl. The Italian was hustled away and everyone assumed that was the end of events, but half an hour later Frankie, wearing a blue towelling dressing-gown, invaded the winner's press conference and accused Foggy of dangerous riding in the fast corners and said he fell because he was so angry. Once again he tried to land a punch on Fogarty. No one could understand why Chili had flipped out, and Carl didn't care. He was now in with a genuine chance of the title, as the top three in the Championship would go to the last

Frankie Chili loses the front end and precipitates the Battle of Assen.

round just six points apart.

What caused Chili's outburst? After all, no one could see anything out of the ordinary about Fogarty's riding. Over the next few weeks more information leaked out about the political situation at Ducati. It transpired that to secure one of the two seats in the 1999 works team, Frankie had to finish in the top three in the Championship and his fall effectively scuppered any hope of that. His team manager Virginio Ferrari was also implicated in fanning the flames as part of his fight with Tardozzi.

Everyone had a month to calm down before the showdown in Sugo and the closest finish to a World Superbike Championship since Tardozzi rode and fought with Fred Merkel in the late 1980s. Corser and Slight started the weekend half a point apart, with Foggy 5½ points further behind in third. Super-Pole showed that the whole works Honda squad was in trouble as Slight dropped from third to tenth with All-Japan Championship leader Itoh's RC45 one place further back and Edwards in 15th. Somehow, Honda and Michelin had failed to give Aaron the tools to do the job.

But the big drama came in Sunday morning warm-up. Troy Corser, who'd been fastest in SuperPole, tipped off at the end of the front straight, apparently after cogging down one gear too many. He landed with his elbow under his body and broke three ribs, but even so was going to race. Then his temperature rocketed and he was taken to hospital with suspected spleen damage. The Championship leader was out of the race after looking stronger than he had all season.

When the green lights came on Haga disappeared, leaving Fogarty fighting with two local Suzuki men, Ryo and Kitagawa. When Haga threw away a certain win the Suzuki men went past Carl and took the factory's first ever one-two finish, leaving the Englishman to fret

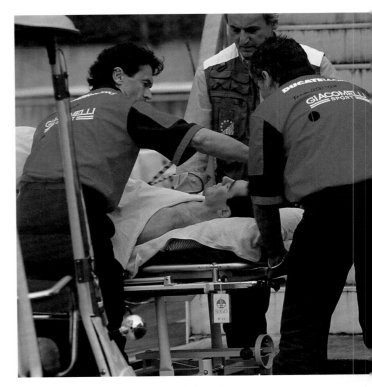

Troy Corser was out of the battle before the race started – he damaged his ribs and spleen in a warm-up crash.

Kitagawa and Ryo celebrate Suzuki's first ever one-two.

Riders' wives and girlfriends don their other halves' kit – and all for charity.

about his rear tyre and a late charge from Yanagawa. Slight could only manage seventh compared to Carl's third place, so the arithmetic was now simple. Carl led the Championship for the first time since the start of the year but with the slimmest of margins – 1½ points. Assuming they ran at the front of the field, whichever of them crossed the line first in Race 2 would be World Champion.

This time Haga didn't make any mistakes and no one saw which way he went. Fogarty got away in second with Slight in touch in fourth, but that was as close as the Kiwi got. Carl reeled off the laps to finish fourth, with Slight four seconds behind in sixth. Carl Fogarty became the first man to win the title three times and the first to regain (as opposed to retain) the crown. On the slow-down lap he stopped the bike and slumped over the tank in tears. It was a title won by sheer bloody-mindedness on a bike that wasn't to his liking at the start of the year.

With hindsight, it was obvious really. When it comes down to a fight the man you want on your side is Carl Fogarty. If the top of the Championship was full of familiar names, it looked as if the politi-

cal landscape was about to change. The first suggestions that the 500cc GP formula be altered to accommodate four-strokes emerged from the factories, and alarmist statements appeared in some Spanish and Italian magazines to the effect that there would be no works bikes in World Superbike after the 2000 season.

What actually happened was that a big meeting held before the Austrian round between the FIM, SBK International, and senior engineers from all four Japanese factories, plus Ducati and Aprilia, decided that for the 2001 Championship each manufacturer would produce at least 30 race kits for their homologated machinery for sale at a fixed price of around £23,000 for four-cylinder machines. All entrants would have to use only original homologated parts or these new kit parts, the idea being to make competitive machinery available to privateers. The meeting also decided that manufacturers entering the Championship for the first time would benefit from a relaxation of the production requirement for homologation. This could be interpreted as a slight move towards the more stringent Supersport regulations, but in no way could it be seen as the end of full works bikes. If, of course, it happened.

chapter twelve

1999
Déjà vu all over again

The similarities between Carl Fogarty's fourth and second World Superbike Championships are almost spooky. With the number one plate on his Ducati, he took a double win in the first round and was never headed in the points table in either year. If anything, this title was even more impressive than those that had gone before, but if you think that would make the season, well, boring, think again. Superbike got a full quota of works teams with the arrival of Aprilia to join the big four Japanese factories and Ducati, and like their fellow-countrymen the Noale company opted for a V-twin. Admittedly, this was a development year for the team, with just one regular rider – the veteran Aussie Peter Goddard – with the occasional help of factory test-rider Antonello, but no other two-wheeled motorsport could boast the official involvement of six factories. Crowds were also up – massively in the case of both Italian races and the USA. The average increase was 30 per cent, with an astonishing 41 per cent being the biggest improvement.

The old problem of the supporting races was well and truly solved with World Championship status for the Supersport class and European Championship for the new Superstock class for under-24s only. British fans were also pleased to see

that the sidecars soldiered on, with the evergreen Steve Webster MBE at the front again. There were lots of new motorbikes, too. As well as the new-from-the-ground-up Aprilia, there was Yamaha's R7 in Superbike and the equally new R6 in Supersport. But yet again it was the

Once again, Carl Fogarty proved that he was at the top of the Superbike food chain.

Honda RC45 that started the season as favourite. Now Colin Edwards had a season on the V4 under his belt he would surely give team-mate Aaron Slight the hurry-up to the benefit of the whole team. It didn't quite work out like that, as Aaron's form faded and he fell out drastically with Colin.

Elsewhere there had been some shuffling of personnel over the close season, and true to their word Ducati fielded just one works team, Ducati Corse. The management struggle from 1998 was well and truly won by Davide Tardozzi, leaving a disgruntled Virginio Ferrari on the sidelines conferring with his lawyers. Troy Corser stayed in the team and was reunited with Tardozzi, who had taken the Aussie to his title as manager of the Power Horse Ducati team in 1996.

Frankie Chili, the man who made way for Foggy at Ducati Corse, signed for the Suzuki team under its new management by Francis Batta's Alstare organisation and with high-profile sponsorship from Corona, the Mexican beer company. Japan insisted that Katsuaki Fujiwara be the second rider. Things did not look good at the start of the year. A despondent Frankie was 38 seconds behind the winner in Round 1, but hard work with his Dunlop tyre technicians reaped dividends, starting with a morale-boosting SuperPole at Round 3. By Round 5 at Monza he was able to finish under a second behind the winner, then win in the rain in Austria – Suzuki's first-ever World Superbike victory outside Japan – and finally win a dry race in Germany.

That may have come after Foggy had wrapped up his title, but the battle with Carl and Aaron Slight on the last lap was as fine a piece of race-craft as you could hope to see. Unfortunately, Fujiwara was no help to Chili, despite being good enough to get on the rostrum at Sugo when he was a Japanese Championship rider and was thought to be a prospect for the Grand Prix team. But after the

first-corner crash he instituted in the 1998 Catalan GP, Superbike was meant to be akin to rehabilitation. At least he stopped crashing, but in '99 he appeared to take more trouble over his haircut and clothes than his racing and looked like he was enjoying himself too much given the paucity of his results. What could Chili have done with some solid back-up from his team-mate? Nevertheless, Frankie's heroics endeared him not just to the team but also to the fans, not least the Brits, who took no time at all in forgiving him for his attacks on Foggy at Assen the previous year.

Neil Hodgson's place in the Kawasaki team was taken by Gregorio Lavilla, who had impressed everyone with his form on a private Ducati in 1998. Unfortunately, the switch to Dunlops didn't suit him and he had a rash of crashes in the second

Aprilia made their first foray into Superbike with the beautiful RSV Mille. Aussie veteran Peter Goddard did the riding.

and third rounds that severely dented his confidence. Akira Yanagawa continued as the number one at Team Green but could only manage one second place before he started crashing. It was debatable whether he was fit to race in Austria and Holland, but race he did, and then got back on the rostrum at Hockenheim where his bike was at a definite disadvantage. When he won the last race of the year everyone in the paddock smiled. However, the Kawasaki was now the last carburetted, as opposed to fuel-injected, bike in the paddock and looked to be struggling against the V-twins and even the newer Suzuki and Yamaha fours.

The other new boy on a works bike, Vitto Guareschi, also struggled early on as Haga's team-mate on the new R7, although he was rewarded with a rostrum finish in that wet Austrian race behind Fogarty. The big question in the Yamaha camp was how would Haga cope not just

Yamaha had a new bike, the R7, with Haga and Guareschi riding.

with the new bike but with racing on Michelins for the first time in his career? Typically he came out with all guns blazing at Kyalami and put the R7 on the front row, rode the wheels off it to finish fourth in the first race, and then crashed it at the chicane in Race 2. When he got to the rostrum it was for first place in Race 1 at Albacete – this time he blew it up in Race 2! His only other visit to the rostrum was at Brands Hatch, his least favourite circuit. Nori-chan never ceased to amaze all season, although it was plain that he sometimes grew weary of fighting against the odds and sometimes didn't show among the leaders all weekend.

So it was left to the usual suspects – Slight, Corser, and Edwards – to battle Foggy for the title, with the other factory riders getting the occasional rostrum but never truly being in the hunt for the crown. Yet just as in 1995, each of the pretenders to the throne suffered injury or misfortune, real or imagined, that held them back. Edwards started the season with torn shoulder muscles from a testing

accident at Laguna Seca barely two weeks before the first round in South Africa, then had his machine fail in Spain when he looked a good bet for the win in Race 1. His tendency to disappear from view at some tracks was less noticeable but still afflicted him at a couple of places, noticeably Laguna Seca.

Troy Corser suffered a similar shoulder injury in SuperPole warm-up at Albacete, but it was his ever more pronounced tendency to fade in the middle of a race that worried observers most. But give him a sniff of the rostrum, or specifically the top step of it, and he was his old self. A scintillating double at home in Phillip Island reminded us just why Troy had won a World Champion-ship, and when Foggy fell from the lead of Race 2 in Germany a previously disinterested Corser awoke to put a stunning move on Slight and take the win. Ducati were not happy and told Troy so – this despite the fact that he was second overall after every race of the year bar two. Unfortunately for Troy one of the two was the final round, something the bosses in Bologna didn't appreciate.

The falling out between the two Castrol Honda riders happened at Donington Park when they came together on the exit of the Melbourne Loop, after Slight outbraked Edwards and Chili but got in the corner too hot. He ran wide on the exit and Edwards cut back underneath him, they touched, and Slight went down. Most observers saw it as a racing incident but the Kiwi was on his feet and gesturing at the disappearing American in a manner that made it clear that he saw it very differently. After a visit to the pits, Slight got back on track and let Edwards through when he lapped him but, as Colin said, 'flipped me off' (made a rude gesture). Slight tucked in behind his team-mate, but in trying to run at Colin's pace fell at Coppice and compounded the damage to his right little

Frankie Chili got his first win on a Suzuki at the A1-Ring. Team boss Francis Batta was quite pleased too.

finger from the first crash. When Edwards went to Slight's motorhome afterwards to check on his team-mate's health he quickly found he wasn't welcome. 'The only reason anyone's interested,' said a puzzled Edwards, 'is because we're on the same make of bike.'

Aaron never really returned to his old form, spending much of the middle of the season complaining of obscure problems with his machinery. Little did anyone know, we were seeing the evidence of a medical condition that would threaten his life.

Colin also got to play a supporting role in what was definitely the race of the year, and a strong candidate for the race of any year. It happened at Monza. Both races came down to three-man dices for the rostrum between Edwards, Foggy, and Chili, although it was obvious that the Italian's Suzuki could stay in the slipstream of the twins but couldn't pass. In Race 1 Foggy somehow magicked extra speed through the awesome Parabolica turn that ends the lap to pass Edwards on the line to win by a tenth of a second. Atypically, Colin threw his toys out of the pram and water over a TV camera.

Although oil and coolant had streamed onto the track, no warning flag was displayed

Race 2 was even closer: this time they went over the line side by side, with Fogarty riding the greatest last lap the Championship has ever seen in which he first dropped to third, repassed Chili, got through the Ascari chicane at impossible angles of lean, then took an impossibly wide line out of the Parabolica that took him out onto the old circuit. Even the electronic timing system was confused. It first gave the race to Edwards, and the marshals at the first chicane signalled to Foggy that he was second. Then the timing screens changed. When Foggy got back to the pit lane he found his crew ecstatically celebrating his win – by five-thousandths of a second. Carl's first words to Tardozzi could serve as the motto for his coat of arms: 'Never give up! Never give up!' Shown a photo of the finish, Carl was his normal dry self: 'Nah, won by miles!' Colin was much happier this time and even had the guts to apologise for being annoyed after the first race. Italian magazine *Moto Sprint*'s race report called Foggy 'a force of nature' and 'the perfect racer'. After those two races, it didn't seem like hyperbole.

Edwards was also central to another major drama, this time at the Nürburgring in Germany. The meeting started under the pall of a personal tragedy for Carl Fogarty after the two-year-old daughter of close friends had a fatal accident at Fogarty's home nine days before the meeting. Little Hannah Walsh's parents told Carl to win for her. He did, pointing to the sky and collapsing over the tank after taking the chequered flag in Race 1. 'I had to win that at all costs,' said a sombre Carl. 'There's a little girl who isn't with us any more. Her dad told me to win it.' There was no champagne on the rostrum.

The race had provided drama of a different type, and it was only by luck that another tragedy was avoided. It started with Igor Jerman's Kawasaki blowing up on the run to turn one. It was a comprehensive bit of self-destruction; coolant and oil were literally flowing out of the belly-pan as the Slovenian pulled off the track. Astoundingly the marshals did not display the oil flag or even the yellow flag.

Leader Fogarty went through okay but Yanagawa went down, still without bringing out the flags. Next time round Haga lost it on the oil, saved the crash, but ran across the gravel for 100 yards before toppling off the Yamaha. Still no flags,

Ducati won both races in the USA, but it was the local Vance & Hines team of Anthony Gobert and Ben Bostrom who shared the victories.

156

despite the crowd shouting at the marshals. Team managers were going berserk in the pit lane, with Tardozzi leading the charge to race control. Then Chili fell, still without the flags coming out, and headed straight for race control, where he threatened to sue everyone in sight for loss of earnings. Tardozzi was screaming for the race to be stopped, despite his riders leading. Then Colin Edwards fell.

Tardozzi was screaming for the race to be stopped, despite his riders leading

Unlike the more stoical Japanese and litigious Chili, Edwards leapt to his feet in a rage, waved his arms, flung gravel on to the track, and yelled at the marshals. He'd assumed the spill had been cleared up and was livid. The marshals did reluctantly put the flags out now, in response to the crowd rather than anything happening in front of their eyes. Edwards's anger didn't subside and for a few weeks he lost faith in the Championship and its organisers. It wasn't just the loss of a rostrum finish: there were echoes of the crash that had fatally injured his team-mate Nagai-san back in 1995, and although Colin never mentioned it in public his racing lost its edge for six weeks.

The second race also looked to be going Foggy's way until he fell as his concentration understandably wavered. But how many World Champions would have done what he did next? He kicked the bike straight, rejoined the race and just snatched the final available point for 15th place. The World Superbike Championship has never been back to the Nürburgring.

Laguna Seca is a track that usually creates controversy but this time all the talk was about the racing, as local riders dominated the Championship regulars for the first time. Actually, local isn't quite the right word, because the man who won Race 1 was racing's wild child, the Australian Anthony Gobert. Superbike had last seen him in 1996 as a leery, permanently sideways Kawasaki rider, yet here he was riding a Ducati as smoothly and consistently as any of the regular men but a good deal faster on his Dunlops. Even his post-race interview was a polished performance.

No one took enough notice of Gobert's Vance & Hines team-mate who finished second – reigning AMA Superbike Champ Ben Bostrom. When Gobert crashed under pressure from Chili in Race 2, Bostrom upheld local honour by taking the victory. Amazingly, it was his first win on a Superbike. Consistency had given him the American title, not race wins. As a Californian, Ben looked and talked the part with his Evel Knievel crash helmet design, designer facial hair, and large collection of classic American motors. His riding was eye-catching too, featuring a wildly snaking entry to the final turn. This man was obviously cool enough to be the next Scott Russell.

The end of the season was a carnival for British bike fans. First, over 120,000 of them turned up for the European round at Brands Hatch and Carl Fogarty promptly had his worst weekend of the year with a non-scoring ride in Race 1, thanks to a chunking tyre, and a fourth place in Race 2. Carl felt he'd let everyone down and asked them to come to Assen, where he'd do the double for them. Instead of their hero dominating as in '95, the massed ranks saw Castrol Honda finish one-two in both races, the first time the team had achieved that feat, and they got to cheer heroic third places from Chili and Haga – who hates the Kent track. A wet weekend in Austria saw Chili notch Suzuki's first-ever win outside of Japan, the first for Suzuki under Alstare management, and his own first on a four-cylinder bike.

King Carl, with crown courtesy of an Italian TV station with a sense of humour.

The Two Kings.

Then came Assen, and it turned into British bike racing's best day out since Foggy's Brands double of '95. At the most conservative estimate there were over 30,000 British fans in the stands, and amazingly they saw not just the double that Foggy had promised them at Brands – which almost assured him of his fourth title – but British winners in every race. Iain MacPherson won the Supersport race, Karl Harris was victorious in Superstock, and the evergreen Steve Webster won the sidecars.

The support classes provided a much more coherent undercard than ever before. Supersport was a real dogfight that eventually went to Suzuki and Stéphane Chambon, but the star was 21-year-old Spaniard Ruben Xaus, the very epitome of a win-or-crash racer. He crashed five times, retired with mechanical problems once, and finished on the rostrum in the other five races. Harris, even younger at 19, won the European Superstock Championship on a 750 Suzuki against a factory supported 1,000cc Aprilia and ran with the fast guys in Supersport when he took over the

injured Yves Briguet's ride at the end of the season. A star in the making, he was even lumbered with the label of the New Fogarty in some quarters.

The Old Fogarty didn't look ready to move over, though. His growing understanding with Davide Tardozzi and the team gave him faith in his own judgement on machine set-up, never previously Carl's strong point. Tardozzi also had other methods of motivating his charge and getting him to do the testing work he wasn't keen on: 'I ask him why he not want to win; I kick his ass.' Dad George Fogarty had no doubts about the situation. He described Tardozzi as Carl's 'gift from God'.

Carl himself was sure he was riding better than ever – including his runaway 1995 Championship. There was no doubt that he was now the greatest four-stroke rider of the modern era. His fourth title in six years showed that, but this year he also took his first pole position since 1995 and won 11 races, equalling his 1993 tally when, ironically, he didn't win the Championship. You only had to try and drive a car in the vicinity of Brands Hatch during the first weekend in August to understand what Carl Fogarty meant to success-starved British sports fans.

chapter thirteen

2000
Twins and drugs and broken bones

Perhaps it was a message from above. Carl Fogarty's pre-season training crash in Valencia all but put him out of the early rounds of the championship as well as knocking him unconscious for the first time he could remember. Dad George later reminded Carl that he had been knocked out way back in his 250 career. But no matter. It was the damage to his son's shoulder that was most worrying and likely to keep him away from early rounds of the millennial World Superbike Championship.

It was a brave man who mentioned the words Fogarty and retirement in the same sentence, but the man himself occasionally let slip that it was a subject he had considered. One more big crash, he once said, would be enough to persuade him to hang up the Daineses.

In the end, he didn't get the choice.

It happened early in Race 2 at Round 2 in Australia. As Carl Fogarty went to pass Robert Ulm, the Austrian's Ducati engine apparently hesitated going into a fast corner – at Phillip Island fast means around 150mph – and caused him to run wide into the path of the World Champion. Carl speared off the track,

Fogarty was already carrying an injury at the first race of the year at Kyalami.

crashed, and did not move. He didn't move for a long time.

Carl regained consciousness back in the medical centre, but the news was not good: a messy fracture of the humerus, the long upper arm bone. The breaks were up at the top where the ball of the shoulder's ball-and-socket joint is joined to the humerus proper by a narrow neck of bone. There was also associated muscle damage and even the possibility of nerves being stretched. Not good, not good at all. And it got worse.

Aaron Slight also fell into the hands of the medical profession, although under very different circumstances. There had been worries about his concentration problems for a good chunk of the previous season, but the peripatetic lifestyle of a racer meant the variety of doctors he consulted in different countries never came to any firm conclusions. Just before the season started his condition deteriorated suddenly and he went for a brain scan in Australia. On the way there Megan Slight ventured to suggest 'I hope they don't find anything.' Aaron's reply, minus the expletives, was a vehement 'I hope they do.' They did. A congenitally weak blood vessel had bled and could have catastrophic consequences. At least it explained the problems he'd been having, but it was obviously serious. He was operated on immediately. No one knew when he'd be back on a bike; in fact no one knew if he'd ever be back.

Exactly 12 weeks later he was on the grid at Donington Park and scored two top-ten finishes. Tough, these Kiwis.

The enforced absences of Slight and Fogarty meant the field had an odd look for much of the year. The immediate consequence of Fogarty's crash was a game of musical saddles involving Ducati teams everywhere. Troy Bayliss, the Aussie who was reigning British Champion, was rid-

The three main players at the start of the millennial season: Edwards, Haga, and Fogarty.

ing for Vance & Hines in the AMA Championship and was drafted in for Round 3 at Sugo, only to be knocked off his bike on the first lap of both races. Luca Cadalora, the factory's official test rider, was on Foggy's bike for Donington but could only manage one paltry 17th place, an embarrassment for a man of his talent. Ducati went back to Bayliss for Round 5. His brace of fourth places confirmed him as Fogarty's full-time replacement in the World Championship, but his erstwhile new team-mate Ben Bostrom, who had been struggling with the Michelin-shod Infostrada bike, was shipped off to the semi-works NCR team. The Championship rookie was at least reunited with familiar Dunlop rubber as Spaniard Juan Borja went the other way to the full works team. The seemingly humiliating exchange worked better for Ben Boz, who promptly beat Borja in

both races then went on to his first rostrum finish of the year next time out in Misano. This was also the first appearance of Ben's Evel Knievel leathers in Europe. The young Californian had just avoided career meltdown and was now starting to enjoy himself.

Honda also went the substitute route, with Simon Crafar deputising for his countryman for the first two rounds but never overcoming his dislike of Michelins. Manabu Kamada took over at Sugo before Slight returned – almost from the dead – at Donington.

It wasn't just the faces that were new on the grid. Honda had a new bike, the VTR1000SP-W. As it was a V-twin there were a few snide remarks about copying Ducati. While it's true that the Big H had never built a sporting V-twin before, the SP was shorter of stroke than the Duke and featured Honda's usual twin-spar aluminium frame, not Ducati's trademark steel lattice or their desmodromic valve-operating system. Winning with a new bike first time out had become very, very difficult, as Honda had found out with the RC45, and they weren't about to make the same mistake twice. Massive resources were poured into pre-season testing and the bike arrived for competition so light it even retained the roadster's starter motor! Colin Edwards duly won the first race of the year on it.

The other Italian V-twin, the Aprilia, got serious this year after its shakedown season. In the black-and-red livery of the factory's GP bikes and with Axo sponsorship, the bike looked the part – and so did the rider. Troy Corser found himself unemployed when Ducati signed Ben Bostrom and wasn't happy about it. The Aprilia ride came along just at the right time, with the team now being run by the

factory using mechanics from their GP efforts. Motivation wasn't a problem for Troy. He duly gave Aprilia their first SuperPole in the first race of the year, their first rostrum in Race 2, and their first win in Round 2. And it was all the sweeter because Ducati was struggling.

Yet another V-twin started the year in the unlikely shape of the Bimota SB8. The Rimini company that was so strong in the early years of Superbike came back with a Suzuki TL1000 V-twin engine in one of their own typically beautiful frames. The personnel involved could boast more arguments with Ducati than even Troy Corser. The rider, Anthony Gobert, was in dispute with his old Vance & Hines Ducati team back in the States, team manager Virginio Ferrari was consulting his lawyers about his removal from the managership of the Ducati Corse team, and tuner Franco Farne, probably the world's most experienced Ducati race mechanic, had been sacked by the company after years of service.

Gobert ran race number 501 in the hope of some big sponsorship from Levi's but it never transpired. Amazingly, a winning tyre gamble in mixed weather conditions landed Bimota and Gobert a win in Phillip Island, making the wayward Aussie only the second man to win World Superbike races on three different makes of motorcycle: Kawasaki, Ducati, and Bimota (the first was Stephane Mertens, on Bimota, Honda, and Ducati). More predictably, the Bimota blew up big-time in Japan, flinging Gobert down the track and following him into the barrier. It was a very fast, very scary crash that left Gobert severely beaten up, with a collection of minor fractures and burns. The team folded shortly afterwards, citing lack of cash.

Down the four-cylinder end of the pit

If UK fans wanted a new hero they need look no further than Hodgson

lane Frankie Chili and Katsuaki Fujiwara kept the Suzuki flag flying with the aid of good work from Dunlop. Kawasaki didn't fare so well; Akira Yanagawa was again consistent without ever scoring a win, while Gregorio Lavilla's season was blighted from the start by a wrist injury picked up in pre-season testing and then ruined by a broken pelvis at Monza. Everyone's favourite sub, Simon Crafar, returned to the green colours for one round at Hockenheim, after which Peter Goddard did the needful for three more races.

It soon became apparent that Carl Fogarty's injuries were going to take a lot longer to heal than first predicted. The brave noises about being back in a few weeks soon turned into disconsolate non-committal announcements. If British fans were looking for a new hero, they had to look no further than Neil Hodgson, who had disappeared from the World Championship radar two seasons earlier. His wild-card win in Race 2 of Round 4 at Donington Park was his first World Superbike victory and – amazingly – Ducati's first of the season.

Home fans were treated to another round of the Hodgson versus Chris Walker battle that raged all year in the British Championship. The pair even managed to scare Noriyuki Haga as they traded places with him in pursuit of leader Frankie Chili. Over 60,000 fans got what they wanted on the last lap when Chili's tyres and motor were both on the verge of throwing in the towel and the home-town heroes went past the Italian for a one-two finish. It was an indication not just of how well the pair rode but of the strength of the British Superbike Championship as a whole. Not surprisingly, both men would find themselves in World Championship paddocks the following season.

The fans went home talking about the racing, but there was only one subject of

Colin Edwards at home in Laguna Seca.

164

Colin Edwards and Aaron Slight got to ride Honda's all-new SP-1 V-twin.

conversation in the paddock. Just before the meeting, the FIM issued one of their regular press releases giving the results of drug tests from earlier rounds. Usually, this would just give a list of riders tested and affirm that no banned substances were detected. This time it was no routine list. The release announced that Noriyuki Haga had tested positive for ephedrine after the second race of the first round in South Africa, a race he had won.

When urine is taken after a race, it is split into A and B samples. The first is sent to an approved laboratory for testing and the second is held by the rider as insurance. Haga and Yamaha immediately asked for the B sample to be tested, which was done by the next race in Monza and confirmed illegal levels of ephedrine. Now ephedrine is a drug much favoured in sports like weight lifting, where its combination of fat-dissolving and stimulating properties is very useful. You only had to look at him to see

that Nori-chan had lost an awful lot of weight over the close season – 15kg was the commonly accepted figure – that's 33lb in old money. It turned out that as part of his winter programme Haga had been taking a herbal formulation back home in Japan and that was the source of the drug.

Standard procedure when a drug test is positive is to exclude the rider from the meeting – that means removing points scored in both races in the case of World Superbike. So Haga found himself 45 points worse off than he thought (he'd won Race 2 and been second in Race 1). There was also the small matter of returning any prize money and trophies, and the much more serious concern of a ban from racing.

In previous years this maybe wouldn't have mattered too much, but now Nori was shaping up as a genuine Championship contender. The Yamaha R7 had improved over the winter and, vitally, the team had switched back to Haga's favoured Dunlop tyres. The Samurai of Slide was back, then he wasn't, and then he was again after Yamaha appealed. Standard legal procedure when this happens is to presume innocence and give the rider all his points back until the appeal is heard.

The FIM Disciplinary Committee couldn't convene until Round 6 at Hockenheim at the start of June, two months after the sample had been taken. For reasons no one had been able to explain satisfactorily, the hearing was held just as the Superbikes, including Haga, were going out for free practice, so neither the man himself nor anyone from Yamaha was present. Not surprisingly the Committee upheld the original decision, stripped Haga of all the points he'd scored at Kyalami, and banned him for a month, which would mean missing two rounds.

Now the legal stuff really hit the fan. Yamaha had gambled on the appeal and lost, and the only chance left was double-or-quits – taking the matter outside of the sport's governing body's jurisdiction to the independent Court of Arbitration in Sport (CAS). First, they had to get leave from the

FIM for this unprecedented move, which they managed just in time for Round 7 at Misano. So yet again Haga raced with his full tally of South African points appearing on the Championship table.

So when did the CAS bring down the curtain on what had inevitably become known as the Haga Saga? Four days before the final round of the year at Brands Hatch, that's when – but as Colin Edwards had hammered out a 52-point advantage with a double win at Oschersleben nearly a month previously, it really didn't matter whether Haga got his 45 points back or not. In the end, he got 20 of them back for the first race because he wasn't tested afterwards. He was tested after Race 2 and therefore lost the 25 points he scored. The CAS also banned him for two weeks with immediate effect so he missed the last round of the year.

That's how long it took to resolve a situation that had its origins at Round 1 of the year – right up until the week of the

Aprilia signed Troy Corser – and won five races.

final round. Could it have been managed any better by any of the parties involved? In view of established practices and precedents the answer is probably yes. In the end Yamaha got exactly the same verdict as Honda did in 1994 when Aaron Slight's fuel sample from Race 2 of Round 1 was found to be illegal – see chapter seven for full details. The difference is, Honda's legal eagles got their verdict from the FIM Disciplinary Court whereas Yamaha said nothing to the Court at Hockenheim and went outside the FIM's orbit. The most cursory examination of doping cases in other sports will have shown one unbendable rule: the authorities don't care how the stuff got in the athlete, only that it was there. Evidence? Remember that Rumanian girl gymnast who lost her medal from the Sydney Olympics thanks to a cold cure given to her by the team doctor; or the Scottish skier at the Salt Lake City Winter Olympics who lost his medal because the medicine he bought in the USA was different in content from the stuff sold under the same label in Europe?

Strangely, it was the removal of Foggy that seemed to de-rail Edwards

Who knows, holding the corporate hands up to the offence and arguing the precedent of Honda's 1994 case, Yamaha might have seen Haga lose just 25 points and escape the ban. How would that have changed the complexion of the season?

It would be grossly unfair to Colin Edwards to suggest that Haga was somehow robbed of a chance of the title. Remember that the Texan had the title sewn up after the penultimate round, before the Haga Saga was resolved. Remember, too, how Colin had to cope with an intensive testing programme for the midseason Suzuka 8 Hours race, which Honda regard as equally important to both the GP and Superbike Championships. Like his riding partner,

Valentino Rossi, Colin found the endurance race a distraction from the main event. Both riders crashed but an SP-1 Honda still won in the hands of Ukawa and Katoh. If you're looking for impressive debuts, the new Honda V-twin won its first Superbike race in Kyalami, its first 24-hour race at Le Mans, its first 8 Hour, and, of course, its first World Superbike Championship. For a brand-new machine, that is some achievement.

It took Colin Edwards a lot longer to win both his first Superbike race and Championship, but that shouldn't be allowed to disguise the grit and determination that took him from a stellar apprenticeship with Yamaha in the States to a fallow three years with the Belgarda Yamaha team in World Superbike. First there was the Dunlop hiatus following the Kobe earthquake, and then the ageing YZF750 simply didn't have the legs any more, a situation illustrated at Phillip Island in 1997 when he came out of the last turn in the lead, rear tyre spinning, front wheel aviating, only to be out-dragged to the line by Aaron Slight's Honda. He may not have won but people still knew he was a contender.

There was even a war of words with Carl Fogarty – and King Carl never stooped to acknowledge those lesser beings whom he considered to be no threat. A truce was declared after Carl had won on the RC45 Honda. Colin went to the Fogarty family motorhome to retract a statement about Foggy not being a true Champion until he won on a four-cylinder machine. Fogarty was duly impressed that someone would have the guts to make such a statement to his face and went so far as to echo Raymond Roche's prophetic statement about himself: 'He'll be World Champion, but not this year.' Then, lest anyone should think he was going soft, Carl hurriedly added:

Haga's season was a mix of the spectacular and the tragicomic.

'Doesn't mean I like him, mind.'

Strangely, it was the removal of Foggy from the picture that seemed to de-rail Colin's season and he seemed in danger of going back to his old habit of having weekends where he was scarcely visible. Misano and Valencia were consecutive low points, but in the last three rounds he won four out of six races as he rediscovered the self-belief that had powered him to what turned out to be a double win in the first round of the season. Nine men won races during the 2000 season but none deserved the title more than Colin Edwards.

Ducati's early season musical chairs following the shock of Fogarty's departure did at least prove that Troy Bayliss was made of the right stuff. The Aussie's battle with Haga at Assen, a track he'd never seen before, was a minor epic, and his win at the first Brands Hatch meeting was reward for his heroics as well as a steadying influence on Ducati. British fans got to cheer Neil Hodgson winning not once but

Ben Bostrom got moved sideways by Ducati, but donned the Evel Knievel leathers and was fast again.

twice (first at Donington, then at Brands), as well as the wily veteran John Reynolds getting his first-ever win at world level in the second Brands meeting.

Second Brands? Yes, the UK got three meetings in 2000, the last being a second dose of the Kent track that ended the season in chilly mid-October nine weeks after the first. The event was originally due to go to Imola but local elections and a massive beer festival (honest) would have stretched the authorities too far and they cancelled. Incredibly, 75,000 fans turned out and fittingly saw Colin Edwards win the last race of the year. They also saw Aaron Slight run his last race for Honda. Embarrassingly, he was presented with all sorts of gifts on Saturday night before he was officially told his services would not be required for 2001. Slight had spent years waiting for a V-twin and thought his time had at last come. He made his feelings plain at Brands, throwing anything he was wearing with a Castrol Honda logo, including his leathers, to the crowd after the second race.

It was a shabby way for Slight to leave Honda. He had ridden hurt more than any other rider in the series to develop

There has never been a more surprising winning combination than Anthony Gobert and the Bimota.

the RC45, been lumbered with a nightmare selection of team-mates, and never broken ranks. It later emerged that his brain operation had been performed in the nick of time: his sight and reactions had been deteriorating rapidly, and when things started going seriously wrong he was lucky to be in Sydney, where one of the few surgeons capable of doing the job was based.

There would obviously have to be a lot of changes off the track as well as on for the 2001 season, and many of them would be informed by the FIM's release of outline plans for the return of four-strokes to the top class of Grand Prix racing first made public on 9 April at the third GP of the year in Japan, after much wrangling between the manufacturers and the FIM itself. From 2002, the 500 class would be opened up to 990cc four-strokes provided they were prototypes.

What would this mean for the future of Superbike? The Japanese factories were already known to be unhappy with the expense of the class and wanted to turn the clock back to what Superbike was meant to be in the late 1980s, when the class originated. Maybe allowing fewer modifications, as in the Supersport class, would be an option. Then there was the ever-increasing problem of the now palpable advantage the 1,000cc twins had over the 750cc fours. The only non-V-twin win of the year was by an inspired Frankie Chili on the Suzuki at home in Monza, where he beat Edwards's Honda by a fraction of a second. Yamaha announced their decision to pull out of the World Superbike Championship before the end of the year after just two seasons with the R7, and there was no new 750 Kawasaki in sight. And the first whispers of the four-stroke GPs had put paid to a plan for kitted engines which were to be made in sufficient numbers to give privateers a chance to be competitive.

Something would have to be done. The question was, what?

chapter fourteen

2001
Brave
new world

Superbike might have lost its two most marketable faces, Carl Fogarty to injury and Noriyuki Haga to Grands Prix, but it got a lot in return including new tracks and a new bike. There were, however, more questions than answers. Such as, how come Troy Corser could win the first two races of the year, in Spain, and never stand on the top box of the podium again? How could Honda's new man Tady Okada, winner of the Suzuka 8 Hours on a Superbike, be so uncompetitive? Would a 750cc four ever win a race again? And how come defending Champ Colin Edwards never scored a pole posi-

Troy Bayliss in the Assen pits after his team had removed the figure 2 from his bike's racing number.

The Benelli Tornado arrived but didn't trouble the leaders.

tion all year? Then there were all the questions over the future of the formula, and by the end of the season the paddock had become a rumour factory.

There were also question marks over the new bike. The Benelli Tornado could claim to be unique in Superbike terms because the racer came before the street-bike. But isn't Superbike by definition a class for machinery based on the road-sters you and I can buy in our local show-rooms? Well, yes, but – and it's a big but – the organisers decided to engineer a loophole to allow first-time entrants to compete, through which the Italian com-pany entered. Experienced Aussie Peter Goddard did the riding under no illu-sions about the bike being competitive; it was, he said, a development year. As the bike wasn't competitive enough to quali-fy in the top 20 any time after its debut at the eighth of 13 rounds, no one was heard complaining too hard about the Benelli's presence. Still, the only three-cylinder bike in the paddock added a dis-tinctive and delectable exhaust note to the scream of the fours and the bark of the twins.

The brand-new circuit was the Lausitzring, an IndyCar-inspired venue of monolithic proportions in Eastern Germany. The monstrous grandstands dwarfed the bikes and safety concerns forced the organisers to mark out a route to Turn 1 with plastic curbing and cones. It looked more like a club race on an ex-airfield than a World Championship event, and paddock wits soon christened the circuit the Lousy Ring. In two years Germany had managed to lose the glorious Hockenheim – probably the best race track in the world – and gain Oschersleben and the Lausitzring; no one thought it was a good deal.

Troy Bayliss emerged from the wreck-age of Ducati's 2000 season as the Bologna factory's undisputed number one and lined up with new-to-Superbike Ruben Xaus, the young, lanky and wild-riding Catalan with a win-it-or-bin-it repu-tation. They formed the official works team – Ducati Infostrada – while Ben Bostrom and his Dunlops were semi-detached and running as Ducati L&M. The really significant change in the red corner was a new bike. Officially it was called the 996R F01 but was soon known to all as the Testastretta, or 'narrow-head'. Sounds better in Italian, doesn't it? This wasn't just Ducati's usual close-season modifications; this was a genuine second-generation of the design that started with the original 851 Superbike built for the start of World Superbike in 1988.

Ducati followed the example of the other V-twin manufacturers, Honda and Aprilia, by shortening the stroke to 63.5mm, which with a 100mm bore actually gives a 998cc motor. This more rev-happy bottom end got a brand new cylinder head design with a significantly narrower valve angle – 25 as opposed to 40 degrees – allowing a much more efficient combustion chamber shape. The problem with the old cylinder head was that all four rockers for the desmodromic valve-operating system that is Ducati's hallmark were positioned between the camshafts, despite Massimo Bordi's original design thesis placing them outside the camshafts and valves. The Testastretta design had the rockers that opened the valves mounted outside the camshafts,

It was wet in Australia: Edwards won the only race and Troy Corser did a lot of talking.

Ben Bostrom did what only Polen and Foggy had done before him, win five in a row.

which allowed the cams to be moved closer together and therefore the valve angle to be narrowed. Camshaft mounting bearings were also done away with and the cams ran directly in the head, saving more space. Overall the result was a great leap forward, with as much as an extra 10hp available to the three factory riders.

Honda had also found extra power but unfortunately lost some reliability. At the opening round at Valencia the new SP-2 failed once under Edwards and three times under Slight's replacement Tadayuki Okada. Edwards promptly won the third race of the year in South Africa, then had his bike break again while shaping up for the double as Okada DNFd twice. That glorious old catch-all phrase 'electrical problems' was dusted off and used straight-faced by Honda people, although one comment about bearing failure did escape the net of secrecy.

Aprilia didn't look like they had any problems. Troy Corser started the season with SuperPole and a double win. His new team-mate Regis Laconi also shone,

briefly leading the first race and netting a creditable fourth despite injuries from a qualifying accident, but it was a false dawn. Corser spent most of the rest of the season complaining about strange vibrations from various parts of the bike, which the team couldn't diagnose. He scored a hatful of podium places but did not win again. It was very apparent that team and rider were not happy with each other, the end result being that RSV Aprilia, which had truly threatened to be the top V-twin in 2000, was reduced to fourth overall in 2001. Since Aprilia was about to launch itself into the US road-

GSE Ducati left the safe waters of British Superbike for the rigours of the World Championship, with Neil Hodgson as lead rider.

bike market, where credibility from Superbike racing on the domestic and world scene is vital, the factory was not happy.

Corser did play a lead role again after Valencia, fittingly at his home race, but it was as a shop steward, not a racer. Phillip Island is in the Bass Strait, the stormy waters that reduced the Sydney to Hobart ocean yacht race to tragic chaos not many years ago. This time the ocean managed to reduce the racing to chaos, fortunately without tragedy. Race 1 went ahead in conditions that were simply appalling; it was like racing inside a storm cloud. (Back in '92, when Carl Fogarty and Terry Rymer clinched their World Endurance title here in a six-hour race, the conditions had been just as bad and several marshals ended up in hospital with hypothermia.) Castrol Honda made the best of the dire conditions and went some way to making up for their dreadful start to the year.

The Supersport race then went ahead in even worse conditions and it was apparent that the track was unraceable thanks to standing water everywhere. Nevertheless, the pit lane was opened on time for Race 2 and a few riders went out. Corser now took matters into his own hands, stationing himself at the pit lane exit and urging his fellow riders not to go out. Public rows with the organisers followed, with Davide Tardozzi also weighing in against Corser because he wanted his riders to make up their own minds. World-wide TV audiences were treated to a bizarre public debate before Colin Edwards, as World Champion, was sent out for an exploratory lap. He returned to state the obvious: Race 2 was cancelled. Good job, or spectators as well as marshals would have been at risk of hypothermia, never mind the riders.

The only notable consequence of the singleton Australian race was that Troy Bayliss went to the lead in the points standings for the first time, and then promptly lost it at Sugo where anyone not on Dunlops was in deep trouble. Colin Edwards could only manage 12th and 13th places behind Dunlop-shod regulars like Corser and the usual crop of local aces, who all – even the Honda men – use Dunlops in their local Championship. Bayliss fared even worse and the Championship lead was handed back to Corser.

The bizarre happenings of the opening four rounds of the season had not revealed any clues about the destination of the title. We had to wait for the fifth round for the picture to come clearly into focus on the awe-inspiring tarmac of Monza, and when the haze cleared it revealed Troy Bayliss. The Aussie took

Ducati got back to business as usual with the works team of Bayliss and Xaus.

SuperPole and then his first-ever double-win at World level.

But there were several other twists to the plot before Troy was able to clinch the crown. The first came from Britain's Neil Hodgson on his return to World Superbike with the GSE Ducati team which had taken him to the 2000 British Championship. Equipped with RS-spec Ducatis – basically last year's works racer – and Dunlop tyres, and with the highly promising youngster

Frankie Chili's Donington win on the GSX-R Suzuki was a landmark victory – probably the last for a 750cc four-cylinder bike.

James Toseland as his team-mate, Neil took a few races to re-adjust to top-level racing, but when he did he was very quick. Quick enough to depose Troy Corser as king of the SuperPole thanks to a stunning run of four of them in five races in the middle of the season, and to win the first race at Donington where the Dunlop runners all had a good day. It was his first rostrum of the season but six more followed in nine races before he faded towards the end of the season.

The second Donington race gave the crowd another favourite to cheer: Frankie Chili. With no Yamaha team in the Championship and the Kawasaki ZX-7R approaching pensionable age, the only hope for a 750cc four-cylinder victory was Chili and the newly fuel-injected Suzuki. The factory's road-going 750 had got injection in 2000 but the Alstare Corona team had stuck with the carburetted version for that season. Now it became apparent why. Chili simply could not get on with the power delivery of the new bike and said so loudly, resulting in an end-of-season bust-up with team-bosses. His team-mate, Frenchman Stephane Chambon, getting his reward for the Supersport crown, wasn't able to give meaningful support, and Frankie's two rostrums at Donington plus Yanagawa's pair at Monza and Lavilla's thirds at Valencia and Misano were the only top-three spots the four-cylinder brigade managed all year. Within the Motor Sports Manufacturers Association (MSMA), the constructors' trade union, there was a move to alter the regulations to allow the 750 fours a ten per cent overbore to 825cc for 2002, which many thought would get them competitive again, but it did not gain the necessary unanimous backing, despite vigorous lobbying by Kawasaki and Suzuki. Note the date: 27 May 2001, the last time a 750cc four won a World Superbike race.

Edwards's title challenge may have been torpedoed at the outset by mechan-

Neil Hodgson leads the field at Laguna Seca.

ical woes, but even his seemingly certain second place overall came under threat from a most unexpected source. Ben Bostrom's introduction to World Superbike had been traumatic to say the least, thanks to Fogarty's exit and the chaos that engulfed Ducati's efforts in 2000, and for the first half of the 2001 season it looked as if things weren't going to get any better. Going into Round 8 at Misano he had one solitary win, at Kyalami, and only one other rostrum, from the opening race in Valencia, plus a dislocated shoulder thanks to the new Mickey Mouse chicane that defaced Monza at the insistence of the F1 cars. Comparisons were being made with the ill-starred career of Mike Hale, the last great hope to emerge from AMA Superbike racing in the States. Then came Misano and, nagging shoulder injury notwithstanding, Bostrum shared the wins with Bayliss at a track where Ducati have always done well. That set him up nicely for a return to the only other track he had ever won on, Laguna Seca. Dunlop runners monopolised the

rostrum as Ben did the double for the first time in his career to make it three wins in a row in front of an ecstatic crowd of fellow Californians.

The big question hanging over Brands Hatch, the next venue, before proceedings got under way, concerned the crowd and how the retirement of Carl Fogarty would affect attendances. On race day it simply looked as if the old red Foggy T-shirts had faded in the wash as the Kent track turned orange, with over 120,000 fans flying the colours of Neil Hodgson's GSE Ducati team. The home favourite couldn't convert yet another SuperPole into a race win, though, as Ben Boz on only his second visit to the complex and intimidating Brands long circuit blitzed to both wins and made it five in a row, something only Doug Polen and Carl Fogarty had achieved in the entire history of the Championship. Bostrom's second half of the season more than made up for his very patchy opening half. Although the Championship was gone and he didn't win another race he still ended the year with six wins, the same number as eventual champion Bayliss.

Ducati's other works rider Ruben Xaus also took some time to get going. True to his win-or-crash reputation he spent a lot of time reducing carbon-fibre bodywork to expensive shrapnel, but at Oschersleben Michelin gave him a front tyre that cured all his problems – or that he believed cured all his problems. He promptly gave Edwards a hard time in Race 1 as his team-mate Bayliss hit mechanical problems, then won Race 2 from the American in a fair fight. It was another historic moment – the first-ever win in World Superbike by a Spanish rider.

It could – should? – have been more at the next round, the penultimate of the year, at Assen, but Xaus did the decent thing and shadowed his team-mate home in both races, having plainly been the

Troy Bayliss's Ducati wears silver at Imola in honour of Paul Smart's landmark win there 30 years earlier.

fastest man out there. No one complained too much about team orders, though, as the two Ducatis were well clear of the field both times and the Championship was at stake. Edwards and the Castrol Honda team conspired with Michelin to make a disastrous tyre choice for the second race, which saw the World Champ come home tenth and lose his crown. Bayliss didn't know that as he came back to the pit lane – like the rest of the paddock he thought the fight would go down to the last round. Only when he saw his team wearing the obligatory celebratory T-shirts did he realise he was World Champion.

All of which left the way clear for a last-round showdown at Imola three weeks later. Superbike's first visit to the historic Italian circuit produced two amazing races, with Ruben Xaus winning the first one to prove a point. Bayliss, his bike resplendent in silver to celebrate Paul Smart's legendary 1972 victory in the Imola 200 – the first race win for a desmo Duke – fell chasing his team-mate, and his bike scooped up Regis

Laconi's Aprilia. It looked horrible. The Frenchman's bike appeared to land on him at one point but the human damage was limited to a broken collarbone for Bayliss. As soon as Laconi stopped rolling he leapt to his feet and rushed to aid the obviously injured Aussie. It was a generous act of spontaneous sportsmanship and earned Laconi a special award from Italian magazine *Moto Sprint* at their end-of-season Casque d'Oro awards. Laconi and Aprilia got their just desserts a few hours later when the Frenchman beat off (almost literally) Xaus to win Race 2. This wasn't just his first win, it was his first rostrum in Superbike and earned him a place alongside the Doohans, Kocinskis and Chilis of this world as one of the very few men to have won a 500 GP and a World Superbike race.

In many ways Laconi's season was symptomatic of much that went on in 2001: initial promise followed by a lengthy period in the wilderness and a moment in the limelight. Some riders, like Bostrom, had longer periods of grace; some, like Okada, hardly troubled the scorers at all. Overall, the departure of Fogarty still seemed to leave a vacuum that was waiting to be filled.

One other feature of the season's last round was the first sight of proposed new technical regulations for the class. The British Superbike Championship had already made a unilateral decision to go to an overall 1,000cc limit, but with Supersport-style regulations on engine modifications to four-cylinder motors that effectively banned any tuning. The proposed World regulations didn't look too different, but there in black and white were the words 'treaded tyres'. No one seemed sure how that had happened, and with both Michelin and Dunlop denying any prior knowledge and pointing out that they didn't have suitable designs to go racing to those regulations confusion reigned.

Clearly the changes were being driven by the MSMA, whose members had seen costs for what was supposed to be a production-based formula spiral out of control to the point where HRC were spending as much keeping an SP-2 on track as they were on an NSR500. That was more than enough motivation to try and row back Superbike to where it was meant to be in 1988, when the class was born. Supersport regs, which forbid almost any modifications to the bottom end of the motor and stipulate that standard forks, brakes and wheels must be used, are an obvious method of cost cutting. Hell, if you look inside the fairing of a factory Honda CBR600 Supersport bike you'll see a hole in the (stock) top yoke where the ignition switch should be; they're that standard. There was also the small matter of the market for 750cc streetbikes collapsing worldwide. Motorcyclists were buying 600 or 1,000cc fours, assuming they were not on big V-twins, of course.

All the puzzling over the future was brought into focus by one cold fact

The need to do something was driven by several causes: money, specifically the severe downturn in the Japanese economy, was, as usual, a major factor, with the rapidly decreasing competitiveness of the 750cc fours another. All the puzzling over the future was brought into sharp relief by one cold fact. In April 2002 the sound of four-strokes would be heard in the Grand Prix paddock for the first time in over 20 years. Honda and Yamaha showcased their new MotoGP machines before the end of the season; Aprilia declared their intention to compete in the new formula; and Ducati, Suzuki, and Kawasaki announced that they would be in MotoGP in 2003. It looked like the time for Superbike to reinvent itself. Honda FireBlade versus Yamaha R1 versus Suzuki GSX-R1000, anyone?

chapter fifteen

2002
A season of two halves

By the end of the 2002 season just about everything in World Superbike had changed, but once again the top men in the Championship gave us a nail-biting finale. In fact they rounded the year off with one of the best races the

Colin Edwards rode a record-breaking season in immaculate style.

Championship has ever seen. Four-stroke Grand Prix bikes were now a reality, with Ducati and Kawasaki waiting to join the new MotoGP class in 2003, while Superbike's 750cc four-cylinder brigade was down to two factory Kawasakis, two Bertocchi Kawasakis and one Suzuki. Pressure for rule changes was extreme but it took a long while for the necessary

unanimity between the manufacturers to be achieved and a decision was only reached halfway through the season.

As traditional Superbike racing companies prepared to put their official efforts into GPs, there was the truly weird sight of one company coming the other way. Malaysian state oil company Petronas had shown a Sauber-engined MotoGP bike at their home Grand Prix at the end of 2001. Now it was announced that the bike would be coming to World Superbike instead and forming the basis for a road bike that would have the name of none other than Carl Fogarty on the tank! The FP1, we were assured by team owner Fogarty, would race by midseason.

While the Japanese four-cylinder teams had either gone, like Yamaha, or were going, Honda signalled their intentions by reducing their team to one man for 2002 – Colin Edwards. For years the Japanese factories had wanted to reduce the costs of Superbike racing, and the severe downturn in their home economy now demanded this. HRC, for instance, said it cost almost as much to run an SP-2 as it did to run an NSR500 two-stroke GP bike. What the factories wanted was to get back to what Superbike was always intended to be – a formula for going racing with modified street bikes. Added pressure came from the market, where sales of 750cc fours had plummeted. The punters wanted 600s, with their obvious relationship to Supersport machinery, or 1000s with two, three or four cylinders.

For a change in the rules, the MSMA had to be unanimous and it took until the Silverstone meeting at the end of May for the Italian manufacturers (mainly Aprilia) to line up with the four Japanese factories. Thus the FIM was able to announce that the Superbike Commission (consisting of Claude Danis of the FIM, Paolo Flammini of SBK International, an MSMA representative and a representative

Bayliss on the way to another early season win – with Edwards close by as usual.

Ruben Xaus contemplates the wreckage down under.

of the teams) had approved new regulations for the 2003 Championship designed to get those 1000cc fours in.

Previous suggestions about treaded tyres were quietly forgotten and the announcement was brief and to the point: 1000cc fours would be allowed in under current regulations but with a minimum weight of 168kg and with air restrictors. The restrictors would be 26.3mm in diameter for a single intake and 18.7mm if the bike had two. The idea of this sort of regulation is to level the playing field for privateers by effectively power-capping motors. If you can only flow so much air you can only make so much power no matter what you do. Theoretically, this is much easier to police than the Supersport regulations, which severely limit engine tuning. Most people were agreed that this was a pretty good compromise, although some asked what the point was of building £20,000 motors and then strangling them.

Meanwhile the show went on with the old rules and one Honda up against the same Ducati teams as last year – Bayliss and Xaus in the Corse team, Hodgson and Toseland in the HM Plant squad and Ben Bostrom in the L&M team. Noriyuki Haga returned after a disgruntled year in GPs to pilot the lone Aprilia, Kawasaki brought in 2000 Sugo double-winner Hitoyasu Izutsu and, to the delight of British fans, Chris Walker – who'd had an even worse 2001 in GPs than Haga. Gregorio Lavilla left Kawasaki to replace Chili on the Suzuki while the Italian found himself on a private NCR Ducati.

Tyres might not have played a part in the new regulations but they did in the racing. Michelin had spent a lot of time and effort developing a fresh generation of S4 slicks to cope with the new MotoGP four-strokes. Happily they also worked on Superbikes, to the tune of around a second a lap improvement. Unhappily, Dunlop hadn't made a similarly great leap forward and Messrs Hodgson, Bostrom and Haga found themselves at an acute disadvantage at most tracks – as did the Michelin runners who didn't have access to the new rubber.

For this and other reasons the Championship quickly became a two-man race between riders with S4 Michelins: reigning champion Troy Bayliss and his predecessor Colin Edwards. Dunlop's qualifiers were as usual on the pace for the one-lap dash of SuperPole which let Hodgson, Bostrom and Haga fight for front-row starts but rarely for the win. The first three rounds of the year were a Bayliss benefit. He won every race, something no-one had done before at the start of the year – but, just as he was eyeing-up Doug Polen's record of seven races on the trot, the circus came to Sugo, the track where Bayliss had crashed twice in 2000 and scored a grand total of four points in 2001. Not surprisingly, the benefit came to an end. Very surprisingly, a Michelin rider won a race in Japan for the first time since Takuma Aoki in '96. That man was Colin Edwards, the Texan sharing the wins with local Honda man and All-Japan Champion Makoto Tamada. It was also the first Sugo win by a non-Japanese rider since '95. Bayliss wasn't fazed by missing out on the record for consecutive wins, and instead seemed happy to escape from his bogey track with fifth and fourth places.

Sugo also gave the World Superbike paddock its first sight of Ben Bostrom's brother Eric away from his home round. Eric, Kawasaki's AMA Superbike star, actually out-scored big brother over the weekend in the first of a series of wild-card rides designed to ease him into world-level competition. Kawasaki needed him, the top four-cylinder man in the Championship, Izutsu, having crashed in qualifying and badly broken his left wrist.

Edwards did hit back occasionally, noticeably at Silverstone where storms of biblical proportions put Bayliss on the floor, not once but twice in the same

It was wet at Silverstone – very wet.

Bayliss may have been winning but no-one could say Edwards wasn't trying.

race. Both times his bike kept going, seemingly in contravention of the regulation that requires a mercury switch to cut the motor if a certain lean angle is exceeded. Both times he got back on and charged towards the front of the field at lap speeds well quicker than anyone else's. In Race 2 Edwards contrived to fall on the warm-up lap, so bad were conditions, but got back on to his spare bike to finish second. A good crowd at the track's first World Superbike round also demonstrated how popular Chris Walker was with British bike fans, even compared with other local riders like Hodgson.

When the two re-enacted their British Championship battle in Race 2 and Walker got a splendid fourth place, both crowd and rider acted like he'd won the Championship.

There were more departures from the form book at Laguna Seca: Bayliss and Edwards scored their maiden wins there but, more significantly, the first race rostrum was 100 per cent Michelin. Local wild cards Bostrom the Younger and Nicky Hayden mixed it up with the regulars with Eboz actually leading the race for a while and scoring a sixth and a fourth. Hayden had been expected to compete for a win but instead took a fighting fourth in Race 1 then crashed and took Haga out in Race 2 before getting back on to finish 13th. Both Americans were obviously well worth tempting away from the domestic scene – but could anyone afford to match the wages they got in AMA racing?

Bayliss now led the Championship by 53 points, despite the fact that Colin Edwards was riding as well as, if not better than, he had ever done and only been off the rostrum once – yes, once – all season. The reigning champ was riding at the top of his form. He looked just as fast and loose as ever and the number-one plate had certainly done nothing to reduce his will to win and that, combined with the latest Ducati, gave him the slightest of advantages over Edwards. Bayliss ruthlessly exploited that edge but the Honda rider never gave up so much as a single point without a fight. Edwards was mentally tough enough to keep the pressure up and every time Troy stood on top of the rostrum there was Colin beside him.

Of the Dunlop runners it was Neil Hodgson who was emerging as the toughest, comfortably outgunning the disappointing Haga and the patchy Bostrom. His motivation was helped by Ducati announcing he would be in the full works Ducati Corse team for 2003 to replace Bayliss who, it was assumed, would go off to Ducati's new MotoGP project. The form of Ruben Xaus was a mystery but it emerged late in the season that he had not had access to the latest Michelins until halfway through the year. Chris Walker was pleasing his hardcore fans by usually, although by no means always, winning the four-cylinder 750cc battle with Lavilla. Young British hopeful James Toseland continued on his learning curve and added steel to his skill, as a spectacular last-corner mugging of Haga at Oschersleben showed. His emotional rostrum finish in Race 2 at Assen was well deserved. Young Aussie Broc Parkes on a Pirelli-shod Ducati also showed promise, as you would expect from a protégé of Wayne Gardner.

As the midseason break approached the question on everyone's lips was could anyone beat Bayliss or would he beat Doug Polen's record of 17 wins in a season? Ironically, the person who nearly cost Bayliss his Championship lead was his team-mate Ruben Xaus. It happened at Brands Hatch on the out-lap of a qualifying session. Both Ducati Corse riders were on the way up the hill to Druids hairpin early in the lap, Xaus weaving to get some heat into his tyres as Bayliss came up considerably faster on the outside. Xaus didn't know his team-mate was coming and moved to the left as Troy was overtaking, with the result that Bayliss was sent onto the grass where he fell and scraped along the Armco barrier. It was a messy crash and the Aussie was obviously hurt. He was still suffering from a sore back thanks to a crash in qualifying at Laguna and this incident aggravated it and added a broken rib for good measure.

Under the circumstances his third and second places were heroic but Edwards did the double for the first time in the season and took a big bite out of the gap at the top of the Championship.

The top three in the order they finished the season: Edwards, Bayliss and Hodgson.

From Bayliss's point of view, the silver lining was the four-week break in the calendar before Oschersleben that enabled him to get back to full fitness.

The other seismic event at Brands was the first public outing of the Foggy Petronas bike in the hands of team riders Troy Corser and James Haydon, as well as a couple of laps from King Carl himself. The bikes had actually been unveiled in June amid assurances that the target of racing at Laguna Seca was attainable. That date was then amended to Brands before the team had to admit defeat and postpone the FP1's race debut until 2003. Producing enough road bikes for homologation was the main stumbling block and the MSMA was in no mood to show the leniency they'd exhibited to Benelli. Typically, Carl brushed aside his earlier statements about how he'd make people eat their words when his team met the deadline by reflecting that perhaps this pressure was necessary to drive the project forward. He probably had a point. The bike certainly showed some very nice detailing and with Petronas bank-rolling things there was no shortage of money, but the team now had to revise their 900cc triple to compete not just with the V-twins but with 1000cc four-cylinder bikes.

The Oschersleben round saw Edwards close the gap even more with another double, making it five wins on the trot. He also passed a few significant milestones. Race 1 gave the Castrol Honda team their 50th World Superbike win and Race 2 took Colin to joint second in the all-time winners table alongside Doug Polen. It was also the 100th win by an

One for the ladies: Frankie Chili gets his kit off.

Neil Hodgson was the season's unsung hero.

American rider and equalled Polen's record of 21 podiums in a year, though Colin had scored them consecutively. Even Foggy in his pomp only managed a dozen consecutive top-three finishes in 1995. All that work and Edwards was still second in the Championship!

Bayliss's Brands crash had obscured the fact that Honda had supplied Edwards with a new motor after the Suzuka 8 Hours race – where Colin teamed with Daijiro Katoh to win. The Texan was on a roll, and all of a sudden Bayliss was looking vulnerable with his Championship lead after Germany reduced to 29 points.

As so often, Assen was the turning point. Race 1 featured the two main men again, with Bayliss following Edwards home. That reduced the lead to 24

points, and with only three more races on the calendar Troy could afford that rate of attrition. But the Aussie was feeling the strain and, according to other riders, making unforced errors. In Race 2 he made several. The first was to run off track, but he stayed on his wheels and set about reeling in the third-place dice between Hodgson and Haga. When Nori punted Neil into the sand Bayliss inherited a safe third place. Inexplicably, he then crashed a couple of laps from the flag and Colin won again to equal Polen's record run of seven consecutive victories. When Edwards got the pit signal telling him that Bayliss was out he couldn't quite believe it and 'used up a year's worth of concentration' getting to the flag. Much more importantly, he also went to the top of the Championship, the first time Troy Bayliss had been deposed all season. The lead? One solitary point, with only the Imola round left.

It was a fitting finale. The two contenders, the men who had so far won all but one of the races in the year, went at it like a six-lap club race. The lap record was shredded time after time and to add to the drama Race 1 was interrupted by a red flag half-way through when Edwards was leading. Conspiracy theorists pointed to the fact that the flag came out very quickly just as the Italian Ducati appeared to be losing touch with the Honda. In truth, it worked to Edwards's advantage as he knew he had a 0.7 second lead and thus was able to follow Bayliss across the line after the restart yet win on corrected time to give him a six-point lead with only one race left.

The last race of the season was a real classic. Bayliss, as usual, gave it everything while Edwards refused to yield up the victory. Despite the fact the title was at stake the last lap involved fairing-bashing and several changes of lead. Fittingly,

Troy Bayliss lost none of his aggression in the defence of his title.

Edwards took the win and the title while Bayliss appeared on the surface to be a lot less upset than he'd been after Assen, maybe because it had been a fair fight and he'd simply been beaten on the day.

In 2002 both men had ridden better than they ever had. Bayliss lost none of his aggression and frightening will to win despite carrying the number-one plate, while Edwards refused to be discouraged by the Aussie's runaway start to the year and maintained his motivation. He also showed, notably at Imola, that he could mix it with the best of them. There was huge pressure on Bayliss, not least because the showdown was at Ducati's home track. Well, the last race wasn't a fight, it was a war – and Edwards won.

The other man who didn't lose his motivation was Neil Hodgson who emerged as clearly the fastest of the Dunlop runners and, as his third place overall showed, he firmly put a few Michelin men in their place too. Knowing that he would be a Ducati factory rider in 2003 must have contributed to his motivation in the final race.

But the statistics tell the story of the season. The year was dominated by just two men – the only other winner all year was Tamada at Sugo. In the first half of the year Troy Bayliss was supreme, but the only time Colin Edwards was off the rostrum was in the first race of the year. Once Bayliss had suffered that unfortunate injury at Brands, Edwards and his new motor took over and shattered the all-time records for consecutive wins, consecutive rostrums and number of rostrums in a season. Anyone who wants to beat those last two marks is going to have to finish in the top three in every race of a season! In the final analysis, Edwards had as near an error-free season as it's possible to imagine. Bayliss made one mistake. That was the difference between them.

Acknowledgements

For those of us who remember earlier short-lived attempts at a production bike-based World Championship it is really pleasing to see the 'fifteen years' on the subtitle of this book. So I'd like to thank the man who started it all, Steve McLaughlin, and the men who picked up the ball and ran with it, Maurizio and Paolo Flammini, for their faith in Superbike. Special thanks to Paolo for his typically charming Foreword.

Motorcycle racing should always be fun and thankfully the people involved in the World Superbike Championship have always remembered that. I hope this book reflects that. Not that this has ever stopped them from competing at the highest level and I hope the book reflects that too.

Thanks also to the Haynes team of Darryl Reach, Mark Hughes and Flora Myer, and to Kay Edge for her eagle-eyed subbing.

Finally, I must say thanks to my wife Wendy who has to put up with my regular excursions to race tracks and other strange motorcycle-connected behaviour. Without her, I couldn't have written this book.

Julian Ryder
Cheshire,
October 2002

I'd like to thank my wife Kay for all her tremendous support and understanding throughout the fifteen years of the Superbike World Championship, and especially for putting up with my frequent excursions. She was one of the few people who didn't think I was mad to leave the Grand Prix scene in 1988 for the unknown joys of World Superbikes.

Special thanks also to my daughter Katie who could do a mean lap-chart from an early age and is now experiencing the joys of travel for herself.

I would also like to thank all the riders, mechanics and team personnel who have made the Superbike scene a great place to work and a good place to have a party. Many a Sunday night has been spent in their company and many of them have become good friends, particularly Fred Merkel – the first Champion. He was a great ambassador for the series when it started, and quickly became a travelling companion and friend of the family.

The series has grown beyond recognition from the early days, but manages to retain the warmth and friendly atmosphere it began with. It might be war on the track, but it's lots of fun off it.

I am happy to have joined the Superbike World Championship at the very beginning and am very happy to be still involved with it at the moment – long may it continue.

Kel Edge
Richmond,
October 2002

Results

1988 season

Round 1 – Great Britain
Donington Park, 3 April
Race 1 & 2, aggregate result
1 Marco Lucchinelli, Ita, Ducati
2 Fred Merkel, USA, Honda
3 Joey Dunlop, GB, Honda
4 Roger Marshall, GB, Suzuki
5 Fabrizio Pirovano, Ita, Yamaha
6 Kenny Irons, GB, Honda
7 Jari Suhonen, Fin, Yamaha
8 Andy McGladdery, GB, Suzuki
9 Steve Williams, GB, Bimota
10 Mark Farmer, GB, Honda
11 Dave Leach, GB, Yamaha
12 Tom Douglas, Can, Yamaha
13 John Lofthouse, GB, Suzuki
14 Asa Moyce, GB, Kawasaki
15 Esko Kuparinen, Fin, Kawasaki

Standings – 1 Lucchinelli 20; 2 Merkel 17;
3 Dunlop 15; 4 Marshall 13; 5 Pirovano 11;
6 Irons 10

Round 2 – Hungary
Hungaroring, 30 April
Race 1
1 Fred Merkel, USA, Honda
2 Davide Tardozzi, Ita, Bimota

3 Stephane Mertens, Bel, Bimota
4 Adrien Morillas, Fra, Kawasaki
5 Fabrizio Pirovano, Ita, Yamaha
6 Joey Dunlop, GB, Honda
7 Rene Rasmussen, Den, Suzuki
8 Roger Burnett, GB, Honda
9 Marco Lucchinelli, Ita, Ducati
10 Ernst Gschwender, Ger, Suzuki
11 Eric Delcamp, Fra, Kawasaki
12 Paul Iddon, GB, Bimota
13 Michael Galinski, Ger, Bimota
14 Jari Suhonen, Fin, Yamaha
15 Andy McGladdery, GB, Suzuki

Race 2
1 Adrien Morillas, Fra, Kawasaki
2 Stephane Mertens, Bel, Bimota
3 Davide Tardozzi, Ita, Bimota
4 Roger Burnett, GB, Honda
5 Fred Merkel, USA, Honda
6 Fabrizio Pirovano, Ita, Yamaha
7 Rene Rasmussen, Den, Suzuki
8 Paul Iddon, GB, Bimota
9 Ernst Gschwender, Ger, Suzuki
10 Jari Suhonen, Fin, Yamaha
11 Virginio Ferrari, Ita, Honda
12 Anders Andersson, Swe, Suzuki
13 Eric Delcamp, Fra, Kawasaki
14 Peter Rubatto, Ger, Bimota
15 Jean-Louis Guignabodet, Fra, Honda

Standings – 1 Merkel 32.5; 2 Lucchinelli 23.5;
3 Pirovano 21.5; 4 Dunlop 20; 5 Morillas 16.5;
6 Mertens & Tardozzi 16

Round 3 – Germany
Hockenheim, 8 May
Race 1
1 Davide Tardozzi, Ita, Bimota
2 Christophe Bouheben, Fra, Honda
3 Alex Vieira, Fra, Honda
4 Edwin Weibel, CH, Honda
5 Roger Burnett, GB, Honda
6 Marco Lucchinelli, Ita, Ducati
7 Joey Dunlop, GB, Honda
8 Andreas Hofmann, Ger, Honda
9 Eric Delcamp, Fra, Kawasaki
10 Virginio Ferrari, Ita, Honda
11 Fabrizio Pirovano, Ita, Yamaha
12 Paul Iddon, GB, Bimota
13 Stephane Mertens, Bel, Bimota
14 Kenny Irons, GB, Honda
15 Peter Rubatto, Ger, Bimota

Race 2
1 Davide Tardozzi, Ita, Bimota
2 Stephane Mertens, Bel, Bimota
3 Alex Vieira, Fra, Honda
4 Roger Burnett, GB, Honda
5 Joey Dunlop, GB, Honda
6 Eric Delcamp, Fra, Kawasaki
7 Kenny Irons, GB, Honda
8 Fabrizio Pirovano, Ita, Yamaha
9 Virginio Ferrari, Ita, Honda
10 Andreas Hofmann, Ger, Honda
11 Marco Lucchinelli, Ita, Ducati
12 Bodo Schmidt, Ger, Bimota
13 Paul Iddon, GB, Bimota
14 Peter Rubatto, Ger, Bimota
15 Michael Galinski, Ger, Bimota

Standings – 1 Tardozzi 36; 2 Merkel 32.5;
3 Lucchinelli 31; 4 Dunlop 30; 5 Pirovano 28;
6 Mertens 26

Round 4 – Austria
Osterreichring, 3 July
Race 1
1 Marco Lucchinelli, Ita, Ducati
2 Fabrizio Pirovano, Ita, Yamaha
3 Mal Campbell, Aus, Honda
4 Alex Vieira, Fra, Honda
5 Davide Tardozzi, Ita, Bimota
6 Edwin Weibel, CH, Honda
7 Adrien Morillas, Fra, Kawasaki
8 Rob Phillis, Aus, Kawasaki
9 Anders Andersson, Swe, Suzuki
10 Ernst Gschwender, Ger, Suzuki
11 Karl-Heinz Reigl, Aut, Bimota
12 Dietmar Kemter, Aut, Honda
13 Udo Mark, Ger, Bimota
14 Dieter Heinen, Bel, Honda
15 Mauro Ricci, Ita, Ducati

Race 2
1 Davide Tardozzi, Ita, Bimota
2 Christophe Bouheben, Fra, Honda
3 Alex Vieira, Fra, Honda
4 Edwin Weibel, CH, Honda
5 Adrien Morillas, Fra, Kawasaki
6 Mal Campbell, Aus, Honda
7 Fabrizio Pirovano, Ita, Yamaha
8 Fred Merkel, USA, Honda
9 Marino Fabbri, Ita, Bimota
10 Ernst Gschwender, Ger, Suzuki
11 Paul Ramon, Bel, Honda
12 Anders Andersson, Swe, Suzuki
13 Jari Suhonen, Fin, Yamaha
14 Udo Mark, Ger, Bimota
15 Dietmar Kemter, Aut, Honda

Standings – 1 Tardozzi 51.5;
2 Lucchinelli & Pirovano 41; 4 Merkel 36.5;
5 Dunlop 30; 6 Vieira 29

Round 5 – Japan
Sugo, 28 August
Race 1
1 Gary Goodfellow, Can, Suzuki
2 Fred Merkel, USA, Honda
3 Yukiya Oshima, Jap, Suzuki
4 Stephane Mertens, Bel, Bimota
5 Mitsuaki Watanabe, Jap, Yamaha
6 Rob Phillis, Aus, Kawasaki
7 Aaron Slight, NZ, Bimota
8 Tadaaki Hanamura, Jap, Honda
9 Koichi Kobayashi, Jap, Honda
10 Virginio Ferrari, Ita, Honda
11 Toshiharu Kaneko, Jap, Yamaha
12 Marco Lucchinelli, Ita, Ducati
13 Hisatomo Nakamura, Jap, Suzuki
14 Satoshi Endo, Jap, Honda
15 Anders Andersson, Swe, Suzuki

Race 2
1 Michael Doohan, Aus, Yamaha
2 Kenichiro Iwahashi, Jap, Honda
3 Gary Goodfellow, Can, Suzuki
4 Davide Tardozzi, Ita, Bimota
5 Edwin Weibel, CH, Honda
6 Rob Phillis, Aus, Kawasaki

7   Brian Morrison, GB, Honda
8   Virginio Ferrari, Ita, Honda
9   Tadaaki Hanamura, Jap, Honda
10   Fabrizio Pirovano, Ita, Yamaha
11   Fred Merkel, USA, Honda
12   Koichi Kobayashi, Jap, Honda
13   Yukiya Oshima, Jap, Suzuki
14   Aaron Slight, NZ, Bimota
15   Mal Campbell, Aus, Honda

Standings – 1 Tardozzi 58; 2 Merkel 47.5;
3 Pirovano 44; 4 Lucchinelli 43; 5 Mertens 32.5;
6 Dunlop 30

Round 6 – France
Le Mans, 4 September
Race 1
1   Fabrizio Pirovano, Ita, Yamaha
2   Eric Delcamp, Fra, Kawasaki
3   Stephane Mertens, Bel, Bimota
4   Alex Vieira, Fra, Honda
5   Christophe Bouheben, Fra, Honda
6   Fred Merkel, USA, Honda
7   Roger Burnett, GB, Honda
8   Terry Rymer, GB, Honda
9   Marino Fabbri, Ita, Bimota
10   Marco Lucchinelli, Ita, Ducati
11   Jari Suhonen, Fin, Yamaha
12   Davide Tardozzi, Ita, Bimota
13   Anders Andersson, Swe, Suzuki
14   Jean-Yves Mounier, Fra, Yamaha
15   Mark Linscott, GB, Honda

Standings – 1 Pirovano 64; 2 Tardozzi 62;
3 Merkel 57.5; 4 Lucchinelli 49; 5 Mertens 47.5;
6 Vieira 42

Round 7 – Portugal
Estoril, 11 September
Race 1
1   Davide Tardozzi, Ita, Bimota
2   Stephane Mertens, Bel, Bimota
3   Marco Lucchinelli, Ita, Ducati
4   Fred Merkel, USA, Honda
5   Terry Rymer, GB, Honda
6   Fabrizio Pirovano, Ita, Yamaha
7   Peter Rubatto, Ger, Bimota
8   Anders Andersson, Swe, Suzuki
9   Paul Iddon, GB, Bimota
10   Robert Dunlop, GB, Honda
11   Mauro Ricci, Ita, Ducati
12   Ernst Gschwender, Ger, Suzuki
13   Anton Grushka, Ger, Honda
14   Jean-Louis Guignabodet, Fra, Honda
15   Andy McGladdery, GB, Honda

Race 2
1   Stephane Mertens, Bel, Bimota
2   Davide Tardozzi, Ita, Bimota
3   Terry Rymer, GB, Honda
4   Marco Lucchinelli, Ita, Ducati
5   Fred Merkel, USA, Honda
6   Fabrizio Pirovano, Ita, Yamaha
7   Robert Dunlop, GB, Honda
8   Paul Iddon, GB, Bimota
9   Anders Andersson, Swe, Suzuki
10   Mauro Ricci, Ita, Ducati
11   Marino Fabbri, Ita, Bimota
12   Andy McGladdery, GB, Honda
13   Jari Suhonen, Fin, Yamaha
14   Anton Grushka, Ger, Honda
15   Jean-Louis Guignabodet, Fra, Honda

Standings – 1 Tardozzi 80.5; 2 Pirovano 74;
3 Merkel 69.5; 4 Mertens 66; 5 Lucchinelli 63;
6 Vieira 42

Round 8 – Australia
Oran Park, 25 September
Race 1
1   Michael Doohan, Aus, Yamaha
2   Michael Dowson, Aus, Yamaha
3   Rob Phillis, Aus, Kawasaki
4   Fred Merkel, USA, Honda
5   Mal Campbell, Aus, Honda
6   Fabrizio Pirovano, Ita, Yamaha
7   Stephane Mertens, Bel, Bimota
8   Gary Goodfellow, Can, Honda
9   Robert Scolyer, Aus, Honda
10   Sean Gallagher, Aus, Honda
11   Davide Tardozzi, Ita, Bimota
12   Andy McGladdery, GB, Honda
13   Robert Dunlop, GB, Honda

14   Terry Rymer, GB, Honda
15   Ian Pero, Aus, Suzuki

Race 2
1   Michael Doohan, Aus, Yamaha
2   Michael Dowson, Aus, Yamaha
3   Fred Merkel, USA, Honda
4   Rob Phillis, Aus, Kawasaki
5   Gary Goodfellow, Can, Honda
6   Stephane Mertens, Bel, Bimota
7   Fabrizio Pirovano, Ita, Yamaha
8   Mal Campbell, Aus, Honda
9   Robert Scolyer, Aus, Honda
10   Davide Tardozzi, Ita, Bimota
11   Terry Rymer, GB, Honda
12   Sean Gallagher, Aus, Honda
13   Andy McGladdery, GB, Honda
14   Robert Dunlop, GB, Honda
15   Len Willing, Aus, Yamaha

Standings – 1 Tardozzi 86;
2 Merkel & Pirovano 83.5; 4 Mertens 75.5;
5 Lucchinelli 63; 6 Vieira 42

Round 9 – New Zealand
Manfeild Park, 2 October,
Race 1
1   Fred Merkel, USA, Honda
2   Fabrizio Pirovano, Ita, Yamaha
3   Gary Goodfellow, Can, Honda
4   Rob Phillis, Aus, Kawasaki
5   Davide Tardozzi, Ita, Bimota

6   Stephane Mertens, Bel, Bimota
7   Tom Douglas, Can, Yamaha
8   Robert Scolyer, Aus, Honda
9   Terry Rymer, GB, Honda
10   Glenn Williams, NZ, Ducati
11   Mal Campbell, Aus, Honda
12   Mike King, NZ, Ducati
13   Andrew Stroud, NZ, Bimota
14   Andy McGladdery, GB, Honda
15   Robert Dunlop, GB, Honda

Race 2
1   Stephane Mertens, Bel, Bimota
2   Mal Campbell, Aus, Honda
3   Rob Phillis, Aus, Kawasaki
4   Robert Scolyer, Aus, Honda
5   Fred Merkel, USA, Honda
6   Gary Goodfellow, Can, Honda
7   Terry Rymer, GB, Honda
8   Glenn Williams, NZ, Ducati
9   Andrew Stroud, NZ, Bimota
10   Andy McGladdery, GB, Honda
11   Tom Douglas, Can, Yamaha
12   Robert Dunlop, GB, Honda
13   Fabrizio Pirovano, Ita, Yamaha
14   Dale Warren, NZ, Honda
15   Mike King, NZ, Ducati

FINAL STANDINGS – 1 Merkel 99;
2 Pirovano 93.5; 3 Tardozzi 91.5;
4 Mertens 90.5; 5 Lucchinelli 63;
6 Phillis & Vieira 42

1989 season

Round 1 – Great Britain
Donington Park, 27 March,
Race 1
1. Fabrizio Pirovano, Ita, Yamaha
2. Roger Burnett, GB, Honda
3. Terry Rymer, GB, Yamaha
4. Fred Merkel, USA, Honda
5. Thierry Crine, Fra, Suzuki
6. Anders Andersson, Swe, Yamaha
7. Carl Fogarty, GB, Honda
8. Brian Morrison, GB, Honda
9. Andreas Hofmann, CH, Honda
10. Patrick Igoa, Fra, Kawasaki
11. Ernst Gschwender, Ger, Suzuki
12. Mark Phillips, GB, Yamaha
13. Peter Rubatto, Ger, Bimota
14. Hervé Moineau, Fra, Suzuki
15. Christophe Bouheben, Fra, Kawasaki

Race 2
1. Giancarlo Falappa, Ita, Bimota
2. Terry Rymer, GB, Yamaha
3. Roger Burnett, GB, Honda
4. Steve Hislop, GB, Honda
5. Anders Andersson, Swe, Yamaha
6. Fred Merkel, USA, Honda
7. Ernst Gschwender, Ger, Suzuki
8. Peter Rubatto, Ger, Bimota
9. Mark Phillips, GB, Yamaha
10. Patrick Igoa, Fra, Kawasaki
11. Andy McGladdery, GB, Honda
12. Paul Iddon, GB, Bimota
13. Carl Fogarty, GB, Honda
14. Rene Rasmussen, Den, Suzuki
15. René Delaby, Lux, Honda

Standings – 1 Burnett & Rymer 32;
3 Merkel 23; 4 Andersson 21;
5 Falappa & Pirovano 20

Round 2 – Hungary
Hungaroring, 30 April
Race 1
1. Fred Merkel, USA, Honda
2. Raymond Roche, Fra, Ducati
3. Fabrizio Pirovano, Ita, Yamaha
4. Rob McElnea, GB, Yamaha
5. Stephane Mertens, Bel, Honda
6. Anders Andersson, Swe, Yamaha
7. Terry Rymer, GB, Yamaha
8. Ernst Gschwender, Ger, Suzuki
9. Giancarlo Falappa, Ita, Bimota
10. Brian Morrison, GB, Honda
11. Andreas Hofmann, CH, Honda
12. Rene Rasmussen, Den, Suzuki
13. Patrick Igoa, Fra, Kawasaki
14. Jari Suhonen, Fin, Yamaha
15. Mal Campbell, Aus, Honda

Race 2
1. Fred Merkel, USA, Honda
2. Fabrizio Pirovano, Ita, Yamaha
3. Rob McElnea, GB, Yamaha
4. Giancarlo Falappa, Ita, Bimota
5. Baldassarre Monti, Ita, Ducati
6. Stephane Mertens, Bel, Honda
7. Anders Andersson, Swe, Yamaha
8. Rene Rasmussen, Den, Suzuki
9. Terry Rymer, GB, Yamaha
10. Peter Rubatto, Ger, Bimota
11. Jari Suhonen, Fin, Yamaha
12. Mal Campbell, Aus, Honda
13. Brian Morrison, GB, Honda
14. Andreas Hofmann, CH, Honda
15. Patrick Igoa, Fra, Kawasaki

Standings – 1 Merkel 63; 2 Pirovano 52;
3 Rymer 48; 4 Andersson & Falappa 40;
6 Burnett 32

Round 3 – Canada
Mosport Park, 4 June
Race 1
1. Fred Merkel, USA, Honda
2. Raymond Roche, Fra, Ducati
3. Rueben McMurter, Can, Honda
4. Stephane Mertens, Bel, Honda
5. Steve Crevier, Can, Yamaha
6. Fabrizio Pirovano, Ita, Yamaha
7. Jari Suhonen, Fin, Yamaha
8. Mike Baldwin, USA, Bimota
9. Anders Andersson, Swe, Yamaha
10. Tommy Douglas, Can, Yamaha

11. Michel Mercier, Can, Suzuki
12. Paul Iddon, GB, Bimota
13. Rene Rasmussen, Den, Suzuki
14. Wolfgang von Muralt, CH, Honda
15. Marino Fabbri, Ita, Bimota

Race 2
1. Giancarlo Falappa, Ita, Bimota
2. Rueben McMurter, Can, Honda
3. Fred Merkel, USA, Honda
4. Fabrizio Pirovano, Ita, Yamaha
5. Stephane Mertens, Bel, Honda
6. Mike Baldwin, USA, Bimota
7. Baldassarre Monti, Ita, Ducati
8. Terry Rymer, GB, Yamaha
9. Jari Suhonen, Fin, Yamaha
10. Gary Goodfellow, Can, Suzuki
11. Anders Andersson, Swe, Yamaha
12. Fabio Biliotti, Ita, Bimota
13. Davide Tardozzi, Ita, Bimota
14. Michel Mercier, Can, Suzuki
15. Rene Rasmussen, Den, Suzuki

Standings – 1 Merkel 98; 2 Pirovano 75;
3 Falappa 60; 4 Rymer 56; 5 Andersson 52;
6 Mertens 45

Round 4 – USA
Brainerd International Raceway, 11 June
Race 1
1. Raymond Roche, Fra, Ducati
2. Fabrizio Pirovano, Ita, Yamaha
3. Stephane Mertens, Bel, Honda
4. Fred Merkel, USA, Honda
5. Terry Rymer, GB, Yamaha
6. Baldassarre Monti, Ita, Ducati
7. Mike Baldwin, USA, Bimota
8. Anders Andersson, Swe, Yamaha
9. Tommy Douglas, Can, Yamaha
10. Richie Arnaiz, USA, Yamaha
11. Rueben McMurter, Can, Honda
12. Fabio Biliotti, Ita, Bimota
13. Gary Goodfellow, Can, Suzuki
14. Marino Fabbri, Ita, Bimota
15. René Delaby, Lux, Honda

Race 2
1. Raymond Roche, Fra, Ducati
2. Stephane Mertens, Bel, Honda
3. Fred Merkel, USA, Honda
4. Fabrizio Pirovano, Ita, Yamaha
5. Terry Rymer, GB, Yamaha
6. Baldassarre Monti, Ita, Ducati
7. Anders Andersson, Swe, Yamaha
8. Fabio Biliotti, Ita, Bimota
9. Tommy Douglas, Can, Yamaha
10. Gary Goodfellow, Can, Suzuki
11. Davide Tardozzi, Ita, Bimota
12. Doug Chandler, USA, Kawasaki
13. René Delaby, Lux, Honda
14. Marino Fabbri, Ita, Bimota
15. Wolfgang von Muralt, CH, Honda

Standings – 1 Merkel 126; 2 Pirovano 105;
3 Rymer 78; 4 Mertens 77; 5 Roche 74;
6 Andersson 69

Round 5 – Austria
Osterreichring, 2 July
Race 1
1. Alex Vieira, Fra, Honda
2. Raymond Roche, Fra, Ducati
3. Stephane Mertens, Bel, Honda
4. Massimo Broccoli, Ita, Ducati
5. Fabrizio Pirovano, Ita, Yamaha
6. Baldassarre Monti, Ita, Ducati
7. Mal Campbell, Aus, Honda
8. Anders Andersson, Swe, Yamaha
9. Terry Rymer, GB, Yamaha
10. Jari Suhonen, Fin, Yamaha
11. Fred Merkel, USA, Honda
12. Patrick Igoa, Fra, Kawasaki
13. Giancarlo Falappa, Ita, Bimota
14. Pierre Bolle, Fra, Kawasaki
15. Ernst Gschwender, Ger, Suzuki

Race 2
1. Stephane Mertens, Bel, Honda
2. Fabrizio Pirovano, Ita, Yamaha
3. Fred Merkel, USA, Honda
4. Massimo Broccoli, Ita, Ducati
5. Patrick Igoa, Fra, Kawasaki
6. Mal Campbell, Aus, Honda

7. Jari Suhonen, Fin, Yamaha
8. Alex Vieira, Fra, Honda
9. Anders Andersson, Swe, Yamaha
10. Raymond Roche, Fra, Ducati
11. Ernst Gschwender, Ger, Suzuki
12. Davide Tardozzi, Ita, Bimota
13. Mauro Ricci, Ita, Kawasaki
14. Baldassarre Monti, Ita, Ducati
15. René Delaby, Lux, Honda

Standings – 1 Merkel 146; 2 Pirovano 133;
3 Mertens 112; 4 Roche 97; 5 Rymer 85;
6 Andersson 84

Round 6 – France
Circuit Paul Ricard, 30 July
Race 1
1. Stephane Mertens, Bel, Honda
2. Mike Baldwin, USA, Bimota
3. Raymond Roche, Fra, Ducati
4. Terry Rymer, GB, Yamaha
5. Giancarlo Falappa, Ita, Bimota
6. Jean-Yves Mounier, Fra, Yamaha
7. Baldassarre Monti, Ita, Ducati
8. Fred Merkel, USA, Honda
9. Davide Tardozzi, Ita, Bimota
10. Anders Andersson, Swe, Yamaha
11. Pierre Bolle, Fra, Kawasaki
12. Rene Rasmussen, Den, Suzuki
13. Jeffry de Vries, Nl, Yamaha
14. Maurice Coq, Fra, Yamaha
15. Didier Handi, Fra, Yamaha

Race 2
1. Giancarlo Falappa, Ita, Bimota
2. Raymond Roche, Fra, Ducati
3. Stephane Mertens, Bel, Honda
4. Fred Merkel, USA, Honda
5. Mike Baldwin, USA, Bimota
6. Baldassarre Monti, Ita, Ducati
7. Anders Andersson, Swe, Yamaha
8. Davide Tardozzi, Ita, Bimota
9. Pierre Bolle, Fra, Kawasaki
10. Paul Iddon, GB, Bimota
11. Maurice Coq, Fra, Yamaha
12. Rene Rasmussen, Den, Suzuki
13. Jean-Yves Mounier, Fra, Yamaha
14. Edwin Weibel, CH, Kawasaki
15. Eric Delcamp, Fra, Yamaha

Standings – 1 Merkel 167; 2 Mertens 147;
3 Pirovano 133; 4 Roche 129; 5 Andersson 99;
6 Rymer 98

Round 7 – Japan
Sugo, 27 August
Race 1
1. Doug Polen, USA, Suzuki
2. Michael Dowson, Aus, Yamaha
3. Rob Phillis, Aus, Kawasaki
4. Giancarlo Falappa, Ita, Bimota
5. Tatsuro Arata, Jap, Yamaha
6. Kenichiro Iwahashi, Jap, Honda
7. Fabrizio Pirovano, Ita, Yamaha
8. Stephane Mertens, Bel, Honda
9. Aaron Slight, NZ, Kawasaki
10. Naoto Abe, Jap, Honda
11. Shoichi Tsukamoto, Jap, Kawasaki
12. Davide Tardozzi, Ita, Bimota
13. Raymond Roche, Fra, Ducati
14. Scott Doohan, Aus, Bimota
15. Mal Campbell, Aus, Honda

Race 2
1. Michael Dowson, Aus, Yamaha
2. Kenichiro Iwahashi, Jap, Honda
3. Giancarlo Falappa, Ita, Bimota
4. Doug Polen, USA, Suzuki
5. Takahiro Sohwa, Jap, Kawasaki
6. Rob Phillis, Aus, Kawasaki
7. Aaron Slight, NZ, Kawasaki
8. Stephane Mertens, Bel, Honda
9. Tatsuro Arata, Jap, Yamaha
10. Mal Campbell, Aus, Honda
11. Shoichi Tsukamoto, Jap, Kawasaki
12. Fred Merkel, USA, Honda
13. Terry Rymer, GB, Yamaha
14. Kochichi Kobayashi, Jap, Honda
15. Koh Takeuchi, Jap, Yamaha

Standings – 1 Merkel 171; 2 Mertens 163;
3 Pirovano 142; 4 Roche 132; 5 Falappa 122;
6 Rymer 101

Round 8 – Germany
Hockenheim, 17 September
Race 1
1 Raymond Roche, Fra, Ducati
2 Stephane Mertens, Bel, Honda
3 Alex Vieira, Fra, Honda
4 Fabrizio Pirovano, Ita, Yamaha
5 Anders Andersson, Swe, Yamaha
6 Mike Baldwin, USA, Bimota
7 Andreas Hofmann, CH, Honda
8 Fred Merkel, USA, Honda
9 Patrick Igoa, Fra, Kawasaki
10 Jari Suhonen, Fin, Yamaha
11 Bodo Schmidt, Ger, Yamaha
12 Roger Burnett, GB, Honda
13 Edwin Weibel, CH, Kawasaki
14 Jean-Yves Mounier, Fra, Yamaha
15 Graeme McGregor, Aus, Honda

Race 2
1 Raymond Roche, Fra, Ducati
2 Giancarlo Falappa, Ita, Bimota
3 Stephane Mertens, Bel, Honda
4 Fred Merkel, USA, Honda
5 Anders Andersson, Swe, Yamaha
6 Fabrizio Pirovano, Ita, Yamaha
7 Mike Baldwin, USA, Bimota
8 Alex Vieira, Fra, Honda
9 Patrick Igoa, Fra, Kawasaki
10 Marco Lucchinelli, Ita, Ducati
11 Bodo Schmidt, Ger, Yamaha
12 Andreas Hofmann, CH, Honda
13 Udo Mark, Ger, Yamaha
14 Jari Suhonen, Fin, Yamaha
15 Christophe Bouheben, Fra, Kawasaki

Standings – 1 Mertens 195; 2 Merkel 192;
3 Roche 172; 4 Pirovano 165; 5 Falappa 139;
6 Andersson 121

Round 9 – Italy
Pergusa, 24 September
Race 1
1 Stephane Mertens, Bel, Honda
2 Fred Merkel, USA, Honda
3 Fabrizio Pirovano, Ita, Yamaha
4 Baldassarre Monti, Ita, Ducati
5 Anders Andersson, Swe, Yamaha
6 Jari Suhonen, Fin, Yamaha
7 Patrick Igoa, Fra, Kawasaki
8 Davide Tardozzi, Ita, Bimota
9 Marco Lucchinelli, Ita, Ducati
10 Piergiorgio Bontempi, Ita, Honda
11 Arpad Harmati, Hun, Honda
12 Corrado Manici, Ita, Ducati
13 Aldeo Presciutti, Ita, Honda
14 Silvano Ricchetti, Ita, Honda
15 Adriano Narducci, Ita, Honda

Race 2
1 Raymond Roche, Fra, Ducati
2 Fred Merkel, USA, Honda
3 Baldassarre Monti, Ita, Ducati
4 Fabrizio Pirovano, Ita, Yamaha
5 Jari Suhonen, Fin, Yamaha
6 Patrick Igoa, Fra, Kawasaki
7 Stephane Mertens, Bel, Honda
8 Christophe Bouheben, Fra, Kawasaki
9 Marino Fabbri, Ita, Bimota
10 Marco dall'Aglio, Ita, Yamaha
11 Arpad Harmati, Hun, Honda
12 Piergiorgio Bontempi, Ita, Honda
13 Aldeo Presciutti, Ita, Honda
14 Corrado Manici, Ita, Ducati
15 Oscar La Ferla, Ita, Yamaha

Standings – 1 Merkel 226; 2 Mertens 224;
3 Pirovano 193; 4 Roche 192; 5 Falappa 139;
6 Andersson 132

Round 10 – Australia
Oran Park, 12 November
Race 1
1 Peter Goddard, Aus, Yamaha
2 Rob Phillis, Aus, Kawasaki
3 Fabrizio Pirovano, Ita, Yamaha
4 Raymond Roche, Fra, Ducati
5 Aaron Slight, NZ, Kawasaki
6 Anders Andersson, Swe, Yamaha
7 Michael Dowson, Aus, Yamaha
8 Stephane Mertens, Bel, Honda
9 Rene Bongers, Aus, Yamaha
10 Scott Doohan, Aus, Suzuki

11 Fred Merkel, USA, Honda
12 Jari Suhonen, Fin, Yamaha
13 John Richards, Aus, Yamaha
14 Takahiro Sohwa, Jap, Kawasaki
15 Steve Martin, Aus, Suzuki

Race 2
1 Michael Dowson, Aus, Yamaha
2 Raymond Roche, Fra, Ducati
3 Rob Phillis, Aus, Kawasaki
4 Stephane Mertens, Bel, Honda
5 Fred Merkel, USA, Honda
6 Aaron Slight, NZ, Kawasaki
7 Takahiro Sohwa, Jap, Kawasaki
8 Rene Bongers, Aus, Yamaha
9 Matt Blair, Aus, Yamaha
10 Graeme Morris, Aus, Ducati
11 Robert Scolyer, Aus, Honda
12 Steve Crevier, Can, Yamaha
13 Andy Roberts, Aus, Yamaha
14 Andy McGladdery, GB, Honda
15 John Richards, Aus, Yamaha

Standings – 1 Mertens 245; 2 Merkel 242;
3 Roche 222; 4 Pirovano 208; 5 Andersson 142;
6 Falappa 139

Round 11 – New Zealand
Manfeild Park, 19 November
Race 1
1 Terry Rymer, GB, Yamaha
2 Aaron Slight, NZ, Kawasaki
3 Fred Merkel, USA, Honda

4 Michael Dowson, Aus, Yamaha
5 Rob Phillis, Aus, Kawasaki
6 Jari Suhonen, Fin, Yamaha
7 Anders Andersson, Swe, Yamaha
8 Glenn Williams, NZ, Ducati
9 Takahiro Sohwa, Jap, Kawasaki
10 Simon Crafar, NZ, Yamaha
11 Eddie Kattenberg, NZ, Suzuki
12 Russell Josiah, NZ, Kawasaki
13 Andy McGladdery, GB, Honda
14 Brian Bernard, NZ, Suzuki
15 Andrew Stroud, NZ, Yamaha

Race 2
1 Stephane Mertens, Bel, Honda
2 Mal Campbell, Aus, Honda
3 Fred Merkel, USA, Honda
4 Terry Rymer, GB, Yamaha
5 Rob Phillis, Aus, Kawasaki
6 Andrew Stroud, NZ, Yamaha
7 Jari Suhonen, Fin, Yamaha
8 Anders Andersson, Swe, Yamaha
9 Takahiro Sohwa, Jap, Kawasaki
10 Simon Crafar, NZ, Yamaha
11 Andy McGladdery, GB, Honda
12 Grant Ramage, NZ, Suzuki
13 Eddie Kattenberg, NZ, Suzuki
14 Russell Josiah, NZ, Kawasaki
15 Glenn Williams, NZ, Ducati

FINAL STANDINGS – 1 Merkel 272;
2 Mertens 265; 3 Roche 222; 4 Pirovano 208;
5 Andersson 159; 6 Falappa 139

1990 season

Round 1 – Spain
Jerez, 18 March
Race 1
1. Raymond Roche, Fra, Ducati
2. Fred Merkel, USA, Honda
3. Stephane Mertens, Bel, Honda
4. Rob Phillis, Aus, Kawasaki
5. Giancarlo Falappa, Ita, Ducati
6. Fabrizio Pirovano, Ita, Yamaha
7. Terry Rymer, GB, Yamaha
8. Rob McElnea, GB, Yamaha
9. Anders Andersson, Swe, Yamaha
10. Ernst Gschwender, Ger, Suzuki
11. Davide Tardozzi, Ita, Ducati
12. Juan Lopez Mella, Spa, Honda
13. Brian Morrison, GB, Honda
14. Carl Fogarty, GB, Honda
15. Edwin Weibel, CH, Kawasaki

Race 2
1. Raymond Roche, Fra, Ducati
2. Giancarlo Falappa, Ita, Ducati
3. Fred Merkel, USA, Honda
4. Stephane Mertens, Bel, Honda
5. Rob Phillis, Aus, Kawasaki
6. Rob McElnea, GB, Yamaha
7. Terry Rymer, GB, Yamaha
8. Fabrizio Pirovano, Ita, Yamaha
9. Ernst Gschwender, Ger, Suzuki
10. Daniel Amatriain, Spa, Honda
11. Baldassarre Monti, Ita, Honda
12. Anders Andersson, Swe, Yamaha
13. Andreas Hofmann, Ger, Honda
14. Jeffry de Vries, Nl, Yamaha
15. Udo Mark, Ger, Yamaha

Standings – 1 Roche 40; 2 Merkel 32;
3 Mertens & Falappa 28; 5 Phillis 24;
6 Rymer, McElnea & Pirovano 18

Round 2 – Great Britain
Donington Park, 16 April
Race 1
1. Fred Merkel, USA, Honda
2. Raymond Roche, Fra, Ducati
3. Stephane Mertens, Bel, Honda
4. Rob Phillis, Aus, Kawasaki
5. Fabrizio Pirovano, Ita, Yamaha
6. Carl Fogarty, GB, Honda
7. Giancarlo Falappa, Ita, Ducati
8. Davide Tardozzi, Ita, Ducati
9. Udo Mark, Ger, Yamaha
10. Baldassarre Monti, Ita, Honda
11. Ray Stringer, GB, Yamaha
12. James Whitham, GB, Honda
13. Niall Mackenzie, GB, Yamaha
14. Brian Morrison, GB, Honda
15. Ernst Gschwender, Ger, Suzuki

Race 2
1. Giancarlo Falappa, Ita, Ducati
2. Raymond Roche, Fra, Ducati
3. Fred Merkel, USA, Honda
4. Niall Mackenzie, GB, Yamaha
5. Fabrizio Pirovano, Ita, Yamaha
6. Carl Fogarty, GB, Honda
7. Rob Phillis, Aus, Kawasaki
8. Stephane Mertens, Bel, Honda
9. Anders Andersson, Swe, Yamaha
10. Udo Mark, Ger, Yamaha
11. Baldassarre Monti, Ita, Honda
12. Ernst Gschwender, Ger, Suzuki
13. Edwin Weibel, CH, Kawasaki
14. Jeffry de Vries, Nl, Yamaha
15. Brian Morrison, GB, Honda

Standings – 1 Roche 74; 2 Merkel 67;
3 Falappa 57; 4 Mertens 51; 5 Phillis 46;
6 Pirovano 40

Round 3 – Hungary
Hungaroring, 30 April
Race 1
1. Fred Merkel, USA, Honda
2. Raymond Roche, Fra, Ducati
3. Fabrizio Pirovano, Ita, Yamaha
4. Mal Campbell, Aus, Honda
5. Rob McElnea, GB, Yamaha
6. Stephane Mertens, Bel, Honda
7. Anders Andersson, Swe, Yamaha
8. Terry Rymer, GB, Yamaha
9. Baldassarre Monti, Ita, Honda
10. Rob Phillis, Aus, Kawasaki
11. Daniel Amatriain, Spa, Honda
12. Juan Lopez Mella, Spa, Honda
13. Ernst Gschwender, Ger, Suzuki
14. Jeffry de Vries, Nl, Yamaha
15. Brian Morrison, GB, Honda

Race 2
1. Raymond Roche, Fra, Ducati
2. Mal Campbell, Aus, Honda
3. Stephane Mertens, Bel, Honda
4. Rob McElnea, GB, Yamaha
5. Terry Rymer, GB, Yamaha
6. Fred Merkel, USA, Honda
7. Giancarlo Falappa, Ita, Ducati
8. Fabrizio Pirovano, Ita, Yamaha
9. Davide Tardozzi, Ita, Ducati
10. Edwin Weibel, CH, Kawasaki
11. Baldassarre Monti, Ita, Honda
12. Daniel Amatriain, Spa, Honda
13. Jeffry de Vries, Nl, Yamaha
14. Jari Suhonen, Fin, Yamaha
15. Michael Galinski, Ger, Kawasaki

Standings – 1 Roche 111; 2 Merkel 97;
3 Mertens 76; 4 Falappa 66; 5 Pirovano 63;
6 Phillis 52

Round 4 – Germany
Hockenheim, 5 May
Race 1
1. Fred Merkel, USA, Honda
2. Rob McElnea, GB, Yamaha
3. Giancarlo Falappa, Ita, Ducati
4. Jari Suhonen, Fin, Yamaha
5. Andreas Hofmann, Ger, Honda
6. Udo Mark, Ger, Yamaha
7. Anders Andersson, Swe, Yamaha
8. Fabrizio Pirovano, Ita, Yamaha
9. Christer Lindholm, Swe, Yamaha
10. Ray Stringer, GB, Yamaha
11. Juan Lopez Mella, Spa, Honda
12. Jeffry de Vries, Nl, Yamaha
13. Huby Meier, CH, Honda
14. Wolfgang Moeckel, Ger, Honda
15. Michael Rudroff, Ger, Bimota

Race 2
1. Stephane Mertens, Bel, Honda
2. Raymond Roche, Fra, Ducati
3. Fred Merkel, USA, Honda
4. Giancarlo Falappa, Ita, Ducati
5. Fabrizio Pirovano, Ita, Yamaha
6. Rob McElnea, GB, Yamaha
7. Terry Rymer, GB, Yamaha
8. Andreas Hofmann, Ger, Honda
9. Mal Campbell, Aus, Honda
10. Jari Suhonen, Fin, Yamaha
11. Udo Mark, Ger, Yamaha
12. Anders Andersson, Swe, Yamaha
13. Edwin Weibel, CH, Kawasaki
14. Baldassarre Monti, Ita, Honda
15. Jeffry de Vries, Nl, Yamaha

Standings – 1 Merkel 132; 2 Roche 128;
3 Mertens 96; 4 Falappa 94; 5 Pirovano 82;
6 McElnea 69

Round 5 – Canada
Mosport, 3 June
Race 1
1. Raymond Roche, Fra, Ducati
2. Jamie James, USA, Ducati
3. Fabrizio Pirovano, Ita, Yamaha
4. Terry Rymer, GB, Yamaha
5. Fred Merkel, USA, Honda
6. Stephane Mertens, Bel, Honda
7. Baldassarre Monti, Ita, Honda
8. Michel Mercier, Can, Yamaha
9. Jari Suhonen, Fin, Yamaha
10. Anders Andersson, Swe, Yamaha
11. Rob McElnea, GB, Yamaha
12. Miguel DuHamel, Can, Suzuki
13. Pascal Picotte, Can, Yamaha
14. Tom Kipp, USA, Yamaha
15. Rene Delaby, Lux, Honda

Race 2
1. Raymond Roche, Fra, Ducati
2. Jamie James, USA, Ducati
3. Stephane Mertens, Bel, Honda
4. Michel Mercier, Can, Yamaha
5. Fabrizio Pirovano, Ita, Yamaha
6. Rob McElnea, GB, Yamaha
7. Terry Rymer, GB, Yamaha
8. Rob Phillis, Aus, Kawasaki
9. Baldassarre Monti, Ita, Honda
10. Fred Merkel, USA, Honda
11. Anders Andersson, Swe, Yamaha
12. Pascal Picotte, Can, Yamaha
13. Jari Suhonen, Fin, Yamaha
14. Tom Kipp, USA, Yamaha
15. Miguel DuHamel, Can, Suzuki

Standings – 1 Roche 168; 2 Merkel 149;
3 Mertens 121; 4 Pirovano 108; 5 Falappa 94;
6 McElnea 84

Round 6 – USA
Brainerd International Raceway, 10 June
Race 1
1. Stephane Mertens, Bel, Honda
2. Raymond Roche, Fra, Ducati
3. Doug Chandler, USA, Kawasaki
4. Terry Rymer, GB, Yamaha
5. Rob McElnea, GB, Yamaha
6. Rob Phillis, Aus, Kawasaki
7. Fred Merkel, USA, Honda
8. Fabrizio Pirovano, Ita, Yamaha
9. David Sadowski, USA, Yamaha
10. Scott Russell, USA, Kawasaki
11. Baldassarre Monti, Ita, Honda
12. Jari Suhonen, Fin, Yamaha
13. Davide Tardozzi, Ita, Ducati
14. Tom Kipp, USA, Yamaha
15. Bruno Bonhuil, Fra, Honda

Race 2
1. Doug Chandler, USA, Kawasaki
2. Stephane Mertens, Bel, Honda
3. Terry Rymer, GB, Yamaha
4. Raymond Roche, Fra, Ducati
5. Rob McElnea, GB, Yamaha
6. Fabrizio Pirovano, Ita, Yamaha
7. Scott Russell, USA, Kawasaki
8. Jari Suhonen, Fin, Yamaha
9. Tom Stevens, USA, Yamaha
10. Fred Merkel, USA, Honda
11. Baldassarre Monti, Ita, Honda
12. Anders Andersson, Swe, Yamaha
13. Tom Kipp, USA, Yamaha
14. Rene Delaby, Lux, Honda
15. Bruno Bonhuil, Fra, Honda

Standings – 1 Roche 198; 2 Merkel 164;
3 Mertens 158; 4 Pirovano 126; 5 McElnea 106;
6 Rymer 96

Round 7 – Austria
Osterreichring, 1 July
Race 1
1. Fabrizio Pirovano, Ita, Yamaha
2. Stephane Mertens, Bel, Honda
3. Rob Phillis, Aus, Kawasaki
4. Anders Andersson, Swe, Yamaha
5. Ernst Gschwender, Ger, Suzuki
6. Rob McElnea, GB, Yamaha
7. Fred Merkel, USA, Honda
8. Raymond Roche, Fra, Ducati
9. Baldassarre Monti, Ita, Honda
10. Daniel Amatriain, Spa, Honda
11. Jean-Michel Mattioli, Fra, Honda
12. Stefano Caracchi, Ita, Ducati
13. Mauro Ricci, Ita, Kawasaki
14. Jean-Yves Mounier, Fra, Yamaha
15. Rene Delaby, Lux, Honda

Race 2
1. Stephane Mertens, Bel, Honda
2. Raymond Roche, Fra, Ducati
3. Fabrizio Pirovano, Ita, Yamaha
4. Fred Merkel, USA, Honda
5. Baldassarre Monti, Ita, Honda
6. Rob McElnea, GB, Yamaha
7. Alex Vieira, Fra, Honda
8. Jean-Yves Mounier, Fra, Yamaha
9. Anders Andersson, Swe, Yamaha
10. Udo Mark, Ger, Yamaha
11. Jari Suhonen, Fin, Yamaha
12. Jean-Michel Mattioli, Fra, Honda
13. Rene Delaby, Lux, Honda
14. Ernst Gschwender, Ger, Suzuki
15. Christian Zwedorn, Aut, Honda

Standings – 1 Roche 223; 2 Mertens 195;
3 Merkel 186; 4 Pirovano 161; 5 McElnea 126;
6 Rymer 96

Round 8 – Japan
Sugo, 26 August
Race 1
1. Raymond Roche, Fra, Ducati
2. Baldassarre Monti, Ita, Honda
3. Doug Chandler, USA, Kawasaki
4. Fabrizio Pirovano, Ita, Yamaha
5. Peter Goddard, Aus, Yamaha
6. Rob Phillis, Aus, Kawasaki
7. Jamie James, USA, Ducati
8. Doug Polen, USA, Suzuki
9. Kenji Osaka, Jap, Yamaha
10. Shingo Kato, Jap, Yamaha
11. Stephane Mertens, Bel, Honda
12. Rob McElnea, GB, Yamaha
13. Mituo Saito, Jap, Yamaha
14. Koichi Kobayashi, Jap, Yamaha
15. Udo Mark, Ger, Yamaha

Race 2
1. Doug Chandler, USA, Kawasaki
2. Peter Goddard, Aus, Yamaha
3. Baldassarre Monti, Ita, Honda
4. Fabrizio Pirovano, Ita, Yamaha
5. Rob Phillis, Aus, Kawasaki
6. Raymond Roche, Fra, Ducati
7. Jamie James, USA, Ducati
8. Stephane Mertens, Bel, Honda
9. Mituo Saito, Jap, Yamaha
10. Brian Morrison, GB, Honda
11. Jari Suhonen, Fin, Yamaha
12. Shigemasa Miwa, Jap, Honda
13. Udo Mark, Ger, Yamaha
14. Tadaaki Hanamura, Jap, Yamaha
15. Mal Campbell, Aus, Honda

Standings – 1 Roche 253; 2 Mertens 208; 3 Pirovano 187; 4 Merkel 186; 5 McElnea 126; 6 Monti 106

Round 9 – France
Le Mans, 9 September
Race 1
1. Raymond Roche, Fra, Ducati
2. Jamie James, USA, Ducati
3. Stephane Mertens, Bel, Honda
4. Baldassarre Monti, Ita, Honda
5. Rob Phillis, Aus, Kawasaki
6. Rob McElnea, GB, Yamaha
7. Christian Lavieille, Fra, Yamaha
8. Jean-Michel Mattioli, Fra, Honda
9. Stefano Caracchi, Ita, Ducati
10. Jari Suhonen, Fin, Yamaha
11. Anders Andersson, Swe, Yamaha
12. Edwin Weibel, CH, Honda
13. Jeffry de Vries, Nl, Yamaha
14. Andeas Hofmann, Ger, Honda
15. Maurice Coq, Fra, Yamaha

Race 2
1. Raymond Roche, Fra, Ducati
2. Fabrizio Pirovano, Ita, Yamaha
3. Stephane Mertens, Bel, Honda
4. Baldassarre Monti, Ita, Honda
5. Rob McElnea, GB, Yamaha
6. Rob Phillis, Aus, Kawasaki
7. Jean-Yves Mounier, Fra, Yamaha
8. Carl Fogarty, GB, Honda
9. Edwin Weibel, CH, Honda
10. Stefano Caracchi, Ita, Ducati
11. Andeas Hofmann, Ger, Honda
12. Jean-Michel Mattioli, Fra, Honda
13. Alex Vieira, Fra, Honda
14. Jari Suhonen, Fin, Yamaha
15. Brian Morrison, GB, Honda

Standings – 1 Roche 293; 2 Mertens 238; 3 Pirovano 204; 4 Merkel 186; 5 McElnea 151; 6 Monti 132

Round 10 – Italy
Monza, 7 October
Race 1
1. Fabrizio Pirovano, Ita, Yamaha
2. Stephane Mertens, Bel, Honda
3. Raymond Roche, Fra, Ducati
4. Rob Phillis, Aus, Kawasaki
5. Rob McElnea, GB, Yamaha
6. Jari Suhonen, Fin, Yamaha
7. Jamie James, USA, Ducati
8. Brian Morrison, GB, Honda
9. Anders Andersson, Swe, Yamaha
10. Edwin Weibel, CH, Honda

11. Alex Vieira, Fra, Honda
12. Fabio Biliotti, Ita, Kawasaki
13. Michel Rudroff, Ger, Bimota
14. Adrian Bosshard, CH, Honda
15. Jeffry de Vries, Nl, Yamaha

Race 2
1. Fabrizio Pirovano, Ita, Yamaha
2. Baldassarre Monti, Ita, Honda
3. Rob McElnea, GB, Yamaha
4. Rob Phillis, Aus, Kawasaki
5. Fred Merkel, USA, Honda
6. Raymond Roche, Fra, Ducati
7. Jari Suhonen, Fin, Yamaha
8. Jamie James, USA, Ducati
9. Brian Morrison, GB, Honda
10. Jeffry de Vries, Nl, Yamaha
11. Anders Andersson, Swe, Yamaha
12. Huby Meier, CH, Honda
13. Adrian Bosshard, CH, Honda
14. Alex Vieira, Fra, Honda
15. Christian Monsch, CH, Honda

Standings – 1 Roche 318; 2 Mertens 255; 3 Pirovano 244; 4 Merkel 197; 5 McElnea 177; 6 Phillis 152

Round 11 – Malaysia
Shah Alam, 4 November
Race 1
1. Fabrizio Pirovano, Ita, Yamaha
2. Rob Phillis, Aus, Kawasaki
3. Stephane Mertens, Bel, Honda
4. Raymond Roche, Fra, Ducati
5. Rob McElnea, GB, Yamaha
6. Peter Goddard, Aus, Yamaha
7. Terry Rymer, GB, Yamaha
8. Mal Campbell, Aus, Honda
9. Jari Suhonen, Fin, Yamaha
10. Rene Bongers, Aus, Yamaha
11. James Knight, Aus, Kawasaki
12. Anders Andersson, Swe, Yamaha
13. Simon Crafar, NZ, Yamaha
14. Sang Kooi Tai, Mal, Honda
15. C. Nattavude, Tld, Kawasaki

Race 2
1. Fabrizio Pirovano, Ita, Yamaha
2. Rob Phillis, Aus, Kawasaki
3. Raymond Roche, Fra, Ducati
4. Stephane Mertens, Bel, Honda
5. Rob McElnea, GB, Yamaha
6. Peter Goddard, Aus, Yamaha
7. Terry Rymer, GB, Yamaha
8. Jari Suhonen, Fin, Yamaha
9. Mal Campbell, Aus, Honda
10. Rene Bongers, Aus, Yamaha
11. James Knight, Aus, Kawasaki
12. Anders Andersson, Swe, Yamaha
13. Simon Crafar, NZ, Yamaha
14. Michael Dowson, Aus, Yamaha
15. C. Nattavude, Tld, Kawasaki

Standings – 1 Roche 346; 2 Pirovano 284; 3 Mertens 283; 4 McElnea 199; 5 Merkel 197; 6 Phillis 152

Round 12 – Australia
Phillip Island, 11 November
Race 1
1. Peter Goddard, Aus, Yamaha
2. Fabrizio Pirovano, Ita, Yamaha
3. Michael Dowson, Aus, Yamaha
4. Mal Campbell, Aus, Honda
5. Raymond Roche, Fra, Ducati
6. Rene Bongers, Aus, Yamaha
7. Scott Doohan, Aus, Honda
8. Aaron Slight, NZ, Kawasaki
9. Terry Rymer, GB, Yamaha
10. Jari Suhonen, Fin, Yamaha
11. Steve Martin, Aus, Suzuki
12. Rob McElnea, GB, Yamaha
13. Brian Morrison, GB, Honda
14. Peter Guest, Aus, Yamaha
15. Ian Short, Aus, Suzuki

Race 2
1. Rob Phillis, Aus, Kawasaki
2. Peter Goddard, Aus, Yamaha
3. Mal Campbell, Aus, Honda
4. Michael Dowson, Aus, Yamaha
5. Fabrizio Pirovano, Ita, Yamaha
6. Scott Doohan, Aus, Honda

7. Aaron Slight, NZ, Kawasaki
8. Raymond Roche, Fra, Ducati
9. Stephane Mertens, Bel, Honda
10. Steve Martin, Aus, Suzuki
11. Brian Morrison, GB, Honda
12. Peter Guest, Aus, Yamaha
13. Michael O'Connor, Aus, Honda
14. Andrew Roberts, Aus, Yamaha
15. Anders Andersson, Swe, Yamaha

Standings – 1 Roche 365; 2 Pirovano 312; 3 Mertens 290; 4 Phillis 206; 5 McElnea 203; 6 Merkel 197

Round 13 – New Zealand
Manfeild Park, 18 November
Race 1
1. Terry Rymer, GB, Yamaha
2. Raymond Roche, Fra, Ducati
3. Rob McElnea, GB, Yamaha
4. Daryl Beattie, Aus, Honda
5. Rob Phillis, Aus, Kawasaki
6. Stephane Mertens, Bel, Honda
7. Anders Andersson, Swe, Yamaha
8. Andrew Stroud, NZ, Yamaha
9. Tony Rees, NZ, Yamaha
10. Brian Morrison, GB, Honda
11. Russell Josiah, NZ, Kawasaki
12. Rob Lewis, NZ, Kawasaki
13. Mark Fissenden, Aus, Honda
14. Brian Billet, NZ, Honda
15. Brent Curtis, NZ, Suzuki

Race 2
1. Rob Phillis, Aus, Kawasaki
2. Terry Rymer, GB, Yamaha
3. Aaron Slight, NZ, Kawasaki
4. Fabrizio Pirovano, Ita, Yamaha
5. Jari Suhonen, Fin, Yamaha
6. Anders Andersson, Swe, Yamaha
7. Andrew Stroud, NZ, Yamaha
8. Brian Morrison, GB, Honda
9. Tony Rees, NZ, Yamaha
10. Russell Josiah, NZ, Kawasaki
11. Rob Lewis, NZ, Kawasaki
12. Mike King, NZ, Ducati
13. Brian Billet, NZ, Honda
14. Brent Curtis, NZ, Suzuki
15. Mark Fissenden, Aus, Honda

FINAL STANDINGS – 1 Roche 382; 2 Pirovano 325; 3 Mertens 300; 4 Phillis 237; 5 McElnea 218; 6 Merkel 197

1991 season

Round 1 – Great Britain
Donington Park, 1 April
Race 1
1   Doug Polen, USA, Ducati
2   Terry Rymer, GB, Yamaha
3   Fabrizio Pirovano, Ita, Yamaha
4   Rob Phillis, Aus, Kawasaki
5   Rob McElnea, GB, Yamaha
6   Brian Morrison, GB, Yamaha
7   Niall Mackenzie, GB, Honda
8   Ray Stringer, GB, Yamaha
9   Jeffry de Vries, Nl, Yamaha
10   John Reynolds, GB, Kawasaki
11   Juan Lopez Mella, Spa, Honda
12   Christian Lavieille, Fra, Ducati
13   Edwin Weibel, CH, Honda
14   Giancarlo Falappa, Ita, Ducati
15   Steve Manley, GB, Bimota

Race 2
1   Stephane Mertens, Bel, Ducati
2   Raymond Roche, Fra, Ducati
3   Rob Phillis, Aus, Kawasaki
4   Terry Rymer, GB, Yamaha
5   Rob McElnea, GB, Yamaha
6   Brian Morrison, GB, Yamaha
7   Niall Mackenzie, GB, Honda
8   Fabrizio Pirovano, Ita, Yamaha
9   Carl Fogarty, GB, Honda
10   Jeffry de Vries, Nl, Yamaha
11   Juan Lopez Mella, Spa, Honda
12   Christian Lavieille, Fra, Ducati
13   Daniel Amatriain, Spa, Honda
14   Edwin Weibel, CH, Honda
15   Luis Maurel, Spa, Yamaha

Standings – 1 Rymer 30; 2 Phillis 28;
3 Pirovano 23; 4 McElnea 22;
5 Mertens, Morrison & Polen 20

Round 2 – Spain
Jarama, 28 April
Race 1
1   Doug Polen, USA, Ducati
2   Rob Phillis, Aus, Kawasaki
3   Juan Lopez Mella, Spa, Honda
4   Daniel Amatriain, Spa, Honda
5   Fabrizio Pirovano, Ita, Yamaha
6   Baldassarre Monti, Ita, Honda
7   Terry Rymer, GB, Yamaha
8   Udo Mark, Ger, Yamaha
9   Carl Fogarty, GB, Honda
10   Bruno Bonhuil, Fra, Yamaha
11   Antonio Moreno, Spa, Honda
12   Peter Rubatto, Ger, Yamaha
13   Walter Amman, CH, Yamaha
14   Aldeo Presciutti, Ita, Kawasaki
15   Jeffry de Vries, Nl, Yamaha

Race 2
1   Doug Polen, USA, Ducati
2   Stephane Mertens, Bel, Ducati
3   Raymond Roche, Fra, Ducati
4   Juan Lopez Mella, Spa, Honda
5   Fabrizio Pirovano, Ita, Yamaha
6   Daniel Amatriain, Spa, Honda
7   Udo Mark, Ger, Yamaha
8   Carl Fogarty, GB, Honda
9   Jari Suhonen, Fin, Yamaha
10   Luis Maurel, Spa, Yamaha
11   Antonio Moreno, Spa, Honda
12   Bruno Bonhuil, Fra, Yamaha
13   Dominique Sarron, Fra, Bimota
14   Massimo Broccoli, Ita, Kawasaki
15   Rene Delaby, Lux, Honda

Standings – 1 Polen 60;
2 Pirovano & Phillis 45; 4 Rymer 39;
5 Mertens 37; 6 Roche 32

Round 3 – Canada
Mosport Park, 2 June
Race 1
1   Pascal Picotte, Can, Yamaha
2   Yves Brisson, Can, Honda
3   Steve Crevier, Can, Kawasaki
4   Linley Clarke, Can, Yamaha
5   Michael Taylor, Can, Kawasaki
6   Benoit Pilon, Can, Yamaha
7   Jimmy Adamo, USA, Ducati
8   John Hopperstad, USA, Yamaha
9   Christian Gardner, USA, Yamaha
10   Tom Etherington, Can, Yamaha

11   Clyde MacDonald, Can, Suzuki
12   Mike Walsh, Can, Yamaha
13   Phil Kress, USA, Kawasaki
14   Frank Mrazek, Can, Ducati
15   Don Vance, Can, Suzuki

Race 2
1   Tom Kipp, USA, Yamaha
2   Linley Clarke, Can, Yamaha
3   Rueben McMurter, Can, Honda
4   Yves Brisson, Can, Honda
5   Steve Crevier, Can, Kawasaki
6   Benoit Pilon, Can, Yamaha
7   John Hopperstad, USA, Yamaha
8   Phil Kress, USA, Kawasaki
9   Tom Etherington, Can, Yamaha
10   Christian Gardner, USA, Yamaha
11   Clyde MacDonald, Can, Suzuki
12   Mike Walsh, Can, Yamaha
13   Frank Mrazek, Can, Ducati

Standings – 1 Polen 60;
2 Pirovano & Phillis 45; 4 Rymer 39;
5 Mertens 37; 6 Roche 32

Round 4 – USA
Brainerd, 9 June
Race 1
1   Doug Polen, USA, Ducati
2   Scott Russell, USA, Kawasaki
3   Stephane Mertens, Bel, Ducati
4   Rob Phillis, Aus, Kawasaki
5   Fabrizio Pirovano, Ita, Yamaha
6   Fred Merkel, USA, Honda
7   Giancarlo Falappa, Ita, Ducati
8   Baldassarre Monti, Ita, Honda
9   Jacques Guenette, Can, Kawasaki
10   Jeffry de Vries, Nl, Yamaha
11   Carl Fogarty, GB, Honda
12   Rueben McMurter, Can, Honda
13   Jean-Yves Mounier, Fra, Yamaha
14   Juan Lopez Mella, Spa, Honda
15   Niall Mackenzie, GB, Honda

Race 2
1   Doug Polen, USA, Ducati
2   Scott Russell, USA, Kawasaki
3   Stephane Mertens, Bel, Ducati
4   Fred Merkel, USA, Honda
5   Rob Phillis, Aus, Kawasaki
6   Fabrizio Pirovano, Ita, Yamaha
7   Baldassarre Monti, Ita, Honda
8   Jacques Guenette, Can, Kawasaki
9   Jean-Yves Mounier, Fra, Yamaha
10   Jeffry de Vries, Nl, Yamaha
11   Carl Fogarty, GB, Honda
12   Bruno Bonhuil, Fra, Yamaha
13   Britt Turkington, USA, Suzuki
14   Niall Mackenzie, GB, Honda
15   Adriano Narducci, Ita, Ducati

Standings – 1 Polen 100; 2 Phillis 69;
3 Mertens 67; 4 Pirovano 66; 5 Rymer 39; 5;
6 Roche 32 & Fogarty 32

Round 5 – Austria
Osterreichring, 30 June
Race 1
1   Stephane Mertens, Bel, Ducati
2   Doug Polen, USA, Ducati
3   Raymond Roche, Fra, Ducati
4   Rob Phillis, Aus, Kawasaki
5   Davide Tardozzi, Ita, Ducati
6   Terry Rymer, GB, Yamaha
7   Udo Mark, Ger, Yamaha
8   Fred Merkel, USA, Honda
9   Jari Suhonen, Fin, Yamaha
10   Jean-Yves Mounier, Fra, Yamaha
11   Jeffry de Vries, Nl, Yamaha
12   Daniel Amatriain, Spa, Honda
13   Fabrizio Furlan, Ita, Honda
14   Bruno Bammert, CH, Yamaha
15   Peter Rubatto, Ger, Yamaha

Race 2
1   Doug Polen, USA, Ducati
2   Stephane Mertens, Bel, Ducati
3   Raymond Roche, Fra, Ducati
4   Rob Phillis, Aus, Kawasaki
5   Fabrizio Pirovano, Ita, Yamaha
6   Davide Tardozzi, Ita, Ducati
7   Giancarlo Falappa, Ita, Ducati
8   Fred Merkel, USA, Honda

9   Terry Rymer, GB, Yamaha
10   Udo Mark, Ger, Yamaha
11   Jari Suhonen, Fin, Yamaha
12   Jeffry de Vries, Nl, Yamaha
13   Peter Rubatto, Ger, Yamaha
14   Jean-Yves Mounier, Fra, Yamaha
15   Russell Wood, Zim, Bimota

Standings – 1 Polen 137; 2 Mertens 104;
3 Phillis 95; 4 Pirovano 77; 5 Roche 62;
6 Rymer 56

Round 6 – San Marino
Misano, 4 August
Race 1
1   Doug Polen, USA, Ducati
2   Rob Phillis, Aus, Kawasaki
3   Davide Tardozzi, Ita, Ducati
4   Raymond Roche, Fra, Ducati
5   Fabrizio Pirovano, Ita, Yamaha
6   Stephane Mertens, Bel, Ducati
7   Carl Fogarty, GB, Honda
8   Terry Rymer, GB, Yamaha
9   Fred Merkel, USA, Honda
10   Giancarlo Falappa, Ita, Ducati
11   Udo Mark, Ger, Yamaha
12   Massimo Broccoli, Ita, Kawasaki
13   Daniel Amatriain, Spa, Honda
14   Russell Wood, Zim, Bimota
15   Jean-Michel Mattioli, Fra, Yamaha

Race 2
1   Doug Polen, USA, Ducati
2   Raymond Roche, Fra, Ducati
3   Rob Phillis, Aus, Kawasaki
4   Fabrizio Pirovano, Ita, Yamaha
5   Davide Tardozzi, Ita, Ducati
6   Giancarlo Falappa, Ita, Ducati
7   Fred Merkel, USA, Honda
8   Carl Fogarty, GB, Honda
9   Terry Rymer, GB, Yamaha
10   Russell Wood, Zim, Bimota
11   Juan Lopez Mella, Spa, Honda
12   Massimo Broccoli, Ita, Kawasaki
13   Daniel Amatriain, Spa, Honda
14   Jean-Michel Mattioli, Fra, Yamaha
15   Jari Suhonen, Fin, Yamaha

Standings – 1 Polen 177; 2 Phillis 127;
3 Mertens 114; 4 Pirovano 101; 5 Roche 92;
6 Rymer 71

Round 7 – Sweden
Anderstorp, 11 August
Race 1
1   Doug Polen, USA, Ducati
2   Rob Phillis, Aus, Kawasaki
3   Fabrizio Pirovano, Ita, Yamaha
4   Carl Fogarty, GB, Honda
5   Jari Suhonen, Fin, Yamaha
6   Giancarlo Falappa, Ita, Ducati
7   Terry Rymer, GB, Yamaha
8   Fred Merkel, USA, Honda
9   Jean-Yves Mounier, Fra, Yamaha
10   Udo Mark, Ger, Yamaha
11   Rob McElnea, GB, Yamaha
12   Jeffry de Vries, Nl, Yamaha
13   Peter Rubatto, Ger, Yamaha
14   Daniel Amatriain, Spa, Honda
15   Rene Rasmussen, Den, Yamaha

Race 2
1   Doug Polen, USA, Ducati
2   Rob Phillis, Aus, Kawasaki
3   Raymond Roche, Fra, Ducati
4   Carl Fogarty, GB, Honda
5   Christer Lindholm, Swe, Yamaha
6   Fred Merkel, USA, Honda
7   Jari Suhonen, Fin, Yamaha
8   Rob McElnea, GB, Yamaha
9   Jean-Yves Mounier, Fra, Yamaha
10   Udo Mark, Ger, Yamaha
11   Daniel Amatriain, Spa, Honda
12   Terry Rymer, GB, Yamaha
13   Giancarlo Falappa, Ita, Ducati
14   Massimo Meregalli, Ita, Yamaha
15   Christophe Guyot, Fra, Honda

Standings – 1 Polen 217; 2 Phillis 161;
3 Pirovano 116; 4 Mertens 114; 5 Roche 107;
6 Rymer 84

Round 8 – Japan
Sugo, 25 August
Race 1
1. Doug Polen, USA, Ducati
2. Rob Phillis, Aus, Kawasaki
3. Aaron Slight, NZ, Kawasaki
4. Peter Goddard, Aus, Yamaha
5. Kevin Magee, Aus, Yamaha
6. Raymond Roche, Fra, Ducati
7. Fabrizio Pirovano, Ita, Yamaha
8. Scott Russell, USA, Kawasaki
9. Davide Tardozzi, Ita, Ducati
10. Giancarlo Falappa, Ita, Ducati
11. Carl Fogarty, GB, Honda
12. Fred Merkel, USA, Honda
13. Ryuji Tsuruta, Jap, Kawasaki
14. Kiyokazu Tada, Jap, Kawasaki
15. Masano Aoki, Jap, Suzuki

Race 2
1. Doug Polen, USA, Ducati
2. Raymond Roche, Fra, Ducati
3. Kevin Magee, Aus, Yamaha
4. Aaron Slight, NZ, Kawasaki
5. Scott Russell, USA, Kawasaki
6. Niall Mackenzie, GB, Yamaha
7. Fabrizio Pirovano, Ita, Yamaha
8. Carl Fogarty, GB, Honda
9. Fred Merkel, USA, Honda
10. Davide Tardozzi, Ita, Ducati
11. Giancarlo Falappa, Ita, Ducati
12. Ryuji Tsuruta, Jap, Kawasaki
13. Kiyokazu Tada, Jap, Kawasaki
14. Terry Rymer, GB, Yamaha
15. Masano Aoki, Jap, Suzuki

Standings – 1 Polen 257; 2 Phillis 178;
3 Pirovano & Roche 134; 5 Mertens 114;
6 Rymer 86

Round 9 – Malaysia
Shah Alam, 1 September
Race 1
1. Raymond Roche, Fra, Ducati
2. Fabrizio Pirovano, Ita, Yamaha
3. Davide Tardozzi, Ita, Ducati
4. Doug Polen, USA, Ducati
5. Rob Phillis, Aus, Kawasaki
6. Giancarlo Falappa, Ita, Ducati
7. Aaron Slight, NZ, Kawasaki
8. Carl Fogarty, GB, Honda
9. Stephane Mertens, Bel, Ducati
10. Terry Rymer, GB, Yamaha
11. Andrew Stroud, NZ, Kawasaki
12. Fred Merkel, USA, Honda
13. Jeffry de Vries, Nl, Yamaha
14. Juan Lopez Mella, Spa, Honda
15. James Knight, Aus, Kawasaki

Race 2
1. Raymond Roche, Fra, Ducati
2. Stephane Mertens, Bel, Ducati
3. Fabrizio Pirovano, Ita, Yamaha
4. Aaron Slight, NZ, Kawasaki
5. Doug Polen, USA, Ducati
6. Davide Tardozzi, Ita, Ducati
7. Carl Fogarty, GB, Honda
8. Simon Crafar, NZ, Yamaha
9. Fred Merkel, USA, Honda
10. Juan Lopez Mella, Spa, Honda
11. James Knight, Aus, Kawasaki
12. Jean-Yves Mounier, Fra, Yamaha
13. Jeffry de Vries, Nl, Yamaha
14. Scott Doohan, Aus, Yamaha
15. M. H. Kuan, Mal, Yamaha

Standings – 1 Polen 281; 2 Phillis 189;
3 Roche 174: 4 Pirovano 166; 5 Mertens 138;
6 Rymer 92

Round 10 – Germany
Hockenheim, 15 September
Race 1
1. Doug Polen, USA, Ducati
2. Raymond Roche, Fra, Ducati
3. Davide Tardozzi, Ita, Ducati
4. Rob Phillis, Aus, Kawasaki
5. Stephane Mertens, Bel, Ducati
6. Giancarlo Falappa, Ita, Ducati
7. Terry Rymer, GB, Yamaha
8. Udo Mark, Ger, Yamaha
9. Carl Fogarty, GB, Honda
10. Edwin Weibel, CH, Ducati
11. Jean-Yves Mounier, Fra, Yamaha
12. Thomas Franz, Ger, Honda
13. Jeffry de Vries, Nl, Yamaha
14. Jari Suhonen, Fin, Yamaha
15. Daniel Amatriain, Spa, Honda

Race 2
1. Raymond Roche, Fra, Ducati
2. Doug Polen, USA, Ducati
3. Giancarlo Falappa, Ita, Ducati
4. Rob Phillis, Aus, Kawasaki
5. Udo Mark, Ger, Yamaha
6. Stephane Mertens, Bel, Ducati
7. Fabrizio Pirovano, Ita, Yamaha
8. Davide Tardozzi, Ita, Ducati
9. Terry Rymer, GB, Yamaha
10. Carl Fogarty, GB, Honda
11. Edwin Weibel, CH, Ducati
12. Jari Suhonen, Fin, Yamaha
13. Peter Rubatto, Ger, Yamaha
14. Bernd Caspers, Ger, Ducati
15. Marcel Kellenberger, CH, Yamaha

Standings – 1 Polen 318; 2 Phillis 215;
3 Roche 211: 4 Pirovano 175; 5 Mertens 159;
6 Rymer 108

Round 11 – France
Magny-Cours, 29 September
Race 1
1. Doug Polen, USA, Ducati
2. Raymond Roche, Fra, Ducati
3. Fred Merkel, USA, Honda
4. Rob Phillis, Aus, Kawasaki
5. Terry Rymer, GB, Yamaha
6. Carl Fogarty, GB, Honda
7. Stephane Mertens, Bel, Ducati
8. Brian Morrison, GB, Yamaha
9. Jari Suhonen, Fin, Yamaha
10. Bruno Bammert, CH, Yamaha
11. Piergiorgio Bontempi, Ita, Kawasaki
12. Jeffry de Vries, Nl, Yamaha
13. Jean-Michel Mattioli, Fra, Kawasaki
14. Edwin Weibel, CH, Ducati
15. Christer Lindholm, Swe, Yamaha

Race 2
1. Doug Polen, USA, Ducati
2. Raymond Roche, Fra, Ducati
3. Stephane Mertens, Bel, Ducati
4. Terry Rymer, GB, Yamaha
5. Rob Phillis, Aus, Kawasaki
6. Fabrizio Pirovano, Ita, Yamaha
7. Carl Fogarty, GB, Honda
8. Giancarlo Falappa, Ita, Ducati
9. Edwin Weibel, CH, Ducati
10. Fred Merkel, USA, Honda
11. Brian Morrison, GB, Yamaha
12. Jari Suhonen, Fin, Yamaha
13. Daniel Amatriain, Spa, Honda
14. Jeffry de Vries, Nl, Yamaha
15. Philippe Mouchet, Fra, Yamaha

Standings – 1 Polen 358; 2 Roche 245;
3 Phillis 239; 4 Pirovano 185; 5 Mertens 183;
6 Rymer 132

Round 12 – Italy
Mugello, 6 October
Race 1
1. Doug Polen, USA, Ducati
2. Raymond Roche, Fra, Ducati
3. Terry Rymer, GB, Yamaha
4. Stephane Mertens, Bel, Ducati
5. Virginio Ferrari, Ita, Ducati
6. Giancarlo Falappa, Ita, Ducati
7. Carl Fogarty, GB, Honda
8. Fred Merkel, USA, Honda
9. Edwin Weibel, CH, Ducati
10. Bruno Bammert, CH, Yamaha
11. Massimo Broccoli, Ita, Kawasaki
12. Vittorio Scatola, Ita, Kawasaki
13. Juan Lopez Mella, Spa, Honda
14. Fabrizio Furlan, Ita, Honda
15. Jeffry de Vries, Nl, Yamaha

Race 2
1. Raymond Roche, Fra, Ducati
2. Doug Polen, USA, Ducati
3. Terry Rymer, GB, Yamaha
4. Piergiorgio Bontempi, Ita, Kawasaki
5. Jeffry de Vries, Nl, Yamaha
6. Fabrizio Pirovano, Ita, Yamaha
7. Edwin Weibel, CH, Ducati
8. Steve Manley, GB, Ducati
9. Vittorio Scatola, Ita, Kawasaki
10. Massimo Broccoli, Ita, Kawasaki
11. Fabrizio Furlan, Ita, Honda
12. Jari Suhonen, Fin, Yamaha
13. Peter Rubatto, Ger, Yamaha
14. Robert Chesaux, CH, Honda
15. Juan Lopez Mella, Spa, Honda

Standings – 1 Polen 395; 2 Roche 282;
3 Phillis 239; 4 Mertens 196; 5 Pirovano 195;
6 Rymer 162

Round 13 – Australia
Phillip Island, 19 October
Race 1
1. Kevin Magee, Aus, Yamaha
2. Doug Polen, USA, Ducati
3. Aaron Slight, NZ, Kawasaki
4. Rob Phillis, Aus, Kawasaki
5. Stephane Mertens, Bel, Ducati
6. Mal Campbell, Aus, Honda
7. Scott Doohan, Aus, Yamaha
8. Steve Martin, Aus, Suzuki
9. Roy Leslie, Aus, Ducati
10. Michael O'Connor, Aus, Honda
11. Andrew Stroud, NZ, Kawasaki
12. Shawn Giles, Aus, Honda
13. Martin Craggill, Aus, Honda
14. Matt Blair, Aus, Suzuki
15. Eddie Kattenberg, NZ, Kawasaki

Race 2
1. Doug Polen, USA, Ducati
2. Kevin Magee, Aus, Yamaha
3. Rob Phillis, Aus, Kawasaki
4. Mal Campbell, Aus, Honda
5. Scott Doohan, Aus, Yamaha
6. Stephane Mertens, Bel, Ducati
7. Steve Martin, Aus, Suzuki
8. Michael O'Connor, Aus, Honda
9. Doug Pitman, Aus, Yamaha
10. Peter Guest, Aus, Yamaha
11. Shawn Giles, Aus, Honda
12. Martin Craggill, Aus, Honda
13. Ian Short, Aus, Suzuki
14. Tony Rees, NZ, Yamaha
15. Andrew Roberts, Aus, Yamaha

FINAL STANDINGS – 1 Polen 432; 2 Roche 282;
3 Phillis 267; 4 Mertens 217; 5 Pirovano 195;
6 Rymer 162

1992 season

Round 1 – Spain
Albacete, 5 April
Race 1
1   Aaron Slight, NZ, Kawasaki
2   Doug Polen, USA, Ducati
3   Fabrizio Pirovano, Ita, Yamaha
4   Giancarlo Falappa, Ita, Ducati
5   Daniel Amatriain, Spa, Ducati
6   Baldassarre Monti, Ita, Honda
7   Raymond Roche, Fra, Ducati
8   Takahiro Sohwa, Jap, Kawasaki
9   Rob Phillis, Aus, Kawasaki
10 Juan Lopez Mella, Spa, Honda
11 Stephane Mertens, Bel, Ducati
12 Carl Fogarty, GB, Ducati
13 Christer Lindholm, Swe, Yamaha
14 Terry Rymer, GB, Kawasaki
15 Jean-Yves Mounier, Fra, Yamaha

Race 2
1   Raymond Roche, Fra, Ducati
2   Rob Phillis, Aus, Kawasaki
3   Daniel Amatriain, Spa, Ducati
4   Fabrizio Pirovano, Ita, Yamaha
5   Giancarlo Falappa, Ita, Ducati
6   Doug Polen, USA, Ducati
7   Scott Russell, USA, Kawasaki
8   John Reynolds, GB, Kawasaki
9   Terry Rymer, GB, Kawasaki
10 Carl Fogarty, GB, Ducati
11 Virginio Ferrari, Ita, Ducati
12 Stephane Mertens, Bel, Ducati
13 Fabrizio Furlan, Ita, Ducati
14 Juan Lopez Mella, Spa, Honda
15 Christer Lindholm, Swe, Yamaha

Standings – 1 Roche 29; 2 Pirovano 28;
3 Polen 27; 4 Amatriain 26;
5 Falappa & Phillis 24

Round 2 – Great Britain
Donington Park, 19 April
Race 1
1   Raymond Roche, Fra, Ducati
2   Fabrizio Pirovano, Ita, Yamaha
3   Scott Russell, USA, Kawasaki
4   Rob Phillis, Aus, Kawasaki
5   Aaron Slight, NZ, Kawasaki
6   Doug Polen, USA, Ducati
7   Stephane Mertens, Bel, Ducati
8   Jean-Yves Mounier, Fra, Yamaha
9   Ray Stringer, GB, Kawasaki
10 Baldassarre Monti, Ita, Honda
11 James Whitham, GB, Suzuki
12 Daniel Amatriain, Spa, Ducati
13 John Reynolds, GB, Kawasaki
14 Jeffry de Vries, Nl, Yamaha
15 Christer Lindholm, Swe, Yamaha

Race 2
1   Carl Fogarty, GB, Ducati
2   Raymond Roche, Fra, Ducati
3   Scott Russell, USA, Kawasaki
4   Doug Polen, USA, Ducati
5   Fabrizio Pirovano, Ita, Yamaha
6   Aaron Slight, NZ, Kawasaki
7   Rob Phillis, Aus, Kawasaki
8   Giancarlo Falappa, Ita, Ducati
9   John Reynolds, GB, Kawasaki
10 Daniel Amatriain, Spa, Ducati
11 Takahiro Sohwa, Jap, Kawasaki
12 Rob McElnea, GB, Yamaha
13 Baldassarre Monti, Ita, Honda
14 James Whitham, GB, Suzuki
15 Christer Lindholm, Swe, Yamaha

Standings – 1 Roche 66; 2 Pirovano 56;
3 Polen 50; 4 Phillis 46; 5 Slight 41;
Russell 39

Round 3 – Germany
Hockenheim, 10 May
Race 1
1   Doug Polen, USA, Ducati
2   Rob Phillis, Aus, Kawasaki
3   Aaron Slight, NZ, Kawasaki
4   Scott Russell, USA, Kawasaki
5   Raymond Roche, Fra, Ducati
6   Stephane Mertens, Bel, Ducati
7   Hervé Moineau, Fra, Suzuki
8   Andreas Hofmann, Ger, Kawasaki
9   Daniel Amatriain, Spa, Ducati
10 Piergiorgio Bontempi, Ita, Kawasaki
11 Virginio Ferrari, Ita, Ducati
12 Klaus Liegibel, Ger, Yamaha
13 Andreas Meklau, Aut, Ducati
14 Jean-Yves Mounier, Fra, Yamaha
15 Sven Seidel, Ger, Suzuki

Race 2
1   Doug Polen, USA, Ducati
2   Rob Phillis, Aus, Kawasaki
3   Giancarlo Falappa, Ita, Ducati
4   Raymond Roche, Fra, Ducati
5   Aaron Slight, NZ, Kawasaki
6   Fabrizio Pirovano, Ita, Yamaha
7   Scott Russell, USA, Kawasaki
8   John Reynolds, GB, Kawasaki
9   Andreas Hofmann, Ger, Kawasaki
10 Hervé Moineau, Fra, Suzuki
11 Carl Fogarty, GB, Ducati
12 Edwin Weibel, D, Ducati
13 Stephane Mertens, Bel, Ducati
14 Massimo Broccoli, Ita, Kawasaki
15 Virginio Ferrari, Ita, Ducati

Standings – 1 Polen & Roche 90;
3 Phillis 80; 4 Slight 67; 5 Pirovano 66;
6 Russell 61

Round 4 – Belgium
Spa-Francorchamps, 24 May
Race 1
1   Rob Phillis, Aus, Kawasaki
2   Stephane Mertens, Bel, Ducati
3   Scott Russell, USA, Kawasaki
4   Giancarlo Falappa, Ita, Ducati
5   Doug Polen, USA, Ducati
6   Aaron Slight, NZ, Kawasaki
7   Daniel Amatriain, Spa, Ducati
8   Andreas Hofmann, Ger, Kawasaki
9   Baldassarre Monti, Ita, Honda
10 Virginio Ferrari, Ita, Ducati
11 Jeffry de Vries, Nl, Yamaha
12 Christer Lindholm, Swe, Yamaha
13 Richard Arnaiz, USA, Honda
14 Piergiorgio Bontempi, Ita, Kawasaki
15 Simon Crafar, NZ, Honda

Race 2
1   Doug Polen, USA, Ducati
2   Giancarlo Falappa, Ita, Ducati
3   Fabrizio Pirovano, Ita, Yamaha
4   Raymond Roche, Fra, Ducati
5   Rob Phillis, Aus, Kawasaki
6   Stephane Mertens, Bel, Ducati
7   Aaron Slight, NZ, Kawasaki
8   Carl Fogarty, GB, Ducati
9   Scott Russell, USA, Kawasaki
10 Hervé Moineau, Fra, Suzuki
11 Daniel Amatriain, Spa, Ducati
12 Davide Tardozzi, Ita, Ducati
13 Piergiorgio Bontempi, Ita, Kawasaki
14 Jeffry de Vries, Nl, Yamaha
15 Christer Lindholm, Swe, Yamaha

Standings – 1 Polen 121; 2 Phillis 111;
3 Roche 103; 4 Slight 86; 5 Russell 83;
6 Pirovano 81

Round 5 – Andorra
Jerez, 21 June
Race 1
1   Rob Phillis, Aus, Kawasaki
2   Raymond Roche, Fra, Ducati
3   Giancarlo Falappa, Ita, Ducati
4   Daniel Amatriain, Spa, Ducati
5   Carl Fogarty, GB, Ducati
6   Aaron Slight, NZ, Kawasaki
7   Christer Lindholm, Swe, Yamaha
8   Davide Tardozzi, Ita, Ducati
9   Baldassarre Monti, Ita, Honda
10 Piergiorgio Bontempi, Ita, Kawasaki
11 Jehan d'Orgeix, Fra, Kawasaki
12 Richard Arnaiz, USA, Honda
13 Jari Suhonen, Fin, Yamaha
14 Fabrizio Furlan, Ita, Ducati
15 Jeffry de Vries, Nl, Yamaha

Race 2
1   Doug Polen, USA, Ducati
2   Rob Phillis, Aus, Kawasaki
3   Fabrizio Pirovano, Ita, Yamaha
4   Stephane Mertens, Bel, Ducati
5   Aaron Slight, NZ, Kawasaki
6   Raymond Roche, Fra, Ducati
7   Giancarlo Falappa, Ita, Ducati
8   Fabrizio Furlan, Ita, Ducati
9   Christer Lindholm, Swe, Yamaha
10 Baldassarre Monti, Ita, Honda
11 Piergiorgio Bontempi, Ita, Kawasaki
12 Richard Arnaiz, USA, Honda
13 Jehan d'Orgeix, Fra, Kawasaki
14 Jari Suhonen, Fin, Yamaha
15 Antonio Moreno, Spa, Yamaha

Standings – 1 Phillis 148; 2 Polen 141;
3 Roche 130; 4 Slight 107; 5 Falappa 101;
6 Pirovano 96

Round 6 – Austria
Osterreichring, 28 June
Race 1
1   Giancarlo Falappa, Ita, Ducati
2   Rob Phillis, Aus, Kawasaki
3   Doug Polen, USA, Ducati
4   Fabrizio Pirovano, Ita, Yamaha
5   Davide Tardozzi, Ita, Ducati
6   Carl Fogarty, GB, Ducati
7   Aaron Slight, NZ, Kawasaki
8   Daniel Amatriain, Spa, Ducati
9   Fred Merkel, USA, Yamaha
10 Simon Crafar, NZ, Honda
11 Ernst Gschwender, Ger, Kawasaki
12 Andreas Meklau, Aut, Ducati
13 Jeffry de Vries, Nl, Yamaha
14 Piergiorgio Bontempi, Ita, Kawasaki
15 Virginio Ferrari, Ita, Ducati

Race 2
1   Giancarlo Falappa, Ita, Ducati
2   Stephane Mertens, Bel, Ducati
3   Raymond Roche, Fra, Ducati
4   Rob Phillis, Aus, Kawasaki
5   Doug Polen, USA, Ducati
6   Fabrizio Pirovano, Ita, Yamaha
7   Carl Fogarty, GB, Ducati
8   Davide Tardozzi, Ita, Ducati
9   Daniel Amatriain, Spa, Ducati
10 Fred Merkel, USA, Yamaha
11 Simon Crafar, NZ, Honda
12 Jeffry de Vries, Nl, Yamaha
13 Andreas Meklau, Aut, Ducati
14 Jari Suhonen, Fin, Yamaha
15 Udo Mark, Ger, Yamaha

Standings – 1 Phillis 178; 2 Polen 167;
3 Roche 145; 4 Falappa 141; 5 Pirovano 119;
6 Slight 116

Round 7 – San Marino
Mugello, 19 July
Race 1
1   Raymond Roche, Fra, Ducati
2   Doug Polen, USA, Ducati
3   Giancarlo Falappa, Ita, Ducati
4   Stephane Mertens, Bel, Ducati
5   Fabrizio Pirovano, Ita, Yamaha
6   Adrien Morillas, Fra, Yamaha
7   Carl Fogarty, GB, Ducati
8   Daniel Amatriain, Spa, Ducati
9   Richard Arnaiz, USA, Honda
10 Christer Lindholm, Swe, Yamaha
11 Piergiorgio Bontempi, Ita, Kawasaki
12 Virginio Ferrari, Ita, Ducati
13 Andreas Hofmann, Ger, Kawasaki
14 Jeffry de Vries, Nl, Yamaha
15 Baldassarre Monti, Ita, Honda

Race 2
1   Raymond Roche, Fra, Ducati
2   Giancarlo Falappa, Ita, Ducati
3   Doug Polen, USA, Ducati
4   Carl Fogarty, GB, Ducati
5   Rob Phillis, Aus, Kawasaki
6   Adrien Morillas, Fra, Yamaha
7   Daniel Amatriain, Spa, Ducati
8   Christer Lindholm, Swe, Yamaha
9   Piergiorgio Bontempi, Ita, Kawasaki
10 Jeffry de Vries, Nl, Yamaha
11 Andreas Hofmann, Ger, Kawasaki
12 Richard Arnaiz, USA, Honda
13 Karl Truchess, Aut, Kawasaki
14 Fabrizio Furlan, Ita, Ducati
15 Massimo Broccoli, Ita, Honda

Standings – 1 Polen 199; 2 Phillis 189;
3 Roche 185; 4 Falappa 173; 5 Pirovano 130;
6 Slight 116

Round 8 – Malaysia
Johor, 23 August

Race 1
1. Raymond Roche, Fra, Ducati
2. Fabrizio Pirovano, Ita, Yamaha
3. Rob Phillis, Aus, Kawasaki
4. Aaron Slight, NZ, Kawasaki
5. Stephane Mertens, Bel, Ducati
6. Giancarlo Falappa, Ita, Ducati
7. Christopher Haldane, NZ, Yamaha
8. Doug Polen, USA, Ducati
9. Piergiorgio Bontempi, Ita, Kawasaki
10. Adrien Morillas, Fra, Yamaha
11. Fred Merkel, USA, Yamaha
12. Steve Hislop, GB, Kawasaki
13. Davide Tardozzi, Ita, Ducati
14. Trevor Jordan, Aus, Kawasaki
15. Andrew Stroud, NZ, Kawasaki

Race 2
1. Doug Polen, USA, Ducati
2. Raymond Roche, Fra, Ducati
3. Aaron Slight, NZ, Kawasaki
4. Giancarlo Falappa, Ita, Ducati
5. Fred Merkel, USA, Yamaha
6. Fabrizio Pirovano, Ita, Yamaha
7. Daniel Amatriain, Spa, Ducati
8. Rob Phillis, Aus, Kawasaki
9. Trevor Jordan, Aus, Kawasaki
10. Piergiorgio Bontempi, Ita, Kawasaki
11. Andrew Stroud, NZ, Kawasaki
12. Christopher Haldane, NZ, Yamaha
13. Adrien Morillas, Fra, Yamaha
14. Virginio Ferrari, Ita, Ducati
15. Jeffry de Vries, Nl, Yamaha

Standings – 1 Polen 227; 2 Roche 222;
3 Phillis 212; 4 Falappa 196; 5 Pirovano 157;
6 Slight 144

Round 9 – Japan
Sugo, 30 August

Race 1
1. Doug Polen, USA, Ducati
2. Kevin Magee, Aus, Yamaha
3. Fabrizio Pirovano, Ita, Yamaha
4. Syouichi Tsukamoto, Jap, Kawasaki
5. Raymond Roche, Fra, Ducati
6. Aaron Slight, NZ, Kawasaki
7. Keiichi Kitagawa, Jap, Kawasaki
8. Stephane Mertens, Bel, Ducati
9. Piergiorgio Bontempi, Ita, Kawasaki
10. Mat Mladin, Aus, Kawasaki
11. Rob Phillis, Aus, Kawasaki
12. Shinichiro Imai, Jap, Kawasaki
13. Davide Tardozzi, Ita, Ducati
14. Adrien Morillas, Fra, Yamaha
15. Tetsuya Shirai, Jap, Honda

Race 2
1. Doug Polen, USA, Ducati
2. Kevin Magee, Aus, Yamaha
3. Fabrizio Pirovano, Ita, Yamaha
4. Aaron Slight, NZ, Kawasaki
5. Syouichi Tsukamoto, Jap, Kawasaki
6. Giancarlo Falappa, Ita, Ducati
7. Keiichi Kitagawa, Jap, Kawasaki
8. Raymond Roche, Fra, Ducati
9. Davide Tardozzi, Ita, Ducati
10. Rob Phillis, Aus, Kawasaki
11. Piergiorgio Bontempi, Ita, Kawasaki
12. Mat Mladin, Aus, Kawasaki
13. Fred Merkel, USA, Yamaha
14. Wataru Yoshikawa, Jap, Yamaha
15. Baldassarre Monti, Ita, Honda

Standings – 1 Polen 267; 2 Roche 241;
3 Phillis 223; 4 Falappa 206; 5 Pirovano 187;
6 Slight 167

Round 10 – Holland
Assen, 13 September

Race 1
1. Doug Polen, USA, Ducati
2. Stephane Mertens, Bel, Ducati
3. Raymond Roche, Fra, Ducati
4. Carl Fogarty, GB, Ducati
5. Rob Phillis, Aus, Kawasaki
6. Piergiorgio Bontempi, Ita, Kawasaki
7. Aaron Slight, NZ, Kawasaki
8. Giancarlo Falappa, Ita, Ducati
9. Fabrizio Pirovano, Ita, Yamaha
10. Adrien Morillas, Fra, Yamaha
11. Terry Rymer, GB, Kawasaki
12. Christer Lindholm, Swe, Yamaha
13. Fred Merkel, USA, Yamaha
14. Daniel Amatriain, Spa, Ducati
15. Roger Kellenberger, CH, Yamaha

Race 2
1. Giancarlo Falappa, Ita, Ducati
2. Carl Fogarty, GB, Ducati
3. Raymond Roche, Fra, Ducati
4. Aaron Slight, NZ, Kawasaki
5. Daniel Amatriain, Spa, Ducati
6. Fabrizio Furlan, Ita, Ducati
7. Adrien Morillas, Fra, Yamaha
8. Fabrizio Pirovano, Ita, Yamaha
9. Roger Kellenberger, CH, Yamaha
10. Jean-Yves Mounier, Fra, Yamaha
11. Mile Pajic, Nl, Kawasaki
12. Johnny Verwijst, Nl, Kawasaki
13. Andreas Meklau, Aut, Ducati
14. Jehan d'Orgeix, Fra, Kawasaki
15. Florian Ferracci, Fra, Ducati

Standings – 1 Polen 287; 2 Roche 271;
3 Phillis & Falappa 234; 5 Pirovano 202;
6 Slight 189

Round 11 – Italy
Monza, 4 October

Race 1
1. Fabrizio Pirovano, Ita, Yamaha
2. Stephane Mertens, Bel, Ducati
3. Rob Phillis, Aus, Kawasaki
4. Piergiorgio Bontempi, Ita, Kawasaki
5. Valerio de Stefanis, Ita, Ducati
6. Daniel Amatriain, Spa, Ducati
7. Jehan d'Orgeix, Fra, Kawasaki
8. Mauro Lucchiari, Ita, Ducati
9. Jari Suhonen, Fin, Yamaha
10. Doug Polen, USA, Ducati
11. Virginio Ferrari, Ita, Ducati
12. Giancarlo Falappa, Ita, Ducati
13. Udo Mark, Ger, Yamaha
14. Patrick Igoa, Fra, Suzuki
15. Vittorio Scatola, Ita, Kawasaki

Race 2
1. Fabrizio Pirovano, Ita, Yamaha
2. Raymond Roche, Fra, Ducati
3. Piergiorgio Bontempi, Ita, Kawasaki
4. Stephane Mertens, Bel, Ducati
5. Doug Polen, USA, Ducati
6. Giancarlo Falappa, Ita, Ducati
7. Jehan d'Orgeix, Fra, Kawasaki
8. Daniel Amatriain, Spa, Ducati
9. Virginio Ferrari, Ita, Ducati
10. Jari Suhonen, Fin, Yamaha
11. Gastone Grassetti, Ita, Ducati
12. Mauro Lucchiari, Ita, Ducati
13. Patrick Igoa, Fra, Suzuki
14. Michel Amalric, Fra, Yamaha
15. Rob Phillis, Aus, Kawasaki

Standings – 1 Polen 304; 2 Roche 288;
3 Phillis 250; 4 Falappa 248; 5 Pirovano 242;
6 Slight 189

Round 12 – Australia
Phillip Island, 18 October

Race 1
1. Kevin Magee, Aus, Yamaha
2. Doug Polen, USA, Ducati
3. Stephane Mertens, Bel, Ducati
4. Aaron Slight, NZ, Kawasaki
5. Giancarlo Falappa, Ita, Ducati
6. Rob Phillis, Aus, Kawasaki
7. Carl Fogarty, GB, Ducati
8. Piergiorgio Bontempi, Ita, Kawasaki
9. Mal Campbell, Aus, Honda
10. Fred Merkel, USA, Yamaha
11. Michael O'Connor, Aus, Honda
12. Fabrizio Pirovano, Ita, Yamaha
13. Martin Craggill, Aus, Kawasaki
14. Jeffry de Vries, Nl, Yamaha
15. Peter Guest, Aus, Yamaha

Race 2
1. Raymond Roche, Fra, Ducati
2. Kevin Magee, Aus, Yamaha
3. Aaron Slight, NZ, Kawasaki
4. Doug Polen, USA, Ducati
5. Mat Mladin, Aus, Kawasaki
6. Fabrizio Pirovano, Ita, Yamaha
7. Piergiorgio Bontempi, Ita, Kawasaki
8. Michael O'Connor, Aus, Honda
9. Rob Phillis, Aus, Kawasaki
10. Scott Doohan, Aus, Yamaha
11. Martin Craggill, Aus, Kawasaki
12. Fred Merkel, USA, Yamaha
13. Jeffry de Vries, Nl, Yamaha
14. Troy Corser, Aus, Yamaha
15. Kirk McCarthy, Aus, Suzuki

Standings – 1 Polen 334; 2 Roche 308;
3 Phillis 267; 4 Falappa 259; 5 Pirovano 256;
6 Slight 217

Round 13 – New Zealand
Manfeild, 25 October

Race 1
1. Doug Polen, USA, Ducati
2. Aaron Slight, NZ, Kawasaki
3. Raymond Roche, Fra, Ducati
4. Rob Phillis, Aus, Kawasaki
5. Fabrizio Pirovano, Ita, Yamaha
6. Fred Merkel, USA, Yamaha
7. Piergiorgio Bontempi, Ita, Kawasaki
8. Scott Doohan, Aus, Yamaha
9. Daniel Amatriain, Spa, Ducati
10. Troy Corser, Aus, Yamaha
11. Tony Rees, NZ, Yamaha
12. Russell Josiah, NZ, Kawasaki
13. Paul McQuilkin, NZ, Suzuki
14. Mike King, NZ, Yamaha
15. Scott Buckley, NZ, Yamaha

Race 2
1. Giancarlo Falappa, Ita, Ducati
2. Doug Polen, USA, Ducati
3. Aaron Slight, NZ, Kawasaki
4. Raymond Roche, Fra, Ducati
5. Fabrizio Pirovano, Ita, Yamaha
6. Fred Merkel, USA, Yamaha
7. Rob Phillis, Aus, Kawasaki
8. Scott Doohan, Aus, Yamaha
9. Daniel Amatriain, Spa, Ducati
10. Troy Corser, Aus, Yamaha
11. Christer Lindholm, Swe, Yamaha
12. Tony Rees, NZ, Yamaha
13. Paul McQuilkin, NZ, Suzuki
14. Russell Josiah, NZ, Kawasaki
15. Scott Buckley, NZ, Yamaha

FINAL STANDINGS – 1 Polen 371; 2 Roche 336;
3 Phillis 289; 4 Falappa 279; 5 Pirovano 278;
6 Slight 249

1993 season

Round 1 – Ireland
9 April, Brands Hatch
Race 1
1. Giancarlo Falappa, Ita, Ducati
2. Scott Russell, USA, Kawasaki
3. Brian Morrison, GB, Kawasaki
4. Adrien Morillas, Fra, Kawasaki
5. Aaron Slight, NZ, Kawasaki
6. Stephane Mertens, Bel, Ducati
7. Fred Merkel, USA, Yamaha
8. Mark Farmer, GB, Kawasaki
9. David Jefferies, GB, Yamaha
10. Tripp Nobles, USA, Honda
11. Juan Garriga, Spa, Ducati
12. Valerio de Stefanis, Ita, Yamaha
13. Mauro Lucchiari, Ita, Ducati
14. Hervé Moineau, Fra, Suzuki
15. Beni Metzger, CH, Yamaha

Race 2
1. Giancarlo Falappa, Ita, Ducati
2. Scott Russell, USA, Kawasaki
3. Fabrizio Pirovano, Ita, Yamaha
4. Stephane Mertens, Bel, Ducati
5. Terry Rymer, GB, Yamaha
6. Aaron Slight, NZ, Kawasaki
7. Fred Merkel, USA, Yamaha
8. Juan Garriga, Spa, Ducati
9. Valerio de Stefanis, Ita, Yamaha
10. Ernst Gschwender, Ger, Kawasaki
11. Adrien Morillas, Fra, Kawasaki
12. Mauro Lucchiari, Ita, Ducati
13. Baldassarre Monti, Ita, Ducati
14. David Jefferies, GB, Yamaha
15. Daniel Amatrain, Spa, Ducati

*Standings – 1 Falappa 40; 2 Russell 34;
3 Mertens 23; 4 Slight 21;
5 Merkel & Morillas 18*

Round 2 – Germany
Hockenheim, 9 May
Race 1
1. Giancarlo Falappa, Ita, Ducati
2. Fabrizio Pirovano, Ita, Yamaha
3. Carl Fogarty, GB, Ducati
4. Aaron Slight, NZ, Kawasaki
5. Adrien Morillas, Fra, Kawasaki
6. Scott Russell, USA, Kawasaki
7. Andreas Hofmann, Ger, Kawasaki
8. Terry Rymer, GB, Yamaha
9. Christer Lindholm, Swe, Yamaha
10. Roger Kellerman, CH, Yamaha
11. Jeffry de Vries, Nl, Yamaha
12. Edwin Weibel, CH, Ducati
13. Dominique Sarron, Fra, Yamaha
14. Udo Mark, Ger, Yamaha
15. Bernhard Schick, Ger, Ducati

Race 2
1. Scott Russell, USA, Kawasaki
2. Juan Garriga, Spa, Ducati
3. Giancarlo Falappa, Ita, Ducati
4. Aaron Slight, NZ, Kawasaki
5. Fabrizio Pirovano, Ita, Yamaha
6. Stephane Mertens, Bel, Ducati
7. Carl Fogarty, GB, Ducati
8. Adrien Morillas, Fra, Kawasaki
9. Piergiorgio Bontempi, Ita, Kawasaki
10. Simon Crafar, NZ, Ducati
11. Edwin Weibel, CH, Ducati
12. Fred Merkel, USA, Yamaha
13. Christer Lindholm, Swe, Yamaha
14. Roger Kellerman, CH, Yamaha
15. Daniel Amatrain, Spa, Ducati

*Standings – 1 Falappa 75; 2 Russell 64;
3 Slight 47; 4 Pirovano 43; 5 Morillas 37;
6 Mertens 33*

Round 3 – Spain
Albacete, 30 May
Race 1
1. Carl Fogarty, GB, Ducati
2. Aaron Slight, NZ, Kawasaki
3. Piergiorgio Bontempi, Ita, Kawasaki
4. Fabrizio Pirovano, Ita, Yamaha
5. Daniel Amatrain, Spa, Ducati
6. Juan Garriga, Spa, Ducati
7. Terry Rymer, GB, Yamaha
8. Simon Crafar, NZ, Ducati
9. Fred Merkel, USA, Yamaha
10. Rob McElnea, GB, Yamaha
11. James Whitham, GB, Yamaha
12. Mauro Lucchiari, Ita, Ducati
13. Christer Lindholm, Swe, Yamaha
14. Fabrizio Furlan, Ita, Kawasaki
15. Aldeo Presciutti, Ita, Ducati

Race 2
1. Carl Fogarty, GB, Ducati
2. Scott Russell, USA, Kawasaki
3. Aaron Slight, NZ, Kawasaki
4. Stephane Mertens, Bel, Ducati
5. Juan Garriga, Spa, Ducati
6. Piergiorgio Bontempi, Ita, Kawasaki
7. Fabrizio Pirovano, Ita, Yamaha
8. Simon Crafar, NZ, Ducati
9. Terry Rymer, GB, Yamaha
10. Mauro Lucchiari, Ita, Ducati
11. James Whitham, GB, Yamaha
12. Fred Merkel, USA, Yamaha
13. Adrien Morillas, Fra, Kawasaki
14. Rob McElnea, GB, Yamaha
15. Jeffry de Vries, Nl, Yamaha

*Standings – 1 Russell 81; 2 Slight 79;
3 Falappa 75; 4 Pirovano 65; 5 Fogarty 64;
6 Garriga 51*

Round 4 – San Marino
Misano, 27 june
Race 1
1. Giancarlo Falappa, Ita, Ducati
2. Mauro Lucchiari, Ita, Ducati
3. Fabrizio Pirovano, Ita, Yamaha
4. Scott Russell, USA, Kawasaki
5. Carl Fogarty, GB, Ducati
6. Aaron Slight, NZ, Kawasaki
7. Juan Garriga, Spa, Ducati
8. Baldassarre Monti, Ita, Ducati
9. Terry Rymer, GB, Yamaha
10. Fred Merkel, USA, Yamaha
11. Jeffry de Vries, Nl, Yamaha
12. Aldeo Presciutti, Ita, Ducati
13. Arpad Harmati, Hun, Yamaha
14. Jean-Marc Deletang, Fra, Yamaha
15. Tripp Nobles, USA, Honda

Race 2
1. Giancarlo Falappa, Ita, Ducati
2. Scott Russell, USA, Kawasaki
3. Carl Fogarty, GB, Ducati
4. Mauro Lucchiari, Ita, Ducati
5. Juan Garriga, Spa, Ducati
6. Aaron Slight, NZ, Kawasaki
7. Piergiorgio Bontempi, Ita, Kawasaki
8. Baldassarre Monti, Ita, Ducati
9. Terry Rymer, GB, Yamaha
10. Stephane Mertens, Bel, Ducati
11. Fabrizio Pirovano, Ita, Yamaha
12. Jeffry de Vries, Nl, Yamaha
13. Daniel Amatrain, Spa, Ducati
14. Udo Mark, Ger, Yamaha
15. Jean-Marc Deletang, Fra, Yamaha

*Standings – 1 Falappa 115; 2 Russell 111;
3 Slight 99; 4 Fogarty 90; 5 Pirovano 85;
6 Garriga 71*

Round 5 – Austria
Osterreichring, 11 July
Race 1
1. Andreas Meklau, Aut, Ducati
2. Aaron Slight, NZ, Kawasaki
3. Scott Russell, USA, Kawasaki
4. Carl Fogarty, GB, Ducati
5. Piergiorgio Bontempi, Ita, Kawasaki
6. Giancarlo Falappa, Ita, Ducati
7. Jeffry de Vries, Nl, Yamaha
8. Ernst Gschwender, Ger, Kawasaki
9. Stephane Mertens, Bel, Ducati
10. Fabrizio Furlan, Ita, Kawasaki
11. Fred Merkel, USA, Yamaha
12. Christer Lindholm, Swe, Yamaha
13. Jean-Marc Deletang, Fra, Yamaha
14. Marcel Ernst, CH, Kawasaki
15. Thierry Rogier, Fra, Ducati

Race 2
1. Giancarlo Falappa, Ita, Ducati
2. Fred Merkel, USA, Yamaha
3. Andreas Meklau, Aut, Ducati
4. Carl Fogarty, GB, Ducati
5. Mauro Lucchiari, Ita, Ducati
6. Ernst Gschwender, Ger, Kawasaki

7. Scott Russell, USA, Kawasaki
8. Tripp Nobles, USA, Honda
9. Jeffry de Vries, Nl, Yamaha
10. Jean-Marc Deletang, Fra, Yamaha
11. Thierry Rogier, Fra, Ducati
12. Hervé Moineau, Fra, Suzuki
13. Marcel Ernst, CH, Kawasaki
14. Udo Mark, Ger, Yamaha
15. Piergiorgio Bontempi, Ita, Kawasaki

*Standings – 1 Falappa 135; 2 Russell 130.5;
3 Slight 116; 4 Fogarty 109.5; 5 Pirovano 85;
6 Garriga 71*

Round 6 – Czech Republic
Brno, 18 July
Race 1
1. Carl Fogarty, GB, Ducati
2. Scott Russell, USA, Kawasaki
3. Aaron Slight, NZ, Kawasaki
4. Fabrizio Pirovano, Ita, Yamaha
5. Giancarlo Falappa, Ita, Ducati
6. Mauro Lucchiari, Ita, Ducati
7. Piergiorgio Bontempi, Ita, Kawasaki
8. Edwin Weibel, CH, Ducati
9. Terry Rymer, GB, Yamaha
10. Stephane Mertens, Bel, Ducati
11. Andreas Hofmann, Ger, Kawasaki
12. Baldassarre Monti, Ita, Ducati
13. Aldeo Presciutti, Ita, Ducati
14. Jeffry de Vries, Nl, Yamaha
15. Ernst Gschwender, Ger, Kawasaki

Race 2
1. Scott Russell, USA, Kawasaki
2. Carl Fogarty, GB, Ducati
3. Stephane Mertens, Bel, Ducati
4. Fabrizio Pirovano, Ita, Yamaha
5. Fred Merkel, USA, Yamaha
6. Piergiorgio Bontempi, Ita, Kawasaki
7. Christer Lindholm, Swe, Yamaha
8. Jeffry de Vries, Nl, Yamaha
9. Aldeo Presciutti, Ita, Ducati
10. Andreas Hofmann, Ger, Kawasaki
11. Bernhard Schick, Ger, Ducati
12. Jean-Marc Deletang, Fra, Yamaha
13. Tripp Nobles, USA, Honda
14. Ernst Gschwender, Ger, Kawasaki
15. Marcel Kellenberger, CH, Kawasaki

*Standings – 1 Russell 167.5; 2 Fogarty 146.5;
3 Falappa 146; 4 Slight 131; 5 Pirovano 111;
6 Mertens 80*

Round 7 – Sweden
Anderstorp, 8 August
Race 1
1. Carl Fogarty, GB, Ducati
2. Giancarlo Falappa, Ita, Ducati
3. Fabrizio Pirovano, Ita, Yamaha
4. Scott Russell, USA, Kawasaki
5. James Whitham, GB, Yamaha
6. Stephane Mertens, Bel, Ducati
7. Piergiorgio Bontempi, Ita, Kawasaki
8. Aaron Slight, NZ, Kawasaki
9. Christer Lindholm, Swe, Yamaha
10. Fabrizio Furlan, Ita, Kawasaki
11. Jean-Marc Deletang, Fra, Yamaha
12. Fred Merkel, USA, Yamaha
13. Jeffry de Vries, Nl, Yamaha
14. Philippe Mouchet, Fra, Ducati
15. Jean-Yves Mounier, Fra, Yamaha

Race 2
1. Carl Fogarty, GB, Ducati
2. Scott Russell, USA, Kawasaki
3. Giancarlo Falappa, Ita, Ducati
4. Fabrizio Pirovano, Ita, Yamaha
5. Aaron Slight, NZ, Kawasaki
6. Stephane Mertens, Bel, Ducati
7. Fabrizio Furlan, Ita, Kawasaki
8. Piergiorgio Bontempi, Ita, Kawasaki
9. Jeffry de Vries, Nl, Yamaha
10. Brian Morrison, GB, Kawasaki
11. Hervé Moineau, Fra, Suzuki
12. Arpad Harmati, Hun, Yamaha
13. Jean-Yves Mounier, Fra, Yamaha
14. Rolf Valderhaug, Nor, Yamaha
15. Christy Rebuttini, Fra, Ducati

*Standings – 1 Russell 197.5; 2 Fogarty 186.5;
3 Falappa 178; 4 Slight 150; 5 Pirovano 139;
6 Mertens 100*

Round 8 – Malaysia
Johor, 22 August
Race 1
1 Carl Fogarty, GB, Ducati
2 Scott Russell, USA, Kawasaki
3 Fabrizio Pirovano, Ita, Yamaha
4 Aaron Slight, NZ, Kawasaki
5 Stephane Mertens, Bel, Ducati
6 Piergiorgio Bontempi, Ita, Kawasaki
7 Mauro Lucchiari, Ita, Ducati
8 Christer Lindholm, Swe, Yamaha
9 Fred Merkel, USA, Yamaha
10 Fabrizio Furlan, Ita, Kawasaki
11 Benn Archibald, Aus, Yamaha
12 Jean-Marc Deletang, Fra, Yamaha
13 Ken Watson, Aus, Kawasaki
14 Cletus Adi Haslam, Mal, Kawasaki
15 Trevor Jordan, Aus, Kawasaki

Race 2
1 Carl Fogarty, GB, Ducati
2 Scott Russell, USA, Kawasaki
3 Fabrizio Pirovano, Ita, Yamaha
4 Piergiorgio Bontempi, Ita, Kawasaki
5 Stephane Mertens, Bel, Ducati
6 Aaron Slight, NZ, Kawasaki
7 Rob Phillis, Aus, Kawasaki
8 Terry Rymer, GB, Yamaha
9 Mauro Lucchiari, Ita, Ducati
10 Christer Lindholm, Swe, Yamaha
11 Hervé Moineau, Fra, Suzuki
12 Jeffry de Vries, Nl, Yamaha
13 Jean-Marc Deletang, Fra, Yamaha
14 Trevor Jordan, Aus, Kawasaki
15 Benn Archibald, Aus, Yamaha

*Standings – 1 Russell 231.5; 2 Fogarty 226.5;
3 Falappa 178; 4 Slight 173; 5 Pirovano 169;
6 Mertens 122*

Round 9 – Japan
Sugo, 29 August
Race 1
1 Carl Fogarty, GB, Ducati
2 Keichi Kitagawa, Jap, Kawasaki
3 Shoichi Tsukamoto, Jap, Kawasaki
4 Stephane Mertens, Bel, Ducati
5 Giancarlo Falappa, Ita, Ducati
6 Aaron Slight, NZ, Kawasaki
7 Fabrizio Pirovano, Ita, Yamaha
8 Scott Russell, USA, Kawasaki
9 Piergiorgio Bontempi, Ita, Kawasaki
10 Terry Rymer, GB, Yamaha
11 Toshiyuki Arakaki, Jap, Ducati
12 Katsuyoshi Takahashi, Jap, Yamaha
13 Aldeo Presciutti, Ita, Ducati
14 Christer Lindholm, Swe, Yamaha
15 Makoto Suzuki, Jap, Ducati

Race 2
1 Scott Russell, USA, Kawasaki
2 Keichi Kitagawa, Jap, Kawasaki
3 Shoichi Tsukamoto, Jap, Kawasaki
4 Aaron Slight, NZ, Kawasaki
5 Fabrizio Pirovano, Ita, Yamaha
6 Toshiyuki Arakaki, Jap, Ducati
7 Terry Rymer, GB, Yamaha
8 Shoji Miyazaki, Jap, Kawasaki
9 Makoto Suzuki, Jap, Ducati
10 Shinichiro Imai, Jap, Kawasaki
11 Fabrizio Furlan, Ita, Kawasaki
12 Christer Lindholm, Swe, Yamaha
13 Masao Nakada, Jap, Yamaha
14 Masato Mogi, Jap, Kawasaki
15 Hideo Senmyo, Jap, Honda

*Standings – 1 Russell 259.5; 2 Fogarty 246.5;
3 Slight 196; 4 Falappa & Pirovano 189;
6 Mertens 135*

Round 10 – Holland
Assen, 12 September
Race 1
1 Carl Fogarty, GB, Ducati
2 Scott Russell, USA, Kawasaki
3 Aaron Slight, NZ, Kawasaki
4 Stephane Mertens, Bel, Ducati
5 James Whitham, GB, Yamaha
6 Piergiorgio Bontempi, Ita, Kawasaki
7 Terry Rymer, GB, Yamaha
8 Andreas Hofmann, Ger, Kawasaki
9 Christer Lindholm, Swe, Yamaha
10 Mauro Lucchiari, Ita, Ducati

11 Fred Merkel, USA, Yamaha
12 Jeffry de Vries, Nl, Yamaha
13 Fabrizio Furlan, Ita, Kawasaki
14 Christian Lavieille, Fra, Ducati
15 Ernst Gschwender, Ger, Kawasaki

Race 2
1 Carl Fogarty, GB, Ducati
2 Scott Russell, USA, Kawasaki
3 Stephane Mertens, Bel, Ducati
4 Fabrizio Pirovano, Ita, Yamaha
5 James Whitham, GB, Yamaha
6 Aaron Slight, NZ, Kawasaki
7 Giancarlo Falappa, Ita, Ducati
8 Christer Lindholm, Swe, Yamaha
9 Terry Rymer, GB, Yamaha
10 Piergiorgio Bontempi, Ita, Kawasaki
11 Jeffry de Vries, Nl, Yamaha
12 Andreas Hofmann, Ger, Kawasaki
13 Fabrizio Furlan, Ita, Kawasaki
14 Mile Pajic, Nl, Kawasaki
15 Alex Vieira, Fra, Yamaha

*Standings – 1 Russell 293.5; 2 Fogarty 286.5;
3 Slight 221; 4 Pirovano 202; 5 Falappa 198;
6 Mertens 163*

Round 11 – Italy
Monza, 26 September
Race 1
1 Aaron Slight, NZ, Kawasaki
2 Scott Russell, USA, Kawasaki
3 Fabrizio Pirovano, Ita, Yamaha
4 Carl Fogarty, GB, Ducati
5 Tripp Nobles, USA, Honda
6 Christer Lindholm, Swe, Yamaha
7 Alex Vieira, Fra, Yamaha
8 Brian Morrison, GB, Kawasaki
9 Fabrizio Furlan, Ita, Kawasaki
10 Marcel Ernst, CH, Kawasaki
11 Dominique Sarron, Fra, Yamaha
12 Mauro Mastrelli, Ita, Yamaha
13 Adrien Morillas, Fra, Kawasaki
14 Hervé Moineau, Fra, Suzuki
15 Denis Bonoris, Fra, Kawasaki

Race 2
1 Giancarlo Falappa, Ita, Ducati
2 Aaron Slight, NZ, Kawasaki
3 Fabrizio Pirovano, Ita, Yamaha
4 Carl Fogarty, GB, Ducati
5 Scott Russell, USA, Kawasaki
6 Mauro Lucchiari, Ita, Ducati
7 Stephane Mertens, Bel, Ducati
8 Piergiorgio Bontempi, Ita, Kawasaki
9 Christer Lindholm, Swe, Yamaha
10 Tripp Nobles, USA, Honda
11 Marcel Ernst, CH, Kawasaki
12 Brian Morrison, GB, Kawasaki
13 Hervé Moineau, Fra, Suzuki
14 Fabrizio Furlan, Ita, Kawasaki
15 Blanc Mugues, CH, Kawasaki

*Standings – 1 Russell 321.5; 2 Fogarty 312.5;
3 Slight 258; 4 Pirovano 232; 5 Falappa 218;
6 Mertens 172*

Round 12 – Great Britain
Donington Park, 3 October
Race 1
1 Scott Russell, USA, Kawasaki
2 Carl Fogarty, GB, Ducati
3 Aaron Slight, NZ, Kawasaki
4 Fabrizio Pirovano, Ita, Yamaha
5 Piergiorgio Bontempi, Ita, Kawasaki
6 Brian Morrison, GB, Kawasaki
7 Andreas Meklau, Aut, Ducati
8 Andreas Hofmann, Ger, Kawasaki
9 Christer Lindholm, Swe, Yamaha
10 Jeremy McWilliams, GB, Ducati
11 Christian Lavieille, Fra, Ducati
12 Steve Hislop, GB, Ducati
13 Michael Rutter, GB, Kawasaki
14 Ray Stringer, GB, Kawasaki
15 M. Uedl, Ger, Kawasaki

Race 2
1 Scott Russell, USA, Kawasaki
2 Aaron Slight, NZ, Kawasaki
3 James Whitham, GB, Yamaha
4 Niall Mackenzie, GB, Ducati
5 Giancarlo Falappa, Ita, Ducati
6 Fabrizio Pirovano, Ita, Yamaha

7 Andreas Meklau, Aut, Ducati
8 Piergiorgio Bontempi, Ita, Kawasaki
9 Brian Morrison, GB, Kawasaki
10 Christer Lindholm, Swe, Yamaha
11 Matt Llewellyn, GB, Kawasaki
12 M. Uedl, Ger, Kawasaki
13 Christian Lavieille, Fra, Ducati
14 Denis Bonoris, Fra, Kawasaki
15 Alex Vieira, Fra, Yamaha

*Standings – 1 Russell 361.5; 2 Fogarty 329.5;
3 Slight 290; 4 Pirovano 255; 5 Falappa 229;
6 Mertens 172*

Round 13 – Portugal
Estoril, 17 October
Race 1
1 Fabrizio Pirovano, Ita, Yamaha
2 Piergiorgio Bontempi, Ita, Kawasaki
3 Aaron Slight, NZ, Kawasaki
4 Giancarlo Falappa, Ita, Ducati
5 Terry Rymer, GB, Yamaha
6 Simon Crafar, NZ, Yamaha
7 Andreas Meklau, Aut, Ducati
8 Brian Morrison, GB, Kawasaki
9 Dominique Sarron, Fra, Yamaha
10 Denis Bonoris, Fra, Kawasaki
11 Fred Merkel, USA, Yamaha
12 Jeffry de Vries, Nl, Yamaha
13 Jean-Marc Deletang, Fra, Yamaha
14 Michel Graziano, Fra, Suzuki
15 Telmo Pereira, Por, Suzuki

Race 2
1 Carl Fogarty, GB, Ducati
2 Scott Russell, USA, Kawasaki
3 Fabrizio Pirovano, Ita, Yamaha
4 Giancarlo Falappa, Ita, Ducati
5 Aaron Slight, NZ, Kawasaki
6 Terry Rymer, GB, Yamaha
7 Andreas Meklau, Aut, Ducati
8 Brian Morrison, GB, Kawasaki
9 Fred Merkel, USA, Yamaha
10 Piergiorgio Bontempi, Ita, Kawasaki
11 Dominique Sarron, Fra, Yamaha
12 Christer Lindholm, Swe, Yamaha
13 Jean-Marc Deletang, Fra, Yamaha
14 Denis Bonoris, Fra, Kawasaki
15 Christian Lavieille, Fra, Ducati

*FINAL STANDINGS – 1 Russell 378.5;
2 Fogarty 349.5; 3 Slight 316; 4 Pirovano 290;
5 Falappa 255; 6 Bontempi 184.5*

1994 season

Round 1 – Great Britain
Donington Park, 2 May,
Race 1
1. Carl Fogarty, GB, Ducati
2. Aaron Slight, NZ, Honda
3. Fabrizio Pirovano, Ita, Ducati
4. Scott Russell, USA, Kawasaki
5. Giancarlo Falappa, Ita, Ducati
6. Simon Crafar, NZ, Honda
7. Piergiorgio Bontempi, Ita, Kawasaki
8. Brian Morrison, GB, Honda
9. Doug Polen, USA, Honda
10. Mauro Moroni, Ita, Kawasaki
11. Valerio de Stefanis, Ita, Ducati
12. Jean-Yves Mounier, Fra, Ducati
13. Michael Rutter, GB, Ducati
14. Jim Moodie, GB, Yamaha
15. Andreas Meklau, Aut, Ducati

Race 2
1. Scott Russell, USA, Kawasaki
2. Carl Fogarty, GB, Ducati
3. Troy Corser, Aus, Ducati
4. Giancarlo Falappa, Ita, Ducati
5. Simon Crafar, NZ, Honda
6. Brian Morrison, GB, Honda
7. Doug Polen, USA, Honda
8. Mauro Lucchiari, Ita, Ducati
9. Jean-Yves Mounier, Fra, Ducati
10. Mauro Moroni, Ita, Kawasaki
11. Nick Hopkins, GB, Yamaha
12. Alex Vieira, Fra, Honda
13. José Kuhn, Fra, Honda
14. Denis Bonoris, Fra, Kawasaki
15. Serafino Foti, Ita, Ducati

Standings – 1 Fogarty 37; 2 Russell 33;
3 Falappa 24; 4 Crafar 21; 5 Morrison 18;
6 Slight 17

Round 2 – Germany
Hockenheim, 8 May
Race 1
1. Scott Russell, USA, Kawasaki
2. Aaron Slight, NZ, Honda
3. Terry Rymer, GB, Kawasaki
4. Adrien Morillas, Fra, Kawasaki
5. Doug Polen, USA, Honda
6. Jean-Yves Mounier, Fra, Ducati
7. Simon Crafar, NZ, Honda
8. Edwin Weibel, CH, Ducati
9. Rob Phillis, Aus, Kawasaki
10. Roger Kellenberger, Ger, Yamaha
11. Alex Vieira, Fra, Honda
12. Andrea Perselli, Ita, Ducati
13. Michael Paquay, Bel, Honda
14. Brian Morrison, GB, Honda
15. Udo Mark, Ger, Ducati

Race 2
1. Scott Russell, USA, Kawasaki
2. Fabrizio Pirovano, Ita, Ducati
3. Doug Polen, USA, Honda
4. Giancarlo Falappa, Ita, Ducati
5. Keiichi Kitagawa, Jap, Kawasaki
6. Terry Rymer, GB, Kawasaki
7. Valerio de Stefanis, Ita, Ducati
8. Edwin Weibel, CH, Ducati
9. Udo Mark, Ger, Ducati
10. Andreas Meklau, Aut, Ducati
11. Mauro Moroni, Ita, Kawasaki
12. Christer Lindholm, Swe, Yamaha
13. Jochen Scmid, Ger, Kawasaki
14. Jean-Yves Mounier, Fra, Ducati
15. Denis Bonoris, Fra, Kawasaki

Standings – 1 Russell 73; 2 Polen 42;
3 Falappa & Fogarty 37; 5 Slight 34;
6 Pirovano 32

Round 3 – Italy
Misano, 29 May
Race 1
1. Scott Russell, USA, Kawasaki
2. Giancarlo Falappa, Ita, Ducati
3. Aaron Slight, NZ, Honda
4. Stephane Mertens, Bel, Ducati
5. Mauro Lucchiari, Ita, Ducati
6. Valerio de Stefanis, Ita, Ducati
7. Simon Crafar, NZ, Honda
8. Gianmaria Liverani, Ita, Honda
9. Massimo Meregalli, Ita, Yamaha
10. Andreas Meklau, Aut, Ducati

11. James Whitham, GB, Ducati
12. Doug Polen, USA, Honda
13. Camillo Mariottini, Ita, Ducati
14. Andrea Perselli, Ita, Ducati
15. Mauro Moroni, Ita, Kawasaki

Race 2
1. Giancarlo Falappa, Ita, Ducati
2. Scott Russell, USA, Kawasaki
3. Mauro Lucchiari, Ita, Ducati
4. Aaron Slight, NZ, Honda
5. Carl Fogarty, GB, Ducati
6. Fabrizio Pirovano, Ita, Ducati
7. Piergiorgio Bontempi, Ita, Kawasaki
8. Valerio de Stefanis, Ita, Ducati
9. Terry Rymer, GB, Kawasaki
10. Andreas Meklau, Aut, Ducati
11. Simon Crafar, NZ, Honda
12. Massimo Meregalli, Ita, Yamaha
13. Serafino Foti, Ita, Ducati
14. Mauro Moroni, Ita, Kawasaki
15. Doug Polen, USA, Honda

Standings – 1 Russell 110; 2 Falappa 74;
3 Slight 62; 4 Fogarty 48; 5 Polen 47;
6 Crafar 44

Round 4 – Spain
Albacete, 19 June
Race 1
1. Carl Fogarty, GB, Ducati
2. Aaron Slight, NZ, Honda
3. James Whitham, GB, Ducati
4. Piergiorgio Bontempi, Ita, Kawasaki
5. Terry Rymer, GB, Kawasaki
6. Doug Polen, USA, Honda
7. Andreas Meklau, Aut, Ducati
8. Simon Crafar, NZ, Honda
9. Stephane Mertens, Bel, Ducati
10. Brian Morrison, GB, Honda
11. Serafino Foti, Ita, Ducati
12. Adrien Morillas, Fra, Kawasaki
13. Carlos Cardus, Spa, Ducati
14. Stefano Caracchi, Ita, Ducati
15. Michel Paquay, Bel, Honda

Race 2
1. Carl Fogarty, GB, Ducati
2. Aaron Slight, NZ, Honda
3. James Whitham, GB, Ducati
4. Andreas Meklau, Aut, Ducati
5. Terry Rymer, GB, Kawasaki
6. Piergiorgio Bontempi, Ita, Kawasaki
7. Doug Polen, USA, Honda
8. Carlos Cardus, Spa, Ducati
9. Adrien Morillas, Fra, Kawasaki
10. Stephane Mertens, Bel, Ducati
11. Fabrizio Pirovano, Ita, Ducati
12. Serafino Foti, Ita, Ducati
13. Brian Morrison, GB, Honda
14. Simon Crafar, NZ, Honda
15. Gianmaria Liverani, Ita, Honda

Standings – 1 Russell 110; 2 Slight 96;
3 Fogarty 88; 4 Falappa 74;
5 Crafar & Rymer 54

Round 5 – Austria
Osterreichring, 17 July
Race 1
1. Carl Fogarty, GB, Ducati
2. Andreas Meklau, Aut, Ducati
3. Doug Polen, USA, Honda
4. Aaron Slight, NZ, Honda
5. Stephane Mertens, Bel, Ducati
6. Simon Crafar, NZ, Honda
7. James Whitham, GB, Ducati
8. Fabrizio Pirovano, Ita, Ducati
9. Roberto Panichi, Ita, Ducati
10. Rob Phillis, Aus, Kawasaki
11. Piergiorgio Bontempi, Ita, Kawasaki
12. Massimo Meregalli, Ita, Yamaha
13. Serafino Foti, Ita, Ducati
14. Scott Russell, USA, Kawasaki
15. Christer Lindholm, Swe, Yamaha

Race 2
1. Carl Fogarty, GB, Ducati
2. Andreas Meklau, Aut, Ducati
3. Doug Polen, USA, Honda
4. Aaron Slight, NZ, Honda
5. Stephane Mertens, Bel, Ducati
6. Simon Crafar, NZ, Honda

7. Paolo Casoli, Ita, Yamaha
8. Jochen Schmid, Ger, Kawasaki
9. Piergiorgio Bontempi, Ita, Kawasaki
10. Serafino Foti, Ita, Ducati
11. Terry Rymer, GB, Kawasaki
12. Scott Russell, USA, Kawasaki
13. Rob Phillis, Aus, Kawasaki
14. Christer Lindholm, Swe, Yamaha
15. Massimo Meregalli, Ita, Yamaha

Standings – 1 Fogarty 128; 2 Slight 122;
3 Russell 116; 4 Polen 96; 5 Meklau 75;
6 Crafar & Falappa 74;

Round 6 – Indonesia
Sentul, 21 August
Race 1
1. James Whitham, GB, Ducati
2. Aaron Slight, NZ, Honda
3. Scott Russell, USA, Kawasaki
4. Doug Polen, USA, Honda
5. Simon Crafar, NZ, Honda
6. Andreas Meklau, Aut, Ducati
7. Adrien Morillas, Fra, Kawasaki
8. Terry Rymer, GB, Kawasaki
9. Stephane Mertens, Bel, Ducati
10. Valerio de Stefanis, Ita, Ducati
11. Piergiorgio Bontempi, Ita, Kawasaki
12. Brian Morrison, GB, Honda
13. Mauro Moroni, Ita, Kawasaki
14. Gérard Muteau, Fra, Ducati
15. Alex Vieira, Fra, Honda

Race 2
1. Carl Fogarty, GB, Ducati
2. Aaron Slight, NZ, Honda
3. Scott Russell, USA, Kawasaki
4. James Whitham, GB, Ducati
5. Andreas Meklau, Aut, Ducati
6. Doug Polen, USA, Honda
7. Terry Rymer, GB, Kawasaki
8. Adrien Morillas, Fra, Kawasaki
9. Stephane Mertens, Bel, Ducati
10. Simon Crafar, NZ, Honda
11. Piergiorgio Bontempi, Ita, Kawasaki
12. Valerio de Stefanis, Ita, Ducati
13. Brian Morrison, GB, Honda
14. Alex Vieira, Fra, Honda
15. Mauro Moroni, Ita, Kawasaki

Standings – 1 Slight 156; 2 Fogarty 148;
3 Russell 146; 4 Polen 119; 5 Meklau 96;
6 Crafar 91

Round 7 – Japan
Sugo, 28 August
Race 1
1. Scott Russell, USA, Kawasaki
2. Fabrizio Pirovano, Ita, Ducati
3. Yasutomo Nagai, Jap, Yamaha
4. Carl Fogarty, GB, Ducati
5. Wataru Yoshikawa, Jap, Yamaha
6. Aaron Slight, NZ, Honda
7. Takuma Aoki, Jap, Honda
8. Anthony Gobert, Aus, Honda
9. Andreas Meklau, Aut, Ducati
10. Doug Polen, USA, Honda
11. Akira Yanagawa, Jap, Suzuki
12. Piergiorgio Bontempi, Ita, Kawasaki
13. Adrien Morillas, Fra, Kawasaki
14. Alex Vieira, Fra, Honda
15. Kenichiro Iwahashi, Jap, Honda

Race 2
1. Scott Russell, USA, Kawasaki
2. Carl Fogarty, GB, Ducati
3. Keiichi Kitagawa, Jap, Kawasaki
4. Wataru Yoshikawa, Jap, Yamaha
5. Yasutomo Nagai, Jap, Yamaha
6. Anthony Gobert, Aus, Honda
7. Aaron Slight, NZ, Honda
8. Takuma Aoki, Jap, Honda
9. Terry Rymer, GB, Kawasaki
10. James Whitham, GB, Ducati
11. Norihiko Fujiwara, Jap, Yamaha
12. Noriyuki Haga, Jap, Ducati
13. Shoichi Tsukamoto, Jap, Kawasaki
14. Simon Crafar, NZ, Honda
15. Shinya Takeishi, Jap, Honda

Standings – 1 Russell 186; 2 Fogarty 178;
3 Slight 175; 4 Polen 125; 5 Meklau 103;
6 Crafar 93

Round 8 – Holland
Assen, 11 September
Race 1
1   Carl Fogarty, GB, Ducati
2   Paolo Casoli, Ita, Yamaha
3   Aaron Slight, NZ, Honda
4   Terry Rymer, GB, Kawasaki
5   James Whitham, GB, Ducati
6   Scott Russell, USA, Kawasaki
7   Simon Crafar, NZ, Honda
8   Jochen Schmid, Ger, Kawasaki
9   Andreas Meklau, Aut, Ducati
10 Stephane Mertens, Bel, Ducati
11 Doug Polen, USA, Honda
12 Jean-Yves Mounier, Fra, Ducati
13 Michael Paquay, Bel, Honda
14 Jeffry de Vries, Nl, Yamaha
15 Arpad Harmati, Hun, Yamaha

Race 2
1   Carl Fogarty, GB, Ducati
2   Aaron Slight, NZ, Honda
3   Mauro Lucchiari, Ita, Ducati
4   Paolo Casoli, Ita, Yamaha
5   James Whitham, GB, Ducati
6   Terry Rymer, GB, Kawasaki
7   Simon Crafar, NZ, Honda
8   Jochen Schmid, Ger, Kawasaki
9   Scott Russell, USA, Kawasaki
10 Christer Lindholm, Swe, Yamaha
11 Fabrizio Pirovano, Ita, Ducati
12 Andreas Meklau, Aut, Ducati
13 Serafino Foti, Ita, Ducati
14 Jean-Yves Mounier, Fra, Ducati
15 Jeffry de Vries, Nl, Yamaha

Standings – 1 Fogarty 218; 2 Slight 207;
3 Russell 203; 4 Polen 130; 5 Meklau 114;
6 Crafar 111

Round 9 – San Marino
Mugello, 25 September
Race 1
1   Scott Russell, USA, Kawasaki
2   Carl Fogarty, GB, Ducati
3   Troy Corser, Aus, Ducati
4   Aaron Slight, NZ, Honda
5   Fabrizio Pirovano, Ita, Ducati
6   Andreas Meklau, Aut, Ducati
7   Paolo Casoli, Ita, Yamaha
8   James Whitham, GB, Ducati
9   Simon Crafar, NZ, Honda
10 Piergiorgio Bontempi, Ita, Kawasaki
11 Doug Polen, USA, Honda
12 Serafino Foti, Ita, Ducati
13 Christer Lindholm, Swe, Yamaha
14 Massimo Meregalli, Ita, Yamaha
15 Stephane Mertens, Bel, Ducati

Race 2
1   Carl Fogarty, GB, Ducati
2   Aaron Slight, NZ, Honda
3   Mauro Lucchiari, Ita, Ducati
4   James Whitham, GB, Ducati
5   Fabrizio Pirovano, Ita, Ducati
6   Piergiorgio Bontempi, Ita, Kawasaki
7   Doug Polen, USA, Honda
8   Jochen Schmid, Ger, Kawasaki
9   Simon Crafar, NZ, Honda
10 Massimo Meregalli, Ita, Yamaha
11 Brian Morrison, GB, Honda
12 Christer Lindholm, Swe, Yamaha
13 Jeffry de Vries, Nl, Yamaha
14 Stephane Mertens, Bel, Ducati
15 Mauro Moroni, Ita, Kawasaki

Standings – 1 Fogarty 255; 2 Slight 237;
3 Russell 223; 4 Polen 144; 5 Whitham 126;
6 Crafar 125

Round 10 – Great Britain
Donington Park, 2 October
Race 1
1   Scott Russell, USA, Kawasaki
2   Troy Corser, Aus, Ducati
3   Paolo Casoli, Ita, Yamaha
4   Alan Carter, GB, Ducati
5   Simon Crafar, NZ, Honda
6   Piergiorgio Bontempi, Ita, Kawasaki
7   Andreas Meklau, Aut, Ducati
8   Aaron Slight, NZ, Honda
9   Brian Morrison, GB, Honda
10 Michael Rutter, GB, Ducati

11 Jochen Schmid, Ger, Kawasaki
12 Doug Polen, USA, Honda
13 Valerio de Stefanis, Ita, Ducati
14 Carl Fogarty, GB, Ducati
15 Massimo Meregalli, Ita, Yamaha

Race 2
1   Scott Russell, USA, Kawasaki
2   Troy Corser, Aus, Ducati
3   Mauro Lucchiari, Ita, Ducati
4   Paolo Casoli, Ita, Yamaha
5   Carl Fogarty, GB, Ducati
6   Alan Carter, GB, Ducati
7   Piergiorgio Bontempi, Ita, Kawasaki
8   Brian Morrison, GB, Honda
9   Andreas Meklau, Aut, Ducati
10 Aaron Slight, NZ, Honda
11 Massimo Meregalli, Ita, Yamaha
12 Fabrizio Pirovano, Ita, Ducati
13 Jeffry de Vries, Nl, Yamaha
14 Matt Llewellyn, GB, Ducati
15 Simon Crafar, NZ, Honda

Standings – 1 Fogarty 268; 2 Russell 263;
3 Slight 251; 4 Polen 148; 5 Meklau 140;
6 Crafar 137

Round 11 – Australia
Phillip Island, 30 October
Race 1
1   Carl Fogarty, GB, Ducati
2   Scott Russell, USA, Kawasaki
3   Anthony Gobert, Aus, Kawasaki

4   Aaron Slight, NZ, Honda
5   Troy Corser, Aus, Ducati
6   Kirk McCarthy, Aus, Honda
7   Mat Mladin, Aus, Kawasaki
8   Shawn Giles, Aus, Ducati
9   Piergiorgio Bontempi, Ita, Kawasaki
10 Simon Crafar, NZ, Honda
11 Doug Polen, USA, Honda
12 Peter Goddard, Aus, Suzuki
13 Roy Leslie, Aus, Ducati
14 Andreas Meklau, Aut, Ducati
15 Steve Martin, Aus, Suzuki

Race 2
1   Anthony Gobert, Aus, Kawasaki
2   Carl Fogarty, GB, Ducati
3   Troy Corser, Aus, Ducati
4   Aaron Slight, NZ, Honda
5   Kirk McCarthy, Aus, Honda
6   Simon Crafar, NZ, Honda
7   Shawn Giles, Aus, Ducati
8   Fabrizio Pirovano, Ita, Ducati
9   Piergiorgio Bontempi, Ita, Kawasaki
10 Andreas Meklau, Aut, Ducati
11 Doug Polen, USA, Honda
12 Stephane Mertens, Bel, Ducati
13 Peter Goddard, Aus, Suzuki
14 Martin Craggill, Aus, Kawasaki
15 Steve Martin, Aus, Suzuki

FINAL STANDINGS – 1 Fogarty 305;
2 Russell 280; 3 Slight 277; 4 Polen 158;
5 Crafar 153; 6 Meklau 148

1995 season

Round 1 – Germany
Hockenheim, 7 May
Race 1
1 Carl Fogarty, GB, Ducati
2 Fabrizio Pirovano, Ita, Ducati
3 Jochen Schmid, Ger, Kawasaki
4 Yasutomo Nagai, Jap, Yamaha
5 Keiichi Kitagawa, Jap, Kawasaki
6 Aaron Slight, NZ, Honda
7 Colin Edwards, USA, Yamaha
8 Scott Russell, USA, Kawasaki
9 Simon Crafar, NZ, Honda
10 Troy Corser, Aus, Ducati
11 Piergiorgio Bontempi, Ita, Kawasaki
12 Massimo Meregalli, Ita, Yamaha
13 Adrien Morillas, Fra, Ducati
14 Edwin Weibel, CH, Ducati
15 Pierfrancesco Chili, Ita, Ducati

Race 2
1 Carl Fogarty, GB, Ducati
2 Jochen Schmid, Ger, Kawasaki
3 Aaron Slight, NZ, Honda
4 Yasutomo Nagai, Jap, Yamaha
5 Colin Edwards, USA, Yamaha
6 Simon Crafar, NZ, Honda
7 Mauro Lucchiari, Ita, Ducati
8 Troy Corser, Aus, Ducati
9 Pierfrancesco Chili, Ita, Ducati
10 Scott Russell, USA, Kawasaki
11 Andreas Meklau, Aut, Ducati
12 Keiichi Kitagawa, Jap, Kawaaki
13 Fabrizio Pirovano, Ita, Ducati
14 Piergiorgio Bontempi, Ita, Kawasaki
15 Paolo Casoli, Ita, Yamaha

Standings – 1 Fogarty 50; 2 Schmid 36;
3 Nagai & Slight 26; 5 Pirovano 23;
6 Edwards 20

Round 2 – Italy
Misano, 21 May
Race 1
1 Mauro Lucchiari, Ita, Ducati
2 Carl Fogarty, GB, Ducati
3 Troy Corser, Aus, Ducati
4 Pierfrancesco Chili, Ita, Ducati
5 Fabrizio Pirovano, Ita, Ducati
6 Anthony Gobert, Aus, Kawasaki
7 John Reynolds, GB, Kawasaki
8 Piergiorgio Bontempi, Ita, Kawasaki
9 Simon Crafar, NZ, Honda
10 Gianmaria Liverani, Ita, Ducati
11 Andreas Meklau, Aut, Ducati
12 Adrien Morillas, Fra, Ducati
13 Yasutomo Nagai, Jap, Yamaha
14 Scott Russell, USA, Kawasaki
15 Jochen Schmid, Ger, Kawasaki

Race 2
1 Mauro Lucchiari, Ita, Ducati
2 Carl Fogarty, GB, Ducati
3 Troy Corser, Aus, Ducati
4 Pierfrancesco Chili, Ita, Ducati
5 Piergiorgio Bontempi, Ita, Kawasaki
6 Fabrizio Pirovano, Ita, Ducati
7 Andreas Meklau, Aut, Ducati
8 Scott Russell, USA, Kawasaki
9 John Reynolds, GB, Kawasaki
10 Simon Crafar, NZ, Honda
11 Gianmaria Liverani, Ita, Ducati
12 Jochen Schmid, Ger, Kawasaki
13 Aaron Slight, NZ, Honda
14 Adrien Morillas, Fra, Ducati
15 Steve Hislop, GB, Ducati

Standings – 1 Fogarty 90; 2 Lucchiari 59;
3 Corser 46; 4 Pirovano 44; 5 Schmid 41;
6 Chili 34

Round 3 – Great Britain
Donington Park, 28 May
Race 1
1 Carl Fogarty, GB, Ducati
2 Troy Corser, Aus, Ducati
3 James Whitham, GB, Ducati
4 Aaron Slight, NZ, Honda
5 Piergiorgio Bontempi, Ita, Kawasaki
6 Scott Russell, USA, Kawasaki
7 John Reynolds, GB, Kawasaki
8 Simon Crafar, NZ, Honda
9 Mauro Lucchiari, Ita, Ducati
10 Anthony Gobert, Aus, Kawasaki

11 Fabrizio Pirovano, Ita, Ducati
12 Adrien Morillas, Fra, Ducati
13 Jochen Schmid, Ger, Kawaski
14 Yasutomo Nagai, Jap, Yamaha
15 Paolo Casoli, Ita, Yamaha

Race 2
1 Carl Fogarty, GB, Ducati
2 Pierfrancesco Chili, Ita, Ducati
3 Aaron Slight, NZ, Honda
4 Piergiorgio Bontempi, Ita, Kawasaki
5 Fabrizio Pirovano, Ita, Ducati
6 Simon Crafar, NZ, Honda
7 Yasutomo Nagai, Jap, Yamaha
8 James Whitham, GB, Ducati
9 Adrien Morillas, Fra, Ducati
10 Mauro Lucchiari, Ita, Ducati
11 John Reynolds, GB, Kawasaki
12 Colin Edwards, USA, Yamaha
13 Paolo Casoli, Ita, Yamaha
14 Andreas Meklau, Aut, Ducati
15 Matt Llewellyn, GB, Ducati

Standings – 1 Fogarty 140; 2 Lucchiari 72;
3 Corser 66; 4 Pirovano 60; 5 Slight 58;
6 Chili 54

Round 4 – San Marino
Monza, 18 June
Race 1
1 Carl Fogarty, GB, Ducati
2 Aaron Slight, NZ, Honda
3 Colin Edwards, USA, Yamaha
4 Simon Crafar, NZ, Honda
5 Yasutomo Nagai, Jap, Yamaha
6 Mauro Lucchiari, Ita, Ducati
7 Piergiorgio Bontempi, Ita, Kawasaki
8 Fabrizio Pirovano, Ita, Ducati
9 John Reynolds, GB, Kawasaki
10 Gianmaria Liverani, Ita, Ducati
11 Sutoshi Tsujimoto, Jap, Honda
12 Michele Gallina, Ita, Ducati
13 David Jefferies, GB, Kawasaki
14 Jean-Yves Mounier, Fra, Ducati
15 Ferdinando di Maso, Ita, Ducati

Race 2
1 Pierfrancesco Chili, Ita, Ducati
2 Carl Fogarty, GB, Ducati
3 Aaron Slight, NZ, Honda
4 Yasutomo Nagai, Jap, Yamaha
5 Colin Edwards, USA, Yamaha
6 Mauro Lucchiari, Ita, Ducati
7 Simon Crafar, NZ, Honda
8 Fabrizio Pirovano, Ita, Ducati
9 Andreas Meklau, Aut, Ducati
10 John Reynolds, GB, Kawasaki
11 Massimo Meregalli, Ita, Yamaha
12 Anthony Gobert, Aus, Kawasaki
13 Paolo Casoli, Ita, Yamaha
14 Sutoshi Tsujimoto, Jap, Honda
15 Ferdinando di Maso, Ita, Ducati

Standings – 1 Fogarty 185; 2 Slight 94;
3 Lucchiari 92; 4 Chili 79; 5 Pirovano 76;
6 Crafar 70

Round 5 – Spain
Albacete, 25 June
Race 1
1 Aaron Slight, NZ, Honda
2 Carl Fogarty, GB, Ducati
3 Troy Corser, Aus, Ducati
4 Pierfrancesco Chili, Ita, Ducati
5 Piergiorgio Bontempi, Ita, Kawasaki
6 Fabrizio Pirovano, Ita, Ducati
7 Anthony Gobert, Aus, Kawasaki
8 Andreas Meklau, Aut, Ducati
9 Yasutomo Nagai, Jap, Yamaha
10 Colin Edwards, USA, Yamaha
11 Simon Crafar, NZ, Honda
12 John Reynolds, GB, Kawasaki
13 Paolo Casoli, Ita, Yamaha
14 Adrien Morillas, Fra, Ducati
15 Gianmaria Liverani, Ita, Ducati

Race 2
1 Carl Fogarty, GB, Ducati
2 Pierfrancesco Chili, Ita, Ducati
3 Aaron Slight, NZ, Honda
4 Fabrizio Pirovano, Ita, Ducati
5 Troy Corser, Aus, Ducati
6 Yasutomo Nagai, Jap, Yamaha

7 Andreas Meklau, Aut, Ducati
8 John Reynolds, GB, Kawasaki
9 Paolo Casoli, Ita, Yamaha
10 Simon Crafar, NZ, Honda
11 Colin Edwards, USA, Yamaha
12 Massimo Meregalli, Ita, Yamaha
13 David Jefferies, GB, Kawasaki
14 Gianmaria Liverani, Ita, Ducati
15 Sutoshi Tsujimoto, Jap, Honda

Standings – 1 Fogarty 230; 2 Slight 135;
3 Chili 112; 4 Pirovano 99; 5 Corser 93;
6 Lucchiari 92

Round 6 – Austria
Salzburgring, 9 July
Race 1
1 Carl Fogarty, GB, Ducati
2 Anthony Gobert, Aus, Kawasaki
3 Troy Corser, Aus, Ducati
4 Aaron Slight, NZ, Honda
5 Yasutomo Nagai, Jap, Yamaha
6 Andreas Meklau, Aut, Ducati
7 Jochen Schmid, Ger, Kawasaki
8 Fabrizio Pirovano, Ita, Ducati
9 Colin Edwards, USA, Yamaha
10 Piergiorgio Bontempi, Ita, Kawasaki
11 Pierfrancesco Chili, Ita, Ducati
12 Paolo Casoli, Ita, Yamaha
13 Mauro Lucchiari, Ita, Ducati
14 Simon Crafar, NZ, Honda
15 Gianmaria Liverani, Ita, Ducati

Race 2
1 Troy Corser, Aus, Ducati
2 Carl Fogarty, GB, Ducati
3 Anthony Gobert, Aus, Kawasaki
4 Aaron Slight, NZ, Honda
5 Fabrizio Pirovano, Ita, Ducati
6 Yasutomo Nagai, Jap, Yamaha
7 Mauro Lucchiari, Ita, Ducati
8 Piergiorgio Bontempi, Ita, Kawasaki
9 Simon Crafar, NZ, Honda
10 Paolo Casoli, Ita, Yamaha
11 Helmut Bradl, Ger, Kawasaki
12 Michael Liedl, Ger, Kawasaki
13 Michael Rudroff, Ger, Ducati
14 Adrien Morillas, Fra, Ducati
15 Massimo Meregalli, Ita, Yamaha

Standings – 1 Fogarty 275; 2 Slight 161;
3 Corser 134; 4 Pirovano 118; 5 Chili 117;
6 Lucchiari 104

Round 7 – USA
Laguna Seca, 23 July
Race 1
1 Anthony Gobert, Aus, Kawasaki
2 Troy Corser, Aus, Ducati
3 Miguel DuHamel, Can, Honda
4 Mike Hale, USA, Honda
5 Carl Fogarty, GB, Ducati
6 Simon Crafar, NZ, Honda
7 Freddie Spencer, USA, Ducati
8 Colin Edwards, USA, Yamaha
9 Aaron Slight, NZ, Honda
10 Yasutomo Nagai, Jap, Yamaha
11 Michael Smith, USA, Ducati
12 Tom Kipp, USA, Yamaha
13 Piergiorgio Bontempi, Ita, Kawasaki
14 Mauro Lucchiari, Ita, Ducati
15 Pascal Picotte, Can, Kawasaki

Race 2
1 Troy Corser, Aus, Ducati
2 Anthony Gobert, Aus, Kawasaki
3 Mike Hale, USA, Honda
4 Miguel DuHamel, Can, Honda
5 Yasutomo Nagai, Jap, Yamaha
6 Simon Crafar, NZ, Honda
7 Carl Fogarty, GB, Ducati
8 Fabrizio Pirovano, Ita, Ducati
9 Colin Edwards, USA, Yamaha
10 Pascal Picotte, Can, Kawasaki
11 Piergiorgio Bontempi, Ita, Kawasaki
12 Steve Crevier, Can, Kawasaki
13 Tom Kipp, USA, Yamaha
14 Mauro Lucchiari, Ita, Ducati
15 Paolo Casoli, Ita, Yamaha

Standings – 1 Fogarty 295; 2 Corser 179;
3 Slight 168; 4 Pirovano 126; 5 Nagai 119;
6 Chili 117

Round 8 – Europe
Brands Hatch, 6 August
Race 1
1 Carl Fogarty, GB, Ducati
2 Troy Corser, Aus, Ducati
3 Anthony Gobert, Aus, Kawasaki
4 John Reynolds, GB, Kawasaki
5 Colin Edwards, USA, Yamaha
6 Pierfrancesco Chili, Ita, Ducati
7 Fabrizio Pirovano, Ita, Ducati
8 Steve Hislop, GB, Ducati
9 Aaron Slight, NZ, Honda
10 Simon Crafar, NZ, Honda
11 Mauro Lucchiari, Ita, Ducati
12 Paolo Casoli, Ita, Yamaha
13 Piergiorgio Bontempi, Ita, Kawasaki
14 David Jefferies, GB, Kawasaki
15 Gianmaria Liverani, Ita, Ducati

Race 2
1 Carl Fogarty, GB, Ducati
2 Colin Edwards, USA, Yamaha
3 John Reynolds, GB, Kawasaki
4 Yasutomo Nagai, Jap, Yamaha
5 Anthony Gobert, Aus, Kawasaki
6 Troy Corser, Aus, Ducati
7 Fabrizio Pirovano, Ita, Ducati
8 Aaron Slight, NZ, Honda
9 Steve Hislop, GB, Ducati
10 Simon Crafar, NZ, Honda
11 Mauro Lucchiari, Ita, Ducati
12 Adrien Morillas, Fra, Ducati
13 Paolo Casoli, Ita, Yamaha
14 Piergiorgio Bontempi, Ita, Kawasaki
15 David Jefferies, GB, Kawasaki

Standings – 1 Fogarty 345; 2 Corser 209;
3 Slight 183; 4 Pirovano 144; 5 Gobert 137;
6 Nagai 132

Round 9 – Japan
Sugo, 27 August
Race 1
1 Troy Corser, Aus, Ducati
2 Aaron Slight, NZ, Honda
3 Yasutomo Nagai, Jap, Yamaha
4 Keiichi Kitagawa, Jap, Kawasaki
5 Anthony Gobert, Aus, Kawasaki
6 Colin Edwards, USA, Yamaha
7 Wataru Yoshikawa, Jap, Yamaha
8 Norihiko Fujiwara, Jap, Yamaha
9 John Reynolds, GB, Kawasaki
10 Simon Crafar, NZ, Honda
11 Akira Ryoh, Jap, Kawasaki
12 Yukio Nukumi, Jap, Ducati
13 Fabrizio Pirovano, Ita, Ducati
14 Piergiorgio Bontempi, Ita, Kawasaki
15 Pierfrancesco Chili, Ita, Ducati

Race 2
1 Carl Fogarty, GB, Ducati
2 Yasutomo Nagai, Jap, Yamaha
3 Katsuaki Fujiwara, Jap, Kawasaki
4 Aaron Slight, NZ, Honda
5 Wataru Yoshikawa, Jap, Yamaha
6 Keiichi Kitagawa, Jap, Kawasaki
7 Takuma Aoki, Jap, Honda
8 Troy Corser, Aus, Ducati
9 Anthony Gobert, Aus, Kawasaki
10 Colin Edwards, USA, Yamaha
11 Shinya Takeishi, Jap, Honda
12 John Reynolds, GB, Kawasaki
13 Piergiorgio Bontempi, Ita, Kawasaki
14 Norihiko Fujiwara, Jap, Yamaha
15 Simon Crafar, NZ, Honda

Standings – 1 Fogarty 370; 2 Corser 242;
3 Slight 216; 4 Nagai 168; 5 Gobert 155;
6 Pirovano 147

Round 10 – Holland
Assen, 10 September
Race 1
1 Carl Fogarty, GB, Ducati
2 Simon Crafar, NZ, Honda
3 Troy Corser, Aus, Ducati
4 Aaron Slight, NZ, Honda
5 Mauro Lucchiari, Ita, Ducati
6 John Reynolds, GB, Kawasaki
7 Yasutomo Nagai, Jap, Yamaha
8 Paolo Casoli, Ita, Yamaha
9 Anthony Gobert, Aus, Kawasaki
10 Fabrizio Pirovano, Ita, Ducati

11 Steve Hislop, GB, Ducati
12 Piergiorgio Bontempi, Ita, Kawasaki
13 Andreas Meklau, Aut, Ducati
14 Jochen Schmid, Ger, Kawasaki
15 Brian Morrison, GB, Ducati

Race 2
1 Carl Fogarty, GB, Ducati
2 Aaron Slight, NZ, Honda
3 John Reynolds, GB, Kawasaki
4 Mauro Lucchiari, Ita, Ducati
5 Yasutomo Nagai, Jap, Yamaha
6 Colin Edwards, USA, Yamaha
7 Anthony Gobert, Aus, Kawasaki
8 Jochen Schmid, Ger, Kawasaki
9 Piergiorgio Bontempi, Ita, Kawasaki
10 Paolo Casoli, Ita, Yamaha
11 Brian Morrison, GB, Ducati
12 Jean-Yves Mounier, Fra, Ducati
13 Mile Pajic, Nl, Kawasaki
14 Gianmaria Liverani, Ita, Ducati
15 Robert Kaufmann, Ger, Yamaha

Standings – 1 Fogarty 420; 2 Corser 258;
3 Slight 249; 4 Nagai 188; 5 Gobert 171;
6 Pirovano 153

Round 11 – Indonesia
Sentul, 15 October
Race 1
1 Carl Fogarty, GB, Ducati
2 Troy Corser, Aus, Ducati
3 Aaron Slight, NZ, Honda
4 Anthony Gobert, Aus, Kawasaki
5 Fabrizio Pirovano, Ita, Ducati
6 Mike Hale, USA, Ducati
7 Mauro Lucchiari, Ita, Ducati
8 Andreas Meklau, Aut, Ducati
9 John Reynolds, GB, Kawasaki
10 Brian Morrison, GB, Ducati
11 Piergiorgio Bontempi, Ita, Kawasaki
12 Peter Goddard, Aus, Suzuki
13 Jochen Schmid, Ger, Kawasaki
14 Freddie Spencer, USA, Ducati
15 Yves Briguet, CH, Honda

Race 2
1 Aaron Slight, NZ, Honda
2 Troy Corser, Aus, Ducati
3 Pierfrancesco Chili, Ita, Ducati
4 Anthony Gobert, Aus, Kawasaki
5 Simon Crafar, NZ, Honda
6 Fabrizio Pirovano, Ita, Ducati
7 Mike Hale, USA, Ducati
8 Piergiorgio Bontempi, Ita, Kawasaki
9 John Reynolds, GB, Kawasaki
10 Andreas Meklau, Aut, Ducati
11 Mauro Lucchiari, Ita, Ducati
12 Jochen Schmid, Ger, Kawasaki
13 Peter Goddard, Aus, Suzuki
14 Yves Briguet, CH, Honda
15 Gianmaria Liverani, Ita, Ducati

Standings – 1 Fogarty 445; 2 Corser 298;
3 Slight 290; 4 Gobert 197; 5 Nagai 188;
6 Pirovano 174

Round 12 – Australia
Phillip Island, 29 October
Race 1
1 Troy Corser, Aus, Ducati
2 Aaron Slight, NZ, Honda
3 Simon Crafar, NZ, Honda
4 Carl Fogarty, GB, Ducati
5 John Reynolds, GB, Kawasaki
6 Pierfrancesco Chili, Ita, Ducati
7 Freddie Spencer, USA, Ducati
8 Kirk McCarthy, Aus, Honda
9 Mat Mladin, Aus, Kawasaki
10 Shawn Giles, Aus, Ducati
11 Jason McEwen, NZ, Ducati
12 Piergiorgio Bontempi, Ita, Kawasaki
13 Marty Craggill, Aus, Kawasaki
14 Mike Hale, USA, Ducati
15 Robert Baird, Aus, Honda

Race 2
1 Anthony Gobert, Aus, Kawasaki
2 Carl Fogarty, GB, Ducati
3 Troy Corser, Aus, Ducati
4 Aaron Slight, NZ, Honda
5 Simon Crafar, NZ, Honda
6 Mike Hale, USA, Ducati

7 John Reynolds, GB, Kawasaki
8 Piergiorgio Bontempi, Ita, Kawasaki
9 Shawn Giles, Aus, Ducati
10 Pierfrancesco Chili, Ita, Ducati
11 Brian Morrison, GB, Ducati
12 Fabrizio Pirovano, Ita, Ducati
13 Marty Craggill, Aus, Kawasaki
14 Robert Baird, Aus, Honda
15 Jochen Schmid, Ger, Kawasaki

FINAL STANDINGS – 1 Fogarty 478;
2 Corser 339; 3 Slight 323; 4 Gobert 222;
5 Nagai 188; 6 Crafar 187

1996 season

Round 1 – San Marino
Misano, 14 April
Race 1
1. John Kocinski, USA, Ducati
2. Troy Corser, Aus, Ducati
3. Pierfrancesco Chili, Ita, Ducati
4. Simon Crafar, NZ, Kawasaki
5. Anthony Gobert, Aus, Kawasaki
6. Aaron Slight, NZ, Honda
7. Carl Fogarty, GB, Honda
8. Christer Lindholm, Swe, Ducati
9. Wataru Yoshikawa, Jap, Yamaha
10. Piergiorgio Bontempi, Ita, Kawasaki
11. Colin Edwards, USA, Yamaha
12. Neil Hodgson, GB, Ducati
13. Mike Hale, USA, Ducati
14. Brian Morrison, GB, Ducati
15. Michel Paquay, Bel, Ducati

Race 2
1. John Kocinski, USA, Ducati
2. Troy Corser, Aus, Ducati
3. Pierfrancesco Chili, Ita, Ducati
4. Simon Crafar, NZ, Kawasaki
5. Aaron Slight, NZ, Honda
6. Carl Fogarty, GB, Honda
7. Colin Edwards, USA, Yamaha
8. Mike Hale, USA, Ducati
9. Christer Lindholm, Swe, Ducati
10. Piergiorgio Bontempi, Ita, Kawasaki
11. Wataru Yoshikawa, Jap, Yamaha
12. Kirk McCarthy, Aus, Suzuki
13. Paolo Casoli, Ita, Yamaha
14. Jochen Schmid, Ger, Kawasaki
15. Michel Paquay, Bel, Ducati

*Standings – 1 Kocinski 50; 2 Corser 40;
3 Chili 32; 4 Crafar 26; 5 Slight 21;
6 Fogarty 19*

Round 2 – Great Britain
Donington Park, 28 April
Race 1
1. Troy Corser, Aus, Ducati
2. Simon Crafar, NZ, Kawasaki
3. Anthony Gobert, Aus, Kawasaki
4. Pierfrancesco Chili, Ita, Ducati
5. Aaron Slight, NZ, Honda
6. Colin Edwards, USA, Yamaha
7. John Kocinski, USA, Ducati
8. Carl Fogarty, GB, Honda
9. Wataru Yoshikawa, Jap, Yamaha
10. Piergiorgio Bontempi, Ita, Kawasaki
11. Paolo Casoli, Ita, Ducati
12. Jochen Schmid, Ger, Kawasaki
13. Kirk McCarthy, Aus, Suzuki
14. Mike Hale, USA, Ducati
15. Stephane Chambon, Fra, Ducati

Race 2
1. Troy Corser, Aus, Ducati
2. Aaron Slight, NZ, Honda
3. Anthony Gobert, Aus, Kawasaki
4. Colin Edwards, USA, Yamaha
5. Pierfrancesco Chili, Ita, Ducati
6. John Kocinski, USA, Ducati
7. Carl Fogarty, GB, Honda
8. Christer Lindholm, Swe, Ducati
9. Paolo Casoli, Ita, Ducati
10. James Whitham, GB, Yamaha
11. Piergiorgio Bontempi, Ita, Kawasaki
12. Wataru Yoshikawa, Jap, Yamaha
13. Niall Mackenzie, GB, Yamaha
14. Kirk McCarthy, Aus, Suzuki
15. Stephane Chambon, Fra, Ducati

*Standings – 1 Corser 90; 2 Kocinski 69;
3 Chili 56; 4 Slight 52; 5 Crafar 46;
6 Gobert 43*

Round 3 – Germany
Hockenheim, 12 May
Race 1
1. Aaron Slight, NZ, Honda
2. John Kocinski, USA, Ducati
3. Colin Edwards, USA, Yamaha
4. Simon Crafar, NZ, Kawasaki
5. Carl Fogarty, GB, Honda
6. Anthony Gobert, Aus, Kawasaki
7. Paolo Casoli, Ita, Ducati
8. Christer Lindholm, Swe, Ducati
9. Jochen Schmid, Ger, Kawasaki
10. Kirk McCarthy, Aus, Suzuki
11. Roger Kellenberger, CH, Honda
12. Piergiorgio Bontempi, Ita, Kawasaki
13. Andreas Meklau, Aut, Ducati
14. Stephane Chambon, Fra, Ducati
15. Michel Paquay, Bel, Ducati

Race 2
1. Carl Fogarty, GB, Honda
2. Aaron Slight, NZ, Honda
3. John Kocinski, USA, Ducati
4. Simon Crafar, NZ, Kawasaki
5. Colin Edwards, USA, Yamaha
6. Paolo Casoli, Ita, Ducati
7. Christer Lindholm, Swe, Ducati
8. Mike Hale, USA, Ducati
9. Kirk McCarthy, Aus, Suzuki
10. Roger Kellenberger, CH, Honda
11. Andreas Meklau, Aut, Ducati
12. Udo Mark, Ger, Yamaha
13. Piergiorgio Bontempi, Ita, Kawasaki
14. Rob Phillis, Aus, Kawasaki
15. Ferdinando di Maso, Ita, Ducati

*Standings – 1 Kocinski 105; 2 Slight 97;
3 Corser 90; 4 Crafar & Fogarty 72;
6 Edwards 64*

Round 4 – Italy
Monza, 16 June
Race 1
1. Carl Fogarty, GB, Honda
2. Aaron Slight, NZ, Honda
3. Colin Edwards, USA, Yamaha
4. Pierfrancesco Chili, Ita, Ducati
5. Troy Corser, Aus, Ducati
6. Neil Hodgson, GB, Ducati
7. James Whitham GB, Yamaha
8. Kirk McCarthy, Aus, Suzuki
9. Simon Crafar, NZ, Kawasaki
10. Christer Lindholm, Swe, Ducati
11. Brian Morrison, GB, Ducati
12. Andreas Meklau, Aut, Ducati
13. Shawn Giles, Aus, Ducati
14. Igor Jerman, Slo, Kawasaki
15. John Reynolds, GB, Suzuki

Race 2
1. Pierfrancesco Chili, Ita, Ducati
2. Aaron Slight, NZ, Honda
3. Carl Fogarty, GB, Honda
4. Troy Corser, Aus, Ducati
5. Colin Edwards, USA, Yamaha
6. James Whitham GB, Yamaha
7. John Reynolds, GB, Suzuki
8. Kirk McCarthy, Aus, Suzuki
9. Neil Hodgson, GB, Ducati
10. Anthony Gobert, Aus, Kawasaki
11. Andreas Meklau, Aut, Ducati
12. Brian Morrison, GB, Ducati
13. Michel Paquay, Bel, Ducati
14. Christer Lindholm, Swe, Ducati
15. Rob Phillis, Aus, Kawasaki

*Standings – 1 Slight 137; 2 Corser 114;
3 Fogarty 113; 4 Kocinski 105; 5 Chili 94;
6 Edwards 91*

Round 5 – Czech Republic
Brno, 30 June
Race 1
1. Troy Corser, Aus, Ducati
2. Carl Fogarty, GB, Honda
3. Aaron Slight, NZ, Honda
4. John Kocinski, USA, Ducati
5. John Reynolds, GB, Suzuki
6. Colin Edwards, USA, Yamaha
7. Mike Hale, USA, Ducati
8. Pierfrancesco Chili, Ita, Ducati
9. Wataru Yoshikawa, Jap, Yamaha
10. Simon Crafar, NZ, Kawasaki
11. Neil Hodgson, GB, Ducati
12. Andreas Meklau, Aut, Ducati
13. Jochen Schmid, Ger, Kawasaki
14. Kirk McCarthy, Aus, Suzuki
15. Rob Phillis, Aus, Kawasaki

Race 2
1. Troy Corser, Aus, Ducati
2. Aaron Slight, NZ, Honda
3. Carl Fogarty, GB, Honda
4. Neil Hodgson, GB, Ducati
5. Mike Hale, USA, Ducati
6. John Kocinski, USA, Ducati
7. Colin Edwards, USA, Yamaha
8. John Reynolds, GB, Suzuki
9. Simon Crafar, NZ, Kawasaki
10. Pierfrancesco Chili, Ita, Ducati
11. Wataru Yoshikawa, Jap, Yamaha
12. Andreas Meklau, Aut, Ducati
13. Christer Lindholm, Swe, Ducati
14. Paolo Casoli, Ita, Ducati
15. Rob Phillis, Aus, Kawasaki

*Standings – 1 Slight 173; 2 Corser 164;
3 Fogarty 149; 4 Kocinski 128; 5 Edwards 110;
6 Chili 108*

Round 6 – USA
Laguna Seca, 21 July
Race 1
1. John Kocinski, USA, Ducati
2. Troy Corser, Aus, Ducati
3. Neil Hodgson, GB, Ducati
4. Colin Edwards, USA, Yamaha
5. Aaron Slight, NZ, Honda
6. Mike Hale, USA, Ducati
7. Simon Crafar, NZ, Kawasaki
8. Carl Fogarty, GB, Honda
9. Wataru Yoshikawa, Jap, Yamaha
10. Kirk McCarthy, Aus, Suzuki
11. Paolo Casoli, Ita, Ducati
12. Larry Pegram, USA, Ducati
13. Piergiorgio Bontempi, Ita, Kawasaki
14. John Boustas, Gre, Ducati
15. Mike Smith, USA, Kawasaki

Race 2
1. Anthony Gobert, Aus, Kawasaki
2. Troy Corser, Aus, Ducati
3. Aaron Slight, NZ, Honda
4. Carl Fogarty, GB, Honda
5. Simon Crafar, NZ, Kawasaki
6. Doug Chandler, USA, Kawasaki
7. Pierfrancesco Chili, Ita, Ducati
8. Wataru Yoshikawa, Jap, Yamaha
9. Neil Hodgson, GB, Ducati
10. Mike Hale, USA, Ducati
11. Paolo Casoli, Ita, Ducati
12. John Kocinski, USA, Ducati
13. Kirk McCarthy, Aus, Suzuki
14. Larry Pegram, USA, Ducati
15. Mike Smith, USA, Kawasaki

*Standings – 1 Corser 204; 2 Slight 200;
3 Fogarty 170; 4 Kocinski 157; 5 Edwards 123;
6 Chili 117*

Round 7 – Europe
Brands Hatch, 4 August
Race 1
1. Pierfrancesco Chili, Ita, Ducati
2. Anthony Gobert, Aus, Kawasaki
3. John Kocinski, USA, Ducati
4. Colin Edwards, USA, Yamaha
5. Carl Fogarty, GB, Honda
6. Aaron Slight, NZ, Honda
7. John Reynolds, GB, Suzuki
8. Neil Hodgson, GB, Ducati
9. Simon Crafar, NZ, Kawasaki
10. Wataru Yoshikawa, Jap, Yamaha
11. Niall Mackenzie, GB, Yamaha
12. Mike Hale, USA, Ducati
13. Piergiorgio Bontempi, Ita, Kawasaki
14. Ian Simpson, GB, Ducati
15. John Boustas, Gre, Ducati

Race 2
1. Troy Corser, Aus, Ducati
2. Pierfrancesco Chili, Ita, Ducati
3. Colin Edwards, USA, Yamaha
4. Anthony Gobert, Aus, Kawasaki
5. Aaron Slight, NZ, Honda
6. Wataru Yoshikawa, Jap, Yamaha
7. Paolo Casoli, Ita, Ducati
8. John Reynolds, GB, Suzuki
9. Piergiorgio Bontempi, Ita, Kawasaki
10. Kirk McCarthy, Aus, Suzuki
11. Mike Hale, USA, Ducati
12. Michel Paquay, Bel, Ducati
13. Jim Moodie, GB, Ducati
14. Shawn Giles, Aus, Ducati
15. Igor Jerman, Slo, Kawasaki

*Standings – 1 Corser 229; 2 Slight 221;
3 Fogarty 181; 4 Kocinski 173; 5 Chili 162;
6 Edwards 152*

Round 8 – Indonesia
Sentul, 18 August
Race 1
1 John Kocinski, USA, Ducati
2 Carl Fogarty, GB, Honda
3 Aaron Slight, NZ, Honda
4 Pierfrancesco Chili, Ita, Ducati
5 Colin Edwards, USA, Yamaha
6 Troy Corser, Aus, Ducati
7 Wataru Yoshikawa, Jap, Yamaha
8 Paolo Casoli, Ita, Ducati
9 John Reynolds, GB, Suzuki
10 Mike Hale, USA, Ducati
11 Piergiorgio Bontempi, Ita, Kawasaki
12 Simon Crafar, NZ, Kawasaki
13 Kirk McCarthy, Aus, Suzuki
14 Dean Thomas, Aus, Honda
15 Rob Phillis, Aus, Kawasaki

Race 2
1 John Kocinski, USA, Ducati
2 Aaron Slight, NZ, Honda
3 Carl Fogarty, GB, Honda
4 Colin Edwards, USA, Yamaha
5 Troy Corser, Aus, Ducati
6 John Reynolds, GB, Suzuki
7 Wataru Yoshikawa, Jap, Yamaha
8 Neil Hodgson, GB, Ducati
9 Mike Hale, USA, Ducati
10 Kirk McCarthy, Aus, Suzuki
11 Simon Crafar, NZ, Kawasaki
12 Piergiorgio Bontempi, Ita, Kawasaki
13 Rob Phillis, Aus, Kawasaki
14 John Boustas, Gre, Ducati
15 Steve Martin, Aus, Suzuki

Standings – 1 Slight 257; 2 Corser 250;
3 Kocinski 223; 4 Fogarty 217; 5 Edwards 176;
6 Chili 175

Round 9 – Japan
Sugo, 25 August
Race 1
1 Yuichi Takeda, Jap, Honda
2 Noriyuki Haga, Jap, Yamaha
3 Wataru Yoshikawa, Jap, Yamaha
4 Troy Corser, Aus, Ducati
5 John Kocinski, USA, Ducati
6 Aaron Slight, NZ, Honda
7 Norihiko Fujiwara, Jap, Yamaha
8 Carl Fogarty, GB, Honda
9 Akira Ryo, Jap, Kawasaki
10 Shinya Takeishi, Jap, Kawasaki
11 Takuma Aoki, Jap, Honda
12 Keiichi Kitagawa, Jap, Suzuki
13 Neil Hodgson, GB, Ducati
14 John Reynolds, GB, Suzuki
15 Tamaki Serizawa, Jap, Suzuki

Race 2
1 Takuma Aoki, Jap, Honda
2 John Kocinski, USA, Ducati
3 Aaron Slight, NZ, Honda
4 Carl Fogarty, GB, Honda
5 Norihiko Fujiwara, Jap, Yamaha
6 Akira Ryo, Jap, Kawasaki
7 Shinya Takeishi, Jap, Kawasaki
8 Wataru Yoshikawa, Jap, Yamaha
9 Troy Corser, Aus, Ducati
10 Keiichi Kitagawa, Jap, Suzuki
11 Simon Crafar, NZ, Kawasaki
12 John Reynolds, GB, Suzuki
13 Yukio Nukumi, Jap, Ducati
14 Neil Hodgson, GB, Ducati
15 Tamaki Serizawa, Jap, Suzuki

Standings – 1 Slight 283; 2 Corser 270;
3 Kocinski 254; 4 Fogarty 238; 5 Edwards 176;
6 Chili 175

Round 10 – Holland
Assen, 8 September
Race 1
1 Carl Fogarty, GB, Honda
2 Pierfrancesco Chili, Ita, Ducati
3 Aaron Slight, NZ, Honda
4 Troy Corser, Aus, Ducati
5 John Kocinski, USA, Ducati
6 James Whitham, GB, Yamaha
7 Neil Hodgson, GB, Ducati
8 Simon Crafar, NZ, Kawasaki
9 Christer Lindholm, Swe, Ducati
10 Wataru Yoshikawa, Jap, Yamaha

11 Mike Hale, USA, Ducati
12 Jeffry de Vries, Nl, Yamaha
13 John Reynolds, GB, Suzuki
14 Kirk McCarthy, Aus, Suzuki
15 Piergiorgio Bontempi, Ita, Kawasaki

Race 2
1 Carl Fogarty, GB, Honda
2 Troy Corser, Aus, Ducati
3 John Kocinski, USA, Ducati
4 Pierfrancesco Chili, Ita, Ducati
5 Aaron Slight, NZ, Honda
6 Neil Hodgson, GB, Ducati
7 Wataru Yoshikawa, Jap, Yamaha
8 Simon Crafar, NZ, Kawasaki
9 Kirk McCarthy, Aus, Suzuki
10 Andreas Meklau, Aut, Ducati
11 Paolo Casoli, Ita, Ducati
12 Mike Hale, USA, Ducati
13 Jeffry de Vries, Nl, Yamaha
14 James Whitham, GB, Yamaha
15 Sean Emmett, GB, Ducati

Standings – 1 Slight 310; 2 Corser 303;
3 Fogarty 288; 4 Kocinski 281; 5 Chili 208;
6 Edwards 176

Round 11 – Spain
Albacete, 6 October
Race 1
1 Troy Corser, Aus, Ducati
2 Colin Edwards, USA, Yamaha
3 John Kocinski, USA, Ducati
4 Simon Crafar, NZ, Kawasaki
5 Carl Fogarty, GB, Honda
6 Wataru Yoshikawa, Jap, Yamaha
7 John Reynolds, GB, Suzuki
8 Neil Hodgson, GB, Ducati
9 Aaron Slight, NZ, Honda
10 Mike Hale, USA, Ducati
11 Gregorio Lavilla, Spa, Yamaha
12 Sean Emmett, GB, Ducati
13 Piergiorgio Bontempi, Ita, Kawasaki
14 Paolo Casoli, Ita, Ducati
15 Jochen Schmid, Ger, Kawasaki

Race 2
1 Troy Corser, Aus, Ducati
2 John Kocinski, USA, Ducati
3 Colin Edwards, USA, Yamaha
4 Simon Crafar, NZ, Kawasaki
5 Wataru Yoshikawa, Jap, Yamaha
6 Aaron Slight, NZ, Honda
7 Carl Fogarty, GB, Honda
8 Neil Hodgson, GB, Ducati
9 John Reynolds, GB, Suzuki
10 Jochen Schmid, Ger, Kawasaki
11 Martin Craggill, Aus, Kawasaki
12 Gregorio Lavilla, Spa, Yamaha
13 Piergiorgio Bontempi, Ita, Kawasaki
14 Sean Emmett, GB, Ducati
15 Kirk McCarthy, Aus, Suzuki

Standings – 1 Corser 353; 2 Slight 327;
3 Kocinski 317; 4 Fogarty 308; 5 Edwards 212;
6 Chili 208

Round 12 – Australia
Phillip Island, 27 October
Race 1
1 Anthony Gobert, Aus, Kawasaki
2 Colin Edwards, USA, Yamaha
3 Troy Corser, Aus, Ducati
4 Carl Fogarty, GB, Honda
5 Peter Goddard, Aus, Suzuki
6 Wataru Yoshikawa, Jap, Yamaha
7 John Kocinski, USA, Ducati
8 Pierfrancesco Chili, Ita, Ducati
9 Mike Hale, USA, Ducati
10 Kirk McCarthy, Aus, Suzuki
11 John Reynolds, GB, Suzuki
12 Piergiorgio Bontempi, Ita, Kawasaki
13 Damon Buckmaster, Aus, Suzuki
14 Steve Martin, Aus, Suzuki
15 Dean Thomas, Aus, Honda

Race 2
1 Anthony Gobert, Aus, Kawasaki
2 Aaron Slight, NZ, Honda
3 Colin Edwards, USA, Yamaha
4 Mike Hale, USA, Ducati
5 John Kocinski, USA, Ducati
6 Carl Fogarty, GB, Honda

7 Wataru Yoshikawa, Jap, Yamaha
8 Peter Goddard, Aus, Suzuki
9 Pierfrancesco Chili, Ita, Ducati
10 John Reynolds, GB, Suzuki
11 Simon Crafar, NZ, Kawasaki
12 Neil Hodgson, GB, Ducati
13 Craig Connell, Aus, Ducati
14 Dean Thomas, Aus, Honda
15 Kirk McCarthy, Aus, Suzuki

FINAL STANDINGS – 1 Corser 369; 2 Slight 347;
3 Kocinski 337; 4 Fogarty 331; 5 Edwards 248;
6 Chili 223

1997 season

Round 1 – Australia
Phillip Island, 23 March
Race 1
1 John Kocinski, USA, Honda
2 Carl Fogarty, GB, Ducati
3 Simon Crafar, NZ, Kawasaki
4 Akira Yanagawa, Jap, Kawasaki
5 Troy Bayliss, Aus, Suzuki
6 Marty Craggill, Aus, Kawasaki
7 Scott Russell, USA, Yamaha
8 Andreas Meklau, Aut, Ducati
9 Shawn Giles, Aus, Honda
10 Pere Riba Cabana, Spa, Honda
11 Jason Love, Aus, Ducati
12 Igor Jerman, Slo, Kawasaki
13 Benn Archibald, Aus, Kawasaki
14 Greg Moss, Aus, Honda
15 Craig Stafford, Aus, Yamaha

Race 2
1 Aaron Slight, NZ, Honda
2 Colin Edwards, USA, Yamaha
3 Simon Crafar, NZ, Kawasaki
4 Carl Fogarty, GB, Ducati
5 Troy Bayliss, Aus, Suzuki
6 Scott Russell, USA, Yamaha
7 John Kocinski, USA, Honda
8 Damon Buckmaster, Aus, Kawasaki
9 Marty Craggill, Aus, Kawasaki
10 Shawn Giles, Aus, Honda
11 Craig Connell, Aus, Ducati
12 Piergiorgio Bontempi, Ita, Kawasaki
13 James Whitham, GB, Suzuki
14 James Haydon, GB, Ducati
15 Andreas Meklau, Aut, Ducati

Standings – 1 Kocinski 34; 2 Fogarty 33;
3 Crafar 32; 4 Slight 25; 5 Bayliss 22;
6 Edwards 20

Round 2 – San Marino
Misano, 20 April
Race 1
1 Pierfrancesco Chili, Ita, Ducati
2 John Kocinski, USA, Honda
3 Carl Fogarty, GB, Ducati
4 Aaron Slight, NZ, Honda
5 Simon Crafar, NZ, Kawasaki
6 Colin Edwards, USA, Yamaha
7 Neil Hodgson, GB, Ducati
8 Piergiorgio Bontempi, Ita, Kawasaki
9 Pere Riba Cabana, Spa, Honda
10 Christian Lavieille, Fra, Honda
11 Giorgio Cantalupo, Ita, Ducati
12 Redamo Assirelli, Ita, Yamaha
13 Igor Jerman, Slo, Kawasaki
14 Jiri Mrkyvka, CZ, Honda
15 Bruno Scatola, Ita, Kawasaki

Race 2
1 John Kocinski, USA, Honda
2 Aaron Slight, NZ, Honda
3 Carl Fogarty, GB, Ducati
4 Neil Hodgson, GB, Ducati
5 Akira Yanagawa, Jap, Kawasaki
6 Scott Russell, USA, Yamaha
7 Simon Crafar, NZ, Kawasaki
8 Colin Edwards, USA, Yamaha
9 Pere Riba Cabana, Spa, Honda
10 Christian Lavieille, Fra, Honda
11 James Haydon, GB, Ducati
12 Mike Hale, USA, Suzuki
13 Giorgio Cantalupo, Ita, Ducati
14 Bruno Scatola, Ita, Kawasaki
15 Jiri Mrkyvka, CZ, Honda

Standings – 1 Kocinski 79; 2 Fogarty 65;
3 Slight 58; 4 Crafar 52; 5 Edwards 38;
6 Russell 29

Round 3 – Great Britain
Donington Park, 4 May
Race 1
1 Aaron Slight, NZ, Honda
2 Carl Fogarty, GB, Ducati
3 Simon Crafar, NZ, Kawasaki
4 Neil Hodgson, GB, Ducati
5 Colin Edwards, USA, Yamaha
6 Scott Russell, USA, Yamaha
7 Niall Mackenzie, GB, Yamaha
8 James Whitham, GB, Suzuki
9 John Reynolds, GB, Ducati
10 John Kocinski, USA, Honda

11 Piergiorgio Bontempi, Ita, Kawasaki
12 Christer Lindholm, Swe, Yamaha
13 Gregorio Lavilla, Spa, Ducati
14 Sean Emmett, GB, Ducati
15 Mike Hale, USA, Suzuki

Race 2
1 Carl Fogarty, GB, Ducati
2 Pierfrancesco Chili, Ita, Ducati
3 Aaron Slight, NZ, Honda
4 Simon Crafar, NZ, Kawasaki
5 John Kocinski, USA, Honda
6 Colin Edwards, USA, Yamaha
7 Scott Russell, USA, Yamaha
8 Niall Mackenzie, GB, Yamaha
9 Neil Hodgson, GB, Ducati
10 James Whitham, GB, Suzuki
11 John Reynolds, GB, Ducati
12 Sean Emmett, GB, Ducati
13 Gregorio Lavilla, Spa, Ducati
14 James Whitham, GB, Suzuki
15 Andreas Meklau, Aut, Ducati

Standings – 1 Fogarty 110; 2 Slight 99;
3 Kocinski 96; 4 Crafar 81; 5 Edwards 59;
6 Russell 48

Round 4 – Germany
Hockenheim, 8 June
Race 1
1 Aaron Slight, NZ, Honda
2 John Kocinski, USA, Honda
3 Scott Russell, USA, Yamaha
4 Carl Fogarty, GB, Ducati
5 Pierfrancesco Chili, Ita, Ducati
6 Neil Hodgson, GB, Ducati
7 Colin Edwards, USA, Yamaha
8 Akira Yanagawa, Jap, Kawasaki
9 Mike Hale, USA, Suzuki
10 Andreas Meklau, Aut, Ducati
11 Piergiorgio Bontempi, Ita, Kawasaki
12 Christer Lindholm, Swe, Yamaha
13 Jochen Schmid, Ger, Kawasaki
14 James Whitham, GB, Suzuki
15 Udo Mark, Ger, Suzuki

Race 2
1 Carl Fogarty, GB, Ducati
2 Akira Yanagawa, Jap, Kawasaki
3 James Whitham, GB, Suzuki
4 Scott Russell, USA, Yamaha
5 Colin Edwards, USA, Yamaha
6 Simon Crafar, NZ, Kawasaki
7 Pierfrancesco Chili, Ita, Ducati
8 Neil Hodgson, GB, Ducati
9 Jochen Schmid, Ger, Kawasaki
10 Andreas Meklau, Aut, Ducati
11 Piergiorgio Bontempi, Ita, Kawasaki
12 Christer Lindholm, Swe, Yamaha
13 Gregorio Lavilla, Spa, Ducati
14 John Kocinski, USA, Honda
15 Udo Mark, Ger, Suzuki

Standings – 1 Fogarty 148; 2 Slight 124;
3 Kocinski 118; 4 Crafar 91; 5 Edwards 79;
6 Russell 77

Round 5 – Italy
Monza, 22 June
Race 1
1 John Kocinski, USA, Honda
2 Aaron Slight, NZ, Honda
3 Carl Fogarty, GB, Ducati
4 Simon Crafar, NZ, Kawasaki
5 Scott Russell, USA, Yamaha
6 James Whitham, GB, Suzuki
7 Pierfrancesco Chili, Ita, Ducati
8 Akira Yanagawa, Jap, Kawasaki
9 Piergiorgio Bontempi, Ita, Kawasaki
10 Mike Hale, USA, Suzuki
11 Andreas Meklau, Aut, Ducati
12 James Haydon, GB, Ducati
13 Jochen Schmid, Ger, Kawasaki
14 Jean-Philippe Ruggia, Fra, Yamaha
15 Igor Jerman, Slo, Kawasaki

Race 2
1 Pierfrancesco Chili, Ita, Ducati
2 John Kocinski, USA, Honda
3 James Whitham, GB, Suzuki
4 Carl Fogarty, GB, Ducati
5 Aaron Slight, NZ, Honda
6 Piergiorgio Bontempi, Ita, Kawasaki

7 Simon Crafar, NZ, Kawasaki
8 Scott Russell, USA, Yamaha
9 Mike Hale, USA, Suzuki
10 Jochen Schmid, Ger, Kawasaki
11 Pere Riba Cabana, Spa, Honda
12 Udo Mark, Ger, Suzuki
13 James Haydon, GB, Ducati
14 Jean-Marc Deletang, Fra, Yamaha
15 Giorgio Cantalupo, Ita, Ducati

Standings – 1 Fogarty 177; 2 Kocinski 163;
3 Slight 155; 4 Crafar 113; 5 Chili 99;
6 Russell 96

Round 6 – USA
Laguna Seca, 13 July
Race 1
1 John Kocinski, USA, Honda
2 Carl Fogarty, GB, Ducati
3 Miguel DuHamel, Can, Honda
4 Simon Crafar, NZ, Kawasaki
5 Doug Chandler, USA, Kawasaki
6 Scott Russell, USA, Yamaha
7 Aaron Slight, NZ, Honda
8 James Whitham, GB, Suzuki
9 Piergiorgio Bontempi, Ita, Kawasaki
10 Akira Yanagawa, Jap, Kawasaki
11 Steve Crevier, Can, Honda
12 Tom Kipp, USA, Yamaha
13 Pascal Picotte, Can, Suzuki
14 Mike Hale, USA, Suzuki
15 Igor Jerman, Slo, Kawasaki

Race 2
1 John Kocinski, USA, Honda
2 Carl Fogarty, GB, Ducati
3 Miguel DuHamel, Can, Honda
4 Scott Russell, USA, Yamaha
5 Akira Yanagawa, Jap, Kawasaki
6 Pierfrancesco Chili, Ita, Ducati
7 Piergiorgio Bontempi, Ita, Kawasaki
8 Tom Kipp, USA, Yamaha
9 Neil Hodgson, GB, Ducati
10 Aaron Slight, NZ, Honda
11 Aaron Yates, USA, Suzuki
12 Steve Crevier, Can, Honda
13 Igor Jerman, Slo, Kawasaki
14 Michael Krynock, USA, Suzuki

Standings – 1 Fogarty 217; 2 Kocinski 213;
3 Slight 170; 4 Crafar 126; 5 Russell 119;
6 Chili 109

Round 7 – Europe
Brands Hatch, 3 August
Race 1
1 Pierfrancesco Chili, Ita, Ducati
2 Scott Russell, USA, Yamaha
3 John Kocinski, USA, Honda
4 Neil Hodgson, GB, Ducati
5 Akira Yanagawa, Jap, Kawasaki
6 Aaron Slight, NZ, Honda
7 James Whitham, GB, Suzuki
8 Piergiorgio Bontempi, Ita, Kawasaki
9 Mike Hale, USA, Suzuki
10 Chris Walker, GB, Yamaha
11 Michael Rutter, GB, Honda
12 Ray Stringer, GB, Kawasaki
13 Pere Riba Cabana, Spa, Honda
14 Brett Sampson, GB, Kawasaki
15 Phil Giles, GB, Kawasaki

Race 2
1 Carl Fogarty, GB, Ducati
2 John Kocinski, USA, Honda
3 Michael Rutter, GB, Honda
4 Akira Yanagawa, Jap, Kawasaki
5 Scott Russell, USA, Yamaha
6 Neil Hodgson, GB, Ducati
7 Simon Crafar, NZ, Kawasaki
8 Aaron Slight, NZ, Honda
9 James Whitham, GB, Suzuki
10 Chris Walker, GB, Yamaha
11 Mike Hale, USA, Suzuki
12 Piergiorgio Bontempi, Ita, Kawasaki
13 Pere Riba Cabana, Spa, Honda
14 Phil Giles, GB, Kawasaki
15 Igor Jerman, Slo, Kawasaki

Standings – 1 Kocinski 249; 2 Fogarty 242;
3 Slight 188; 4 Russell 150; 5 Crafar 135;
6 Chili 134

Round 8 – Austria
A1-Ring, 17 August
Race 1
1 Carl Fogarty, GB, Ducati
2 Akira Yanagawa, Jap, Kawasaki
3 Aaron Slight, NZ, Honda
4 Pierfrancesco Chili, Ita, Ducati
5 John Kocinski, USA, Honda
6 Simon Crafar, NZ, Kawasaki
7 Scott Russell, USA, Yamaha
8 Neil Hodgson, GB, Ducati
9 Piergiorgio Bontempi, Ita, Kawasaki
10 James Whitham, GB, Suzuki
11 Mike Hale, USA, Suzuki
12 Chris Walker, GB, Yamaha
13 Udo Mark, Ger, Suzuki
14 Jochen Schmid, Ger, Kawasaki
15 Andreas Meklau, Aut, Ducati

Race 2
1 Akira Yanagawa, Jap, Kawasaki
2 Aaron Slight, NZ, Honda
3 John Kocinski, USA, Honda
4 Scott Russell, USA, Yamaha
5 Piergiorgio Bontempi, Ita, Kawasaki
6 James Whitham, GB, Suzuki
7 Mike Hale, USA, Suzuki
8 Andreas Meklau, Aut, Ducati
9 Udo Mark, Ger, Suzuki
10 Chris Walker, GB, Yamaha
11 Jochen Schmid, Ger, Kawasaki
12 Pere Riba Cabana, Spa, Honda
13 Igor Jerman, Slo, Kawasaki
14 Anton Gruschka, Ger, Yamaha
15 Gibson Scudeler, Bra, Ducati

Standings – 1 Kocinski 276; 2 Fogarty 267;
3 Slight 224; 4 Russell 172; 5 Chili 147;
6 Yanagawa 146

Round 9 – Holland
Assen, 31 August
Race 1
1 John Kocinski, USA, Honda
2 Carl Fogarty, GB, Ducati
3 Pierfrancesco Chili, Ita, Ducati
4 Aaron Slight, NZ, Honda
5 Neil Hodgson, GB, Ducati
6 Scott Russell, USA, Yamaha
7 James Whitham, GB, Suzuki
8 Akira Yanagawa, Jap, Kawasaki
9 Simon Crafar, NZ, Kawasaki
10 Chris Walker, GB, Yamaha
11 Mike Hale, USA, Suzuki
12 Pere Riba Cabana, Spa, Honda
13 Jochen Schmid, Ger, Kawasaki
14 Udo Mark, Ger, Suzuki
15 Erkka Korpiaho, Fin, Kawasaki

Race 2
1 Carl Fogarty, GB, Ducati
2 Pierfrancesco Chili, Ita, Ducati
3 John Kocinski, USA, Honda
4 Aaron Slight, NZ, Honda
5 Neil Hodgson, GB, Ducati
6 Simon Crafar, NZ, Kawasaki
7 Akira Yanagawa, Jap, Kawasaki
8 Scott Russell, USA, Yamaha
9 Chris Walker, GB, Yamaha
10 Piergiorgio Bontempi, Ita, Kawasaki
11 James Whitham, GB, Suzuki
12 Jochen Schmid, Ger, Kawasaki
13 Udo Mark, Ger, Suzuki
14 Igor Jerman, Slo, Kawasaki
15 Pere Riba Cabana, Spa, Honda

Standings – 1 Kocinski 317; 2 Fogarty 312;
3 Slight 250; 4 Russell 190; 5 Chili 183;
6 Yanagawa 163

Round 10 – Spain
Albacete, 21 September
Race 1
1 John Kocinski, USA, Honda
2 Aaron Slight, NZ, Honda
3 Simon Crafar, NZ, Kawasaki
4 Akira Yanagawa, Jap, Kawasaki
5 Pierfrancesco Chili, Ita, Ducati
6 Piergiorgio Bontempi, Ita, Kawasaki
7 Gregorio Lavilla, Spa, Ducati
8 Mike Hale, USA, Suzuki
9 Jochen Schmid, Ger, Kawasaki
10 Chris Walker, GB, Yamaha

11 Pere Riba Cabana, Spa, Honda
12 Udo Mark, Ger, Suzuki
13 Igor Jerman, Slo, Kawasaki
14 Giorgio Cantalupo, Ita, Ducati
15 Jiri Mrkyvka, Cz, Honda

Race 2
1 John Kocinski, USA, Honda
2 Simon Crafar, NZ, Kawasaki
3 Aaron Slight, NZ, Honda
4 Akira Yanagawa, Jap, Kawasaki
5 Scott Russell, USA, Yamaha
6 Piergiorgio Bontempi, Ita, Kawasaki
7 Pierfrancesco Chili, Ita, Ducati
8 Neil Hodgson, GB, Ducati
9 Mike Hale, USA, Suzuki
10 James Whitham, GB, Suzuki
11 Chris Walker, GB, Yamaha
12 Jochen Schmid, Ger, Kawasaki
13 Pere Riba Cabana, Spa, Honda
14 Udo Mark, Ger, Suzuki
15 James Haydon, GB, Ducati

Standings – 1 Kocinski 367; 2 Fogarty 312;
3 Slight 286; 4 Chili 203; 5 Russell 201;
6 Crafar 198

Round 11 – Japan
Sugo, 5 October
Race 1
1 Akira Yanagawa, Jap, Kawasaki
2 Noriyuki Haga, Jap, Yamaha
3 Simon Crafar, NZ, Kawasaki
4 Keiichi Kitagawa, Jap, Suzuki
5 Wataru Yoshikawa, Jap, Yamaha
6 Aaron Slight, NZ, Honda
7 Shin'ya Takeishi, Jap, Kawasaki
8 Katsuaki Fujiwara, Jap, Suzuki
9 John Kocinski, USA, Honda
10 Tamaki Serizawa, Jap, Suzuki
11 Shinichi Itoh, Jap, Honda
12 Pierfrancesco Chili, Ita, Ducati
13 Carl Fogarty, GB, Ducati
14 Scott Russell, USA, Yamaha
15 Norihiko Fujiwara, Jap, Yamaha

Race 2
1 Noriyuki Haga, Jap, Yamaha
2 Simon Crafar, NZ, Kawasaki
3 John Kocinski, USA, Honda
4 Aaron Slight, NZ, Honda
5 Katsuaki Fujiwara, Jap, Suzuki
6 Tamaki Serizawa, Jap, Suzuki
7 Yuichi Takeda, Jap, Honda
8 Akira Ryo, Jap, Kawasaki
9 Sean Emmett, GB, Ducati
10 Mike Hale, USA, Suzuki
11 Makato Suzuki, Jap, Ducati
12 Ichiro Asai, Jap, Honda
13 Manabu Kamada, Jap, Honda
14 Igor Jerman, Slo, Kawasaki
15 Pere Riba Cabana, Spa, Honda

Standings – 1 Kocinski 391; 2 Fogarty 317;
3 Slight 310; 4 Crafar 234; 5 Yanagawa 214;
6 Chili 209

Round 12 – Indonesia
Sentul, 12 October
Race 1
1 John Kocinski, USA, Honda
2 Aaron Slight, NZ, Honda
3 Carl Fogarty, GB, Ducati
4 Akira Yanagawa, Jap, Kawasaki
5 Noriyuki Haga, Jap, Yamaha
6 Scott Russell, USA, Yamaha
7 John Reynolds, GB, Ducati
8 Mike Hale, USA, Suzuki
9 James Whitham, GB, Suzuki
10 Igor Jerman, Slo, Kawasaki
11 Pere Riba Cabana, Spa, Honda
12 Makato Suzuki, Jap, Ducati
13 Yudhe Kusuma, Ind, Kawasaki

Race 2
1 Carl Fogarty, GB, Ducati
2 Akira Yanagawa, Jap, Kawasaki
3 Noriyuki Haga, Jap, Yamaha
4 Aaron Slight, NZ, Honda
5 Scott Russell, USA, Yamaha
6 James Whitham, GB, Suzuki
7 Neil Hodgson, GB, Ducati
8 Sean Emmett, GB, Ducati

9 Igor Jerman, Slo, Kawasaki
10 Makato Suzuki, Jap, Ducati
11 Pere Riba Cabana, Spa, Honda
12 Christian Lavieille, Fra, Honda
13 Yudhe Kusuma, Ind, Kawasaki

FINAL STANDINGS – 1 Kocinski 416;
2 Fogarty 358; 3 Slight 343; 4 Yanagawa 247;
5 Crafar 234; 6 Russell 226

1998 season

Round 1 – Australia
Phillip Island, 22 March
Race 1
1. Carl Fogarty, GB, Ducati
2. Troy Corser, Aus, Ducati
3. Noriyuki Haga, Jpn, Yamaha
4. Pierfrancesco Chili, Ita, Ducati
5. Akira Yanagawa, Jpn, Kawasaki
6. Mark Willis, Aus, Suzuki
7. Colin Edwards, USA, Honda
8. Neil Hodgson, GB, Kawasaki
9. Aaron Slight, NZ, Honda
10. Scott Russell, USA, Yamaha
11. Gregorio Lavilla, Spa, Ducati
12. Piergiorgio Bontempi, Ita, Kawasaki
13. Lucio Pedercini, Ita, Ducati
14. Mal Campbell, Aus, Ducati
15. Igor Jerman, Slo, Kawasaki

Race 2
1. Noriyuki Haga, Jpn, Yamaha
2. Aaron Slight, NZ, Honda
3. Carl Fogarty, GB, Ducati
4. Peter Goddard, Aus, Suzuki
5. Akira Yanagawa, Jpn, Kawasaki
6. Troy Corser, Aus, Ducati
7. Colin Edwards, USA, Honda
8. Scott Russell, USA, Yamaha
9. Mark Willis, Aus, Suzuki
10. Steve Martin, Aus, Ducati
11. Gregorio Lavilla, Spa, Ducati
12. James Whitham, GB, Suzuki
13. Shawn Giles, Aus, Honda
14. Craig Connell, Aus, Ducati
15. Alessandro Gramigni, Ita, Ducati

Standings – 1 Haga & Fogarty 41;
3 Corser 30; 4 Slight 27; 5 Yanagawa 22;
6 Edwards 18

Round 2 – Great Britain
Donington Park, 13 April
Race 1
1. Noriyuki Haga, Jpn, Yamaha
2. Troy Corser, Aus, Ducati
3. Pierfrancesco Chili, Ita, Ducati
4. Aaron Slight, NZ, Honda
5. Akira Yanagawa, Jpn, Kawasaki
6. Colin Edwards, USA, Honda
7. Carl Fogarty, GB, Ducati
8. James Whitham, GB, Suzuki
9. Peter Goddard, Aus, Suzuki
10. Steve Hislop, GB, Yamaha
11. Chris Walker, GB, Kawasaki
12. Neil Hodgson, GB, Kawasaki
13. Scott Russell, USA, Yamaha
14. Piergiorgio Bontempi, Ita, Kawasaki
15. James Haydon, GB, Suzuki

Race 2
1. Noriyuki Haga, Jpn, Yamaha
2. Troy Corser, Aus, Ducati
3. Carl Fogarty, GB, Ducati
4. Aaron Slight, NZ, Honda
5. Pierfrancesco Chili, Ita, Ducati
6. Niall Mackenzie, GB, Yamaha
7. Colin Edwards, USA, Honda
8. James Whitham, GB, Suzuki
9. Steve Hislop, GB, Yamaha
10. Peter Goddard, Aus, Suzuki
11. Scott Russell, USA, Yamaha
12. Chris Walker, GB, Kawasaki
13. Piergiorgio Bontempi, Ita, Kawasaki
14. James Haydon, GB, Suzuki
15. Terry Rymer, GB, Suzuki

Standings – 1 Haga 91; 2 Corser 70;
3 Fogarty 66; 4 Slight 53; 5 Chili 40;
6 Edwards 37

Round 3 – Italy
Monza, 10 May
Race 1
1. Colin Edwards, USA, Honda
2. Aaron Slight, NZ, Honda
3. Troy Corser, Aus, Ducati
4. Neil Hodgson, GB, Kawasaki
5. Pierfrancesco Chili, Ita, Ducati
6. Carl Fogarty, GB, Ducati
7. Peter Goddard, Aus, Suzuki
8. James Whitham, GB, Suzuki
9. Noriyuki Haga, Jpn, Yamaha
10. Gregorio Lavilla, Spn, Ducati
11. Andy Meklau, Aut, Ducati
12. Alessandro Gramigni, Ita, Ducati
13. Igor Jerman, Slo, Kawasaki
14. Lucio Pedercini, Ita, Ducati
15. Erkka Korpiaho, Fin, Kawasaki

Race 2
1. Colin Edwards, USA, Honda
2. Carl Fogarty, GB, Ducati
3. Pierfrancesco Chili, Ita, Ducati
4. Troy Corser, Aus, Ducati
5. James Whitham, GB, Suzuki
6. Akira Yanagawa, Jpn, Kawasaki
7. Neil Hodgson, GB, Kawasaki
8. Peter Goddard, Aus, Suzuki
9. Andy Meklau, Aut, Ducati
10. Noriyuki Haga, Jpn, Yamaha
11. Piergiorgio Bontempi, Ita, Kawasaki
12. Igor Jerman, Slo, Kawasaki
13. Alessandro Gramigni, Ita, Ducati
14. Lucio Pedercini, Ita, Ducati
15. Erkka Korpiaho, Fin, Kawasaki

Standings – 1 Haga 104; 2 Corser 99;
3 Fogarty 96; 4 Edwards 87; 5 Slight 73;
6 Chili 67

Round 4 – Spain
Albacete, 24 May
Race 1
1. Pierfrancesco Chili, Ita, Ducati
2. Troy Corser, Aus, Ducati
3. Gregorio Lavilla, Spa, Ducati
4. Aaron Slight, NZ, Honda
5. Colin Edwards, USA, Honda
6. Scott Russell, USA, Yamaha
7. Neil Hodgson, GB, Kawasaki
8. Alessandro Gramigni, Ita, Ducati
9. Carl Fogarty, GB, Ducati
10. Noriyuki Haga, Jpn, Yamaha
11. James Whitham, GB, Suzuki
12. Piergiorgio Bontempi, Ita, Kawasaki
13. Akira Yanagawa, Jpn, Kawasaki
14. Peter Goddard, Aus, Suzuki
15. Erkka Korpiaho, Fin, Kawasaki

Race 2
1. Carl Fogarty, GB, Ducati
2. Aaron Slight, NZ, Honda
3. Troy Corser, Aus, Ducati
4. Noriyuki Haga, Jpn, Yamaha
5. Pierfrancesco Chili, Ita, Ducati
6. Piergiorgio Bontempi, Ita, Kawasaki
7. Akira Yanagawa, Jpn, Kawasaki
8. Peter Goddard, Aus, Suzuki
9. Scott Russell, USA, Yamaha
10. James Whitham, GB, Suzuki
11. Jean-Marc Deletang, Fra, Yamaha
12. Igor Jerman, Slo, Kawasaki
13. Frederic Protat, Fra, Honda
14. Neil Hodgson, GB, Kawasaki
15. Jiri Mrkyvka, CZ, Honda

Standings – 1 Corser 135; 2 Fogarty 128;
3 Haga 123; 4 Slight 106; 5 Chili 103;
6 Edwards 98

Round 5 – Germany
Nürburgring, 7 June
Race 1
1. Aaron Slight, NZ, Honda
2. Colin Edwards, USA, Honda
3. Pierfrancesco Chili, Ita, Ducati
4. Akira Yanagawa, Jpn, Kawasaki
5. Noriyuki Haga, Jpn, Yamaha
6. Peter Goddard, Aus, Suzuki
7. Troy Corser, Aus, Ducati
8. Piergiorgio Bontempi, Ita, Kawasaki
9. James Whitham, GB, Suzuki
10. Alessandro Gramigni, Ita, Ducati
11. Scott Russell, USA, Yamaha
12. Lucio Pedercini, Ita, Ducati
13. Carl Fogarty, GB, Ducati
14. Igor Jerman, Slo, Kawasaki
15. Ruben Xaus, Spa, Suzuki

Race 2
1. Pierfrancesco Chili, Ita, Ducati
2. Colin Edwards, USA, Honda
3. Troy Corser, Aus, Ducati
4. Aaron Slight, NZ, Honda
5. Akira Yanagawa, Jpn, Kawasaki
6. Gregorio Lavilla, Spa, Ducati
7. Noriyuki Haga, Jpn, Yamaha
8. Peter Goddard, Aus, Suzuki
9. Piergiorgio Bontempi, Ita, Kawasaki
10. James Whitham, GB, Suzuki
11. Neil Hodgson, GB, Kawasaki
12. Udo Mark, Ger, Suzuki
13. Carl Fogarty, GB, Ducati
14. Lucio Pedercini, Ita, Ducati
15. Igor Jerman, Slo, Kawasaki

Standings – 1 Corser 160;
2 Chili & Slight 144; 4 Haga 143;
5 Edwards 138; 6 Fogarty 134

Round 6 – San Marino
Misano, 21 June
Race 1
1. Aaron Slight, NZ, Honda
2. Troy Corser, Aus, Ducati
3. Colin Edwards, USA, Honda
4. Carl Fogarty, GB, Ducati
5. Akira Yanagawa, Jpn, Kawasaki
6. James Whitham, GB, Suzuki
7. Neil Hodgson, GB, Kawasaki
8. Scott Russell, USA, Yamaha
9. Andy Meklau, Aut, Ducati
10. Udo Mark, Ger, Suzuki
11. Alessandro Gramigni, Ita, Ducati
12. Lucio Pedercini, Ita, Ducati
13. Paolo Blora, Ita, Ducati
14. Andy Stroud, NZ, Kawasaki
15. Igor Jerman, Slo, Kawasaki

Race 2
1. Aaron Slight, NZ, Honda
2. Troy Corser, Aus, Ducati
3. Carl Fogarty, GB, Ducati
4. Colin Edwards, USA, Honda
5. Akira Yanagawa, Jpn, Kawasaki
6. Scott Russell, USA, Yamaha
7. Gregorio Lavilla, Spa, Ducati
8. Neil Hodgson, GB, Kawasaki
9. Andy Meklau, Aut, Ducati
10. Igor Jerman, Slo, Kawasaki
11. Piergiorgio Bontempi, Ita, Kawasaki
12. Alessandro Gramigni, Ita, Ducati
13. Udo Mark, Ger, Suzuki
14. Lucio Pedercini, Ita, Ducati
15. Andy Stroud, NZ, Kawasaki

Standings – 1 Corser 200; 2 Slight 194;
3 Edwards 167; 4 Fogarty 163; 5 Chili 144;
6 Haga 143

Round 7 – South Africa
Kyalami, 5 July
Race 1
1. Pierfrancesco Chili, Ita, Ducati
2. Carl Fogarty, GB, Ducati
3. Gregorio Lavilla, Spa, Ducati
4. James Whitham, GB, Suzuki
5. Peter Goddard, Aus, Suzuki
6. Akira Yanagawa, Jpn, Kawasaki
7. Noriyuki Haga, Jpn, Yamaha
8. Aaron Slight, NZ, Honda
9. Colin Edwards, USA, Honda
10. Scott Russell, USA, Yamaha
11. Alessandro Gramigni, Ita, Ducati
12. Piergiorgio Bontempi, Ita, Kawasaki
13. Igor Jerman, Slo, Kawasaki
14. Andy Stroud, NZ, Kawasaki
15. Frederic Protat, Fra, Ducati

Race 2
1. Pierfrancesco Chili, Ita, Ducati
2. Carl Fogarty, GB, Ducati
3. Noriyuki Haga, Jpn, Yamaha
4. Colin Edwards, USA, Honda
5. Akira Yanagawa, Jpn, Kawasaki
6. Peter Goddard, Aus, Suzuki
7. Troy Corser, Aus, Ducati
8. Aaron Slight, NZ, Honda
9. Scott Russell, USA, Yamaha
10. Piergiorgio Bontempi, Ita, Kawasaki
11. Igor Jerman, Slo, Kawasaki
12. Andy Stroud, NZ, Kawasaki
13. Lucio Pedercini, Ita, Ducati
14. Alessandro Gramigni, Ita, Ducati
15. Frederic Protat, Fra, Ducati

Standings – 1 Slight 210; 2 Corser 209;
3 Fogarty 203; 4 Chili 194; 5 Edwards 187;
6 Haga 168

Round 8 – USA
Laguna Seca, 12 July
Race 1
1 Troy Corser, Aus, Ducati
2 Akira Yanagawa, Jpn, Kawasaki
3 Doug Chandler, USA, Kawasaki
4 Ben Bostrom, USA, Honda
5 Carl Fogarty, GB, Ducati
6 James Whitham, GB, Suzuki
7 Pierfrancesco Chili, Ita, Ducati
8 Aaron Slight, NZ, Honda
9 Neil Hodgson, GB, Kawasaki
10 Jamie Hacking, USA, Yamaha
11 Colin Edwards, USA, Honda
12 Aaron Yates, USA, Suzuki
13 Gregorio Lavilla, Spa, Ducati
14 Peter Goddard, Aus, Suzuki
15 Scott Russell, USA, Yamaha

Race 2
1 Noriyuki Haga, Jpn, Yamaha
2 Troy Corser, Aus, Ducati
3 Ben Bostrom, USA, Honda
4 Pierfrancesco Chili, Ita, Ducati
5 James Whitham, GB, Suzuki
6 Neil Hodgson, GB, Kawasaki
7 Jamie Hacking, USA, Yamaha
8 Peter Goddard, Aus, Suzuki
9 Alessandro Gramigni, Ita, Ducati
10 Colin Edwards, USA, Honda
11 Igor Jerman, Slo, Kawasaki
12 Lucio Pedercini, Ita, Ducati
13 Ricky Orlando, USA, Kawasaki

*Standings – 1 Corser 241.5; 2 Slight 214;
3 Chili 211.5; 4 Fogarty 208.5; 5 Edwards 195.5;
6 Haga 193*

Round 9 – Europe
Brands Hatch, 2 August
Race 1
1 Colin Edwards, USA, Honda
2 Aaron Slight, NZ, Honda
3 Scott Russell, USA, Yamaha
4 Carl Fogarty, GB, Ducati
5 James Whitham, GB, Suzuki
6 Niall Mackenzie, GB, Yamaha
7 Troy Corser, Aus, Ducati
8 Steve Hislop, GB, Yamaha
9 Pierfrancesco Chili, Ita, Ducati
10 Peter Goddard, Aus, Suzuki
11 Sean Emmett, GB, Ducati
12 Noriyuki Haga, Jpn, Yamaha
13 Troy Bayliss, Aus Ducati
14 Matt Llewellyn, GB, Ducati
15 Alessandro Gramigni, Ita, Ducati

Race 2
1 Troy Corser, Aus, Ducati
2 Carl Fogarty, GB, Ducati
3 James Whitham, GB, Suzuki
4 Colin Edwards, USA, Honda
5 Aaron Slight, NZ, Honda
6 Pierfrancesco Chili, Ita, Ducati
7 Noriyuki Haga, Jpn, Yamaha
8 Scott Russell, USA, Yamaha
9 Neil Hodgson, GB, Kawasaki
10 Niall Mackenzie, GB, Yamaha
11 Steve Hislop, GB, Yamaha
12 James Haydon, GB, Suzuki
13 Peter Goddard, Aus, Suzuki
14 John Reynolds, GB, Ducati
15 Troy Bayliss, Aus, Ducati

*Standings – 1 Corser 275.5; 2 Slight 245;
3 Fogarty 241.5; 4 Edwards 233.5; 5 Chili 228.5
6 Haga 206*

Round 10 – Austria
A1-Ring, 30 August
Race 1
1 Aaron Slight, NZ, Honda
2 Pierfrancesco Chili, Ita, Ducati
3 Carl Fogarty, GB, Ducati
4 Akira Yanagawa, Jpn, Kawasaki
5 James Whitham, GB, Suzuki
6 Troy Corser, Aus, Ducati
7 Colin Edwards, USA, Honda
8 Neil Hodgson, GB, Kawasaki
9 Noriyuki Haga, Jpn, Yamaha
10 Peter Goddard, Aus, Suzuki
11 Gregorio Lavilla, Spn, Ducati
12 Scott Russell, USA, Yamaha

13 Alessandro Gramigni, Ita, Ducati
14 Andy Meklau, Aut, Ducati
15 Igor Jerman, Slo, Kawasaki

Race 2
1 Aaron Slight, NZ, Honda
2 Carl Fogarty, GB, Ducati
3 Pierfrancesco Chili, Ita, Ducati
4 Akira Yanagawa, Jpn, Kawasaki
5 Troy Corser, Aus, Ducati
6 James Whitham, GB, Suzuki
7 Gregorio Lavilla, Spa, Ducati
8 Peter Goddard, Aus, Suzuki
9 Colin Edwards, USA, Honda
10 Neil Hodgson, GB, Kawasaki
11 Scott Russell, USA, Yamaha
12 Noriyuki Haga, Jpn, Yamaha
13 Andy Meklau, Aut, Ducati
14 Alessandro Gramigni, Ita, Ducati
15 Igor Jerman, Slo, Kawasaki

*Standings – 1 Corser 296.5; 2 Slight 295;
3 Fogarty 277.5; 4 Chili 264.5; 5 Edwards 249.5;
6 Haga 217*

Round 11 – Holland
Assen, 6 September
Race 1
1 Pierfrancesco Chili, Ita, Ducati
2 Carl Fogarty, GB, Ducati
3 Troy Corser, Aus, Ducati
4 Aaron Slight, NZ, Honda
5 Colin Edwards, USA, Honda
6 Peter Goddard, Aus, Suzuki
7 Akira Yanagawa, Jpn, Kawasaki
8 Noriyuki Haga, Jpn, Yamaha
9 Scott Russell, USA, Yamaha
10 Neil Hodgson, GB, Kawasaki
11 Alessandro Gramigni, Ita, Ducati
12 Igor Jerman, Slo, Kawasaki
13 Mario Innamorati, Ita, Kawasaki
14 Erkka Korpiaho, Fin, Kawasaki
15 Andy Stroud, NZ, Kawasaki

Race 2
1 Carl Fogarty, GB, Ducati
2 Aaron Slight, NZ, Honda
3 Troy Corser, Aus, Ducati
4 Colin Edwards, USA, Honda
5 James Whitham, GB, Suzuki
6 Akira Yanagawa, Jpn, Kawasaki
7 Peter Goddard, Aus, Suzuki
8 Noriyuki Haga, Jpn, Yamaha
9 Neil Hodgson, GB, Kawasaki
10 Igor Jerman, Slo, Kawasaki
11 Mario Innamorati, Ita, Kawasaki
12 Erkka Korpiaho, Fin, Kawasaki
13 Andy Stroud, NZ, Kawasaki
14 Heinz Platacis, Ger, Kawasaki

*Standings – 1 Corser 328.5; 2 Slight 328;
3 Fogarty 322.5; 4 Chili 289.5; 5 Edwards 273.5;
6 Haga 233*

Round 12 – Japan
Sugo, 4 October
Race 1
1 Keiichi Kitagawa, Jpn, Suzuki
2 Akira Ryo, Jpn, Suzuki
3 Carl Fogarty, GB, Ducati
4 Akira Yanagawa, Jpn, Kawasaki
5 Scott Russell, USA, Yamaha
6 Neil Hodgson, GB, Kawasaki
7 Aaron Slight, NZ, Honda
8 Shinichi Itoh, Jpn, Honda
9 Wataru Yoshikawa, Jpn, Yamaha
10 Peter Goddard, Aus, Suzuki
11 James Whitham, GB, Suzuki
12 Pierfrancesco Chili, Ita, Ducati
13 Colin Edwards, USA, Honda
14 Shinya Takeishi, Jpn, Kawasaki
15 Yuichi Takeda, Jpn, Honda

Race 2
1 Noriyuki Haga, Jpn, Yamaha
2 Akira Yanagawa, Jpn, Kawasaki
3 Akira Ryo, Jpn, Suzuki
4 Carl Fogarty, GB, Ducati
5 Keiichi Kitagawa, Jpn, Suzuki
6 Aaron Slight, NZ, Honda
7 Wataru Yoshikawa, Jpn, Yamaha
8 Kensuke Haga, Jpn, Yamaha
9 James Whitham, GB, Suzuki

10 Peter Goddard, Aus, Suzuki
11 Shinya Takeishi, Jpn, Kawasaki
12 Scott Russell, USA, Yamaha
13 Colin Edwards, USA, Honda
14 Yuichi Takeda, Jpn, Honda
15 Gregorio Lavilla, Spn, Ducati

*FINAL STANDINGS – 1 Fogarty 351.5;
2 Slight 347; 3 Corser 328.5; 4 Chili 293.5;
5 Edwards 279.5; 6 Haga 258*

1999 season

Round 1 – South Africa
Kyalami, 28 March
Race 1
1 Carl Fogarty, GB, Ducati
2 Troy Corser, Aus, Ducati
3 Aaron Slight, NZ, Honda
4 Noriyuki Haga, Jpn, Yamaha
5 Colin Edwards, USA, Honda
6 Akira Yanagawa, Jpn, Kawasaki
7 Pierfrancesco Chili, Ita, Suzuki
8 Gregorio Lavilla, Spn, Kawasaki
9 Doriano Romboni, Ita, Ducati
10 Robert Ulm, Aut, Kawasaki
11 Katsuaki Fujiwara, Jpn, Suzuki
12 Vitto Guareschi, Ita, Yamaha
13 Andy Meklau, Aut, Ducati
14 Lance Isaacs, RSA, Ducati
15 Alessandro Gramigni, Ita, Yamaha

Race 2
1 Carl Fogarty, GB, Ducati
2 Aaron Slight, NZ, Honda
3 Troy Corser, Aus, Ducati
4 Colin Edwards, USA, Honda
5 Akira Yanagawa, Jpn, Kawasaki
6 Gregorio Lavilla, Spn, Kawasaki
7 Peter Goddard, Aus, Aprilia
8 Pierfrancesco Chili, Ita, Suzuki
9 Doriano Romboni, Ita, Ducati
10 Katsuaki Fujiwara, Jpn, Suzuki
11 Robert Ulm, Aut, Kawasaki
12 Lucio Pedercini, Ita, Ducati
13 Vitto Guareschi, Ita, Yamaha
14 Lance Isaacs, RSA, Ducati
15 Igor Jerman, Slo, Kawasaki

Standings – 1 Fogarty 50;
2 Slight & Corser 36; 4 Edwards 24;
5 Yanagawa 21; 6 Lavilla 18

Round 2 – Australia
Phillip Island, 18 April
Race 1
1 Troy Corser, Aus, Ducati
2 Carl Fogarty, GB, Ducati
3 Colin Edwards, USA, Honda
4 Aaron Slight, NZ, Honda
5 Akira Yanagawa, Jpn, Kawasaki
6 Noriyuki Haga, Jpn, Yamaha
7 Doriano Romboni, Ita, Ducati
8 Craig Connell, Aus, Ducati
9 Katsuaki Fujiwara, Jpn, Suzuki
10 Andy Meklau, Aut, Ducati
11 Shawn Giles, Aus, Suzuki
12 Igor Jerman, Slo, Kawasaki
13 Vitto Guareschi, Ita, Yamaha
14 Robert Ulm, Aut, Kawasaki
15 Jiri Mrkyvka, CZ, Ducati

Race 2
1 Troy Corser, Aus, Ducati
2 Carl Fogarty, GB, Ducati
3 Colin Edwards, USA, Honda
4 Aaron Slight, NZ, Honda
5 Noriyuki Haga, Jpn, Yamaha
6 Akira Yanagawa, Jpn, Kawasaki
7 Steve Martin, Aus, Ducati
8 Doriano Romboni, Ita, Ducati
9 Craig Connell, Aus, Ducati
10 Katsuaki Fujiwara, Jpn, Suzuki
11 Andy Meklau, Aut, Ducati
12 Shawn Giles, Aus, Suzuki
13 Pierfrancesco Chili, Ita, Suzuki
14 Lucio Pedercini, Ita, Ducati
15 Vitto Guareschi, Ita, Yamaha

Standings – 1 Fogarty 90; 2 Corser 86;
3 Slight 62; 4 Edwards 56; 5 Yanagawa 42;
6 Haga 34

Round 3 – Great Britain
Donington Park, 2 May
Race 1
1 Carl Fogarty, GB, Ducati
2 Aaron Slight, NZ, Honda
3 Colin Edwards, USA, Honda
4 Chris Walker, GB, Kawasaki
5 Akira Yanagawa, Jpn, Kawasaki
6 Troy Corser, Aus, Ducati
7 John Reynolds, GB, Ducati
8 Steve Hislop, GB, Kawasaki
9 Sean Emmett, GB, Ducati
10 Noriyuki Haga, Jpn, Yamaha

11 Doriano Romboni, Ita, Ducati
12 Niall Mackenzie, GB, Yamaha
13 Katsuaki Fujiwara, Jpn, Suzuki
14 Igor Jerman, Slo, Kawasaki
15 Frederic Protat, Fra, Ducati

Race 2
1 Colin Edwards, USA, Honda
2 Carl Fogarty, GB, Ducati
3 Troy Corser, Aus, Ducati
4 Akira Yanagawa, Jpn, Kawasaki
5 Pierfrancesco Chili, Ita, Suzuki
6 Noriyuki Haga, Jpn, Yamaha
7 John Reynolds, GB, Ducati
8 Doriano Romboni, Ita, Ducati
9 Steve Hislop, GB, Kawasaki
10 Niall Mackenzie, GB, Yamaha
11 Katsuaki Fujiwara, Jpn, Suzuki
12 Robert Ulm, Aut, Kawasaki
13 Martin Craggill, Aus, Suzuki
14 Alessandro Gramigni, Ita, Yamaha
15 Frederic Protat, Fra, Ducati

Standings – 1 Fogarty 135; 2 Corser 112;
3 Edwards 97; 4 Slight 82; 5 Yanagawa 66;
6 Haga 50

Round 4 – Spain
Albacete, 16 May
Race 1
1 Noriyuki Haga, Jpn, Yamaha
2 Akira Yanagawa, Jpn, Kawasaki
3 Carl Fogarty, GB, Ducati
4 Aaron Slight, NZ, Honda
5 Pierfrancesco Chili, Ita, Suzuki
6 Gregorio Lavilla, Spa, Kawasaki
7 Troy Corser, Aus, Ducati
8 Katsuaki Fujiwara, Jpn, Suzuki
9 Vitto Guareschi, Ita, Yamaha
10 Peter Goddard, Aus, Aprilia
11 Igor Jerman, Slo, Kawasaki
12 Andy Meklau, Aut, Ducati
13 Robert Ulm, Aut, Kawasaki
14 Alessandro Gramigni, Ita, Yamaha
15 Lucio Pedercini, Ita, Ducati

Race 2
1 Colin Edwards, USA, Honda
2 Akira Yanagawa, Jpn, Kawasaki
3 Carl Fogarty, GB, Ducati
4 Gregorio Lavilla, Spa, Kawasaki
5 Pierfrancesco Chili, Ita, Suzuki
6 Troy Corser, Aus, Ducati
7 Aaron Slight, NZ, Honda
8 Katsuaki Fujiwara, Jpn, Suzuki
9 Vitto Guareschi, Ita, Yamaha
10 Peter Goddard, Aus, Aprilia
11 Andy Meklau, Aut, Ducati
12 Igor Jerman, Slo, Kawasaki
13 Robert Ulm, Aut, Kawasaki
14 Alessandro Gramigni, Ita, Yamaha
15 Lucio Pedercini, Ita, Ducati

Standings – 1 Fogarty 167; 2 Corser 131;
3 Edwards 122; 4 Yanagawa 106; 5 Slight 104;
6 Haga 75

Round 5 – Italy
Monza, 30 May
Race 1
1 Carl Fogarty, GB, Ducati
2 Colin Edwards, USA, Honda
3 Pierfrancesco Chili, Ita, Suzuki
4 Troy Corser, Aus, Ducati
5 Aaron Slight, NZ, Honda
6 Noriyuki Haga, Jpn, Yamaha
7 Akira Yanagawa, Jpn, Kawasaki
8 Gregorio Lavilla, Spn, Kawasaki
9 Peter Goddard, Aus, Aprilia
10 Andy Meklau, Aut, Ducati
11 Vitto Guareschi, Ita, Yamaha
12 Igor Jerman, Slo, Kawasaki
13 Lucio Pedercini, Ita, Ducati
14 Robert Ulm, Aut, Kawasaki
15 Lance Isaacs, RSA, Ducati

Race 2
1 Carl Fogarty, GB, Ducati
2 Colin Edwards, USA, Honda
3 Pierfrancesco Chili, Ita, Suzuki
4 Troy Corser, Aus, Ducati
5 Akira Yanagawa, Jpn, Kawasaki
6 Noriyuki Haga, Jpn, Yamaha

7 Gregorio Lavilla, Spn, Kawasaki
8 Andy Meklau, Aut, Ducati
9 Katsuaki Fujiwara, Jpn, Suzuki
10 Vitto Guareschi, Ita, Yamaha
11 Peter Goddard, Aus, Aprilia
12 Alessandro Gramigni, Ita, Yamaha
13 Alessandro Antonello, Ita, Aprilia
14 Lance Isaacs, RSA, Ducati
15 Mauro Lucchiari, Ita, Yamaha

Standings – 1 Fogarty 217; 2 Edwards 162;
3 Corser 157; 4 Yanagawa 126; 5 Slight 115;
6 Haga 95

Round 6 – Germany
Nürburgring, 13 June
Race 1
1 Carl Fogarty, GB, Ducati
2 Aaron Slight, NZ, Honda
3 Troy Corser, Aus, Ducati
4 Gregorio Lavilla, Spn, Kawasaki
5 Peter Goddard, Aus, Aprilia
6 Katsuaki Fujiwara, Jpn, Suzuki
7 Vitto Guareschi, Ita, Yamaha
8 Andy Meklau, Aut, Ducati
9 Christer Lindholm, Swe, Yamaha
10 Jochen Schmid, Ger, Kawasaki
11 Lucio Pedercini, Ita, Ducati
12 Alessandro Gramigni, Ita, Yamaha
13 Giovanni Bussei, Ita, Suzuki
14 Jonnie Ekerold, RSA, Kawasaki
15 Frederic Protat, Fra, Ducati

Race 2
1 Troy Corser, Aus, Ducati
2 Aaron Slight, NZ, Honda
3 Akira Yanagawa, Jpn, Kawasaki
4 Colin Edwards, USA, Honda
5 Pierfrancesco Chili, Ita, Suzuki
6 Noriyuki Haga, Jpn, Yamaha
7 Katsuaki Fujiwara, Jpn, Suzuki
8 Peter Goddard, Aus, Aprilia
9 Vitto Guareschi, Ita, Yamaha
10 Andy Meklau, Aut, Ducati
11 Robert Ulm, Aut, Kawasaki
12 Igor Jerman, Slo, Kawasaki
13 Lucio Pedercini, Ita, Ducati
14 Christer Lindholm, Swe, Yamaha
15 Carl Fogarty, GB, Ducati

Standings – 1 Fogarty 243; 2 Corser 198;
3 Edwards 175; 4 Slight 155; 5 Yanagawa 142;
6 Haga 105

Round 7 – San Marino
Misano, 27 June
Race 1
1 Carl Fogarty, GB, Ducati
2 Troy Corser, Aus, Ducati
3 Akira Yanagawa, Jpn, Kawasaki
4 Pierfrancesco Chili, Ita, Suzuki
5 Aaron Slight, NZ, Honda
6 Colin Edwards, USA, Honda
7 Gregorio Lavilla, Spa, Kawasaki
8 Noriyuki Haga, Jpn, Yamaha
9 Vitto Guareschi, Ita, Yamaha
10 Peter Goddard, Aus, Aprilia
11 Lucio Pedercini, Ita, Ducati
12 Lance Isaacs, RSA, Ducati
13 Mauro Lucchiari, Ita, Yamaha
14 Katsuaki Fujiwara, Jpn, Suzuki
15 Igor Jerman, Slo, Kawasaki

Race 2
1 Carl Fogarty, GB, Ducati
2 Troy Corser, Aus, Ducati
3 Akira Yanagawa, Jpn, Kawasaki
4 Aaron Slight, NZ, Honda
5 Gregorio Lavilla, Spa, Kawasaki
6 Pierfrancesco Chili, Ita, Suzuki
7 Colin Edwards, USA, Honda
8 Vitto Guareschi, Ita, Yamaha
9 Katsuaki Fujiwara, Jpn, Suzuki
10 Robert Ulm, Aut, Kawasaki
11 Mauro Lucchiari, Ita, Yamaha
12 Igor Jerman, Slo, Kawasaki
13 Alessandro Gramigni, Ita, Yamaha
14 Lucio Pedercini, Ita, Ducati
15 Lance Isaacs, RSA, Ducati

Standings – 1 Fogarty 293; 2 Corser 238;
3 Edwards 194; 4 Slight 179; 5 Yanagawa 174;
6 Chili 119

Round 8 – USA
Laguna Seca, 11 July
Race 1
1 Anthony Gobert, Aus, Ducati
2 Ben Bostrom, USA, Ducati
3 Akira Yanagawa, Jpn, Kawasaki
4 Colin Edwards, USA, Honda
5 Carl Fogarty, GB, Ducati
6 Troy Corser, Aus, Ducati
7 Pierfrancesco Chili, Ita, Suzuki
8 Jamie Hacking, USA, Yamaha
9 Aaron Slight, NZ, Honda
10 Eric Bostrom, USA, Honda
11 Katsuaki Fujiwara, Jpn, Suzuki
12 Gregorio Lavilla, Spa, Kawasaki
13 Igor Jerman, Slo, Kawasaki
14 Lance Isaacs, RSA, Ducati
15 Alessandro Gramigni, Ita, Yamaha

Race 2
1 Ben Bostrom, USA, Ducati
2 Troy Corser, Aus, Ducati
3 Pierfrancesco Chili, Ita, Suzuki
4 Carl Fogarty, GB, Ducati
5 Colin Edwards, USA, Honda
6 Aaron Slight, NZ, Honda
7 Eric Bostrom, USA, Honda
8 Gregorio Lavilla, Spa, Kawasaki
9 Peter Goddard, Aus, Aprilia
10 Noriyuki Haga, Jpn, Yamaha
11 Katsuaki Fujiwara, Jpn, Suzuki
12 Akira Yanagawa, Jpn, Kawasaki
13 Jamie Hacking, USA, Yamaha
14 Frederic Protat, Fra, Ducati
15 Alessandro Gramigni, Ita, Yamaha

Standings – 1 Fogarty 317; 2 Corser 268;
3 Edwards 218; 4 Slight 196; 5 Yanagawa 194;
6 Chili 144

Round 9 – Europe
Brands Hatch, 1 August
Race 1
1 Colin Edwards, USA, Honda
2 Aaron Slight, NZ, Honda
3 Pierfrancesco Chili, Ita, Suzuki
4 John Reynolds, GB, Ducati
5 Troy Corser, Aus, Ducati
6 Akira Yanagawa, Jpn, Kawasaki
7 Noriyuki Haga, Jpn, Yamaha
8 Niall Mackenzie, GB, Yamaha
9 James Haydon, GB, Suzuki
10 Chris Walker, GB, Kawasaki
11 Andy Meklau, Aut, Ducati
12 Peter Goddard, Aus, Aprilia
13 Igor Jerman, Slo, Kawasaki
14 Katsuaki Fujiwara, Jpn, Suzuki
15 Vitto Guareschi, Ita, Yamaha

Race 2
1 Colin Edwards, USA, Honda
2 Aaron Slight, NZ, Honda
3 Noriyuki Haga, Jpn, Yamaha
4 Carl Fogarty, GB, Ducati
5 Akira Yanagawa, Jpn, Kawasaki
6 Sean Emmett, GB, Ducati
7 Niall Mackenzie, GB, Yamaha
8 John Reynolds, GB, Ducati
9 Peter Goddard, Aus, Aprilia
10 Gregorio Lavilla, Spa, Kawasaki
11 James Haydon, GB, Suzuki
12 Andy Meklau, Aut, Ducati
13 Troy Corser, Aus, Ducati
14 Vitto Guareschi, Ita, Yamaha
15 Katsuaki Fujiwara, Jpn, Suzuki

Standings – 1 Fogarty 330; 2 Corser 282;
3 Edwards 268; 4 Slight 236; 5 Yanagawa 215;
6 Chili 160

Round 10 – Austria
A1-Ring, 29 August
Race 1
1 Colin Edwards, USA, Honda
2 Carl Fogarty, GB, Ducati
3 Vitto Guareschi, Ita, Yamaha
4 Robert Ulm, Aut, Kawasaki
5 Gregorio Lavilla, Spa, Kawasaki
6 Brian Morrison, GB, Yamaha
7 Mauro Lucchiari, Ita, Yamaha
8 Alessandro Gramigni, Ita, Yamaha
9 Frederic Protat, Fra, Ducati
10 Lucio Pedercini, Ita, Ducati
11 Jiri Mrkyvka, CZ, Ducati
12 Anton Rechberger, Aut, Suzuki
13 Carlos Macias, Col, Ducati

Race 2
1 Pierfrancesco Chili, Ita, Suzuki
2 Troy Corser, Aus, Ducati
3 Aaron Slight, NZ, Honda
4 Carl Fogarty, GB, Ducati
5 Roger Kellenberger, Ger, Honda
6 Giovanni Bussei, Ita, Suzuki
7 Andy Meklau, Aut, Ducati
8 Colin Edwards, USA, Honda
9 Mauro Lucchiari, Ita, Yamaha
10 Brian Morrison, GB, Yamaha
11 Robert Ulm, Aut, Kawasaki
12 Igor Jerman, Slo, Kawasaki
13 Frederic Protat, Fra, Ducati
14 Vladimir Karban, Svk, Suzuki
15 Lance Isaacs, RSA, Ducati

Standings – 1 Fogarty 363; 2 Corser 302;
3 Edwards 301; 4 Slight 252; 5 Yanagawa 215;
6 Chili 185

Round 11 – Holland
Assen, 5 September
Race 1
1 Carl Fogarty, GB, Ducati
2 Troy Corser, Aus, Ducati
3 Aaron Slight, NZ, Honda
4 Pierfrancesco Chili, Ita, Suzuki
5 Colin Edwards, USA, Honda
6 Akira Yanagawa, Jpn, Kawasaki
7 Noriyuki Haga, Jpn, Yamaha
8 Andy Meklau, Aut, Ducati
9 Gregorio Lavilla, Spa, Kawasaki
10 Chris Walker, GB, Kawasaki
11 Igor Jerman, Slo, Kawasaki
12 Katsuaki Fujiwara, Jpn, Suzuki
13 Vitto Guareschi, Ita, Yamaha
14 Robert Ulm, Aut, Kawasaki
15 Alessandro Gramigni, Ita, Yamaha

Race 2
1 Carl Fogarty, GB, Ducati
2 Troy Corser, Aus, Ducati
3 Aaron Slight, NZ, Honda
4 Akira Yanagawa, Jpn, Kawasaki
5 Colin Edwards, USA, Honda
6 Pierfrancesco Chili, Ita, Suzuki
7 Gregorio Lavilla, Spa, Kawasaki
8 Noriyuki Haga, Jpn, Yamaha
9 Andy Meklau, Aut, Ducati
10 Chris Walker, GB, Kawasaki
11 Igor Jerman, Slo, Kawasaki
12 Katsuaki Fujiwara, Jpn, Suzuki
13 Michele Malatesta, Ita, Ducati
14 Alessandro Gramigni, Ita, Yamaha
15 Lucio Pedercini, Ita, Ducati

Standings – 1 Fogarty 413; 2 Corser 342;
3 Edwards 323; 4 Slight 284; 5 Yanagawa 238;
6 Chili 208

Round 12 – Germany
Hockenheim, 12 September
Race 1
1 Carl Fogarty, GB, Ducati
2 Aaron Slight, NZ, Honda
3 Akira Yanagawa, Jpn, Kawasaki
4 Colin Edwards, USA, Honda
5 Noriyuki Haga, Jpn, Yamaha
6 Gregorio Lavilla, Spa, Kawasaki
7 Katsuaki Fujiwara, Jpn, Suzuki
8 Peter Goddard, Aus, Aprilia
9 Igor Jerman, Slo, Kawasaki
10 Vitto Guareschi, Ita, Yamaha
11 Michele Malatesta, Ita, Ducati
12 Alessandro Gramigni, Ita, Yamaha
13 Robert Ulm, Aut, Kawasaki
14 Lucio Pedercini, Ita, Ducati
15 Frederic Protat, Fra, Ducati

Race 2
1 Pierfrancesco Chili, Ita, Suzuki
2 Carl Fogarty, GB, Ducati
3 Aaron Slight, NZ, Honda
4 Akira Yanagawa, Jpn, Kawasaki
5 Colin Edwards, USA, Honda
6 Andy Meklau, Aut, Ducati
7 Troy Corser, Aus, Ducati
8 Gregorio Lavilla, Spa, Kawasaki
9 Noriyuki Haga, Jpn, Yamaha
10 Katsuaki Fujiwara, Jpn, Suzuki
11 Michele Malatesta, Ita, Ducati
12 Vitto Guareschi, Ita, Yamaha
13 Jochen Schmid, Ger, Kawasaki
14 Alessandro Gramigni, Ita, Yamaha
15 Lance Isaacs, RSA, Ducati

Standings – 1 Fogarty 458; 2 Corser 351;
3 Edwards 347; 4 Slight 320; 5 Yanagawa 267;
6 Chili 233

Round 13 – Japan
Sugo, 10 October
Race 1
1 Akira Ryo, Jpn, Suzuki
2 Carl Fogarty, GB, Ducati
3 Akira Yanagawa, Jpn, Kawasaki
4 Keiichi Kitagawa, Jpn, Suzuki
5 Wataru Yoshikawa, Jpn, Yamaha
6 Tamaki Serizawa, Jpn, Kawasaki
7 Pierfrancesco Chili, Ita, Suzuki
8 Troy Corser, Aus, Ducati
9 Colin Edwards, USA, Honda
10 Makoto Tamada, Jpn, Honda
11 Shinichi Itoh, Jpn, Honda
12 Noriyuki Haga, Jpn, Yamaha
13 Takeshi Tsujimura, Jpn, Yamaha
14 Gregorio Lavilla, Spa, Kawasaki
15 Yuichi Takeda, Jpn, Honda

Race 2
1 Akira Yanagawa, Jpn, Kawasaki
2 Akira Ryo, Jpn, Suzuki
3 Keiichi Kitagawa, Jpn, Suzuki
4 Noriyuki Haga, Jpn, Yamaha
5 Carl Fogarty, GB, Ducati
6 Wataru Yoshikawa, Jpn, Yamaha
7 Pierfrancesco Chili, Ita, Suzuki
8 Tamaki Serizawa, Jpn, Kawasaki
9 Colin Edwards, USA, Honda
10 Makoto Tamada, Jpn, Honda
11 Shinya Takeishi, Jpn, Kawasaki
12 Takeshi Tsujimura, Jpn, Yamaha
13 Aaron Slight, NZ, Honda
14 Troy Corser, Aus, Ducati
15 Hitoyasu Izutsu, Jpn, Kawasaki

FINAL STANDINGS – 1 Fogarty 489;
2 Edwards 361; 3 Corser 361; 4 Slight 323;
5 Yanagawa 308; 6 Chili 251

2000 season

Round 1 – South Africa
Kyalami, 2 April
Race 1
1 Colin Edwards, USA, Honda
2 Noriyuki Haga, Jap, Yamaha
3 Carl Fogarty, GB, Ducati
4 Troy Corser, Aus, Aprilia
5 Pierfrancesco Chili, Ita, Suzuki
6 Gregorio Lavilla, Spn, Kawasaki
7 Haruchika Aoki, Jpn, Ducati
8 Katsuaki Fujiwara, Jpn, Suzuki
9 Ben Bostrom, USA, Ducati
10 Juan Borja, Spn, Ducati
11 Andy Meklau, Aut, Ducati
12 Giovanni Bussei, Ita, Kawasaki
13 Lance Isaacs, RSA, Ducati
14 Simon Crafar, NZ, Honda
15 Vitto Guareschi, Ita, Yamaha

Race 2
1 Colin Edwards, USA, Honda
2 Pierfrancesco Chili, Ita, Suzuki
3 Troy Corser, Aus, Aprilia
4 Haruchika Aoki, Jpn, Ducati
5 Gregorio Lavilla, Spa, Kawasaki
6 Juan Borja, Spn, Ducati
7 Ben Bostrom, USA, Ducati
8 Katsuaki Fujiwara, Jpn, Suzuki
9 Alessandro Antonello, Ita, Aprilia
10 Giovanni Bussei, Ita, Kawasaki
11 Anthony Gobert, Aus, Bimota
12 Andy Meklau, Aut, Ducati
13 Simon Crafar, NZ, Honda
14 Alessandro Gramigni, Ita, Yamaha
15 Mauro Sanchini, Ita, Ducati

Standings – 1 Edwards 50; 2 Chili 31;
3 Corser 29; 4 Aoki 22; 5 Lavilla 21;
6 Haga 20

Round 2 – Australia
Phillip Island, 23 April
Race 1
1 Anthony Gobert, Aus, Bimota
2 Carl Fogarty, GB, Ducati
3 Vitto Guareschi, Ita, Yamaha
4 Lucio Pedercini, Ita, Ducati
5 Colin Edwards, USA, Honda
6 Robert Ulm, Aut, Ducati
7 Gregorio Lavilla, Spa, Kawasaki
8 Giovanni Bussei, Ita, Kawasaki
9 Akira Yanagawa, Jpn, Kawasaki
10 Noriyuki Haga, Jpn, Yamaha
11 Alistair Maxwell, Aus, Kawasaki
12 Mauro Sanchini, Ita, Ducati
13 Katsuaki Fujiwara, Jpn, Suzuki
14 Lance Isaacs, RSA, Ducati
15 Ben Bostrom, USA, Ducati

Race 2
1 Troy Corser, Aus, Aprilia
2 Noriyuki Haga, Jpn, Yamaha
3 Pierfrancesco Chili, Ita, Suzuki
4 Gregorio Lavilla, Spn, Kawasaki
5 Colin Edwards, USA, Honda
6 Akira Yanagawa, Jpn, Kawasaki
7 Katsuaki Fujiwara, Jpn, Suzuki
8 Simon Crafar, NZ, Honda
9 Anthony Gobert, Aus, Bimota
10 Haruchika Aoki, Jpn, Ducati
11 Robert Ulm, Aut, Ducati
12 Mauro Sanchini, Ita, Ducati
13 Lucio Pedercini, Ita, Ducati
14 Ben Bostrom, USA, Ducati
15 Igor Antonelli, Ita, Kawasaki

Standings – 1 Edwards 72; 2 Corser 54;
3 Chili 47; 4 Haga 46; 5 Lavilla 43;
6 Gobert 37

Round 3 – Japan
Sugo, 30 April
Race 1
1 Hitoyasu Izutsu, Jpn, Kawasaki
2 Noriyuki Haga, Jpn, Yamaha
3 Pierfrancesco Chili, Ita, Suzuki
4 Akira Ryo, Jpn, Suzuki
5 Colin Edwards, USA, Honda
6 Keiichi Kitagawa, Jpn, Suzuki
7 Makoto Tamada, Jpn, Honda
8 Wataru Yoshikawa, Jpn, Yamaha
9 Troy Corser, Aus, Aprilia
10 Gregorio Lavilla, Spa, Kawasaki

11 Andy Meklau, Aut, Ducati
12 Robert Ulm, Aut, Ducati
13 Yuichi Takeda, Jpn, Honda
14 Juan Borja, Spa, Ducati
15 Giovanni Bussei, Ita, Kawasaki

Race 2
1 Hitoyasu Izutsu, Jpn, Kawasaki
2 Wataru Yoshikawa, Jpn, Yamaha
3 Colin Edwards, USA, Honda
4 Noriyuki Haga, Jpn, Yamaha
5 Troy Corser, Ita, Aprilia
6 Akira Yanagawa, Jpn, Kawasaki
7 Tamaki Serizawa, Jpn, Kawasaki
8 Keiichi Kitagawa, Jpn, Suzuki
9 Akira Ryo, Jpn, Suzuki
10 Gregorio Lavilla, Spa, Kawasaki
11 Juan Borja, Spa, Ducati
12 Andy Meklau, Aut, Ducati
13 Ben Bostrom, USA, Ducati
14 Robert Ulm, Aut, Ducati
15 Manabu Kamada, Jpn, Honda

Standings – 1 Edwards 99; 2 Haga 79;
3 Corser 72; 4 Chili 63; 5 Lavilla 55;
6 Izutsu 50

Round 4 – Great Britain
Donington Park, 14 May
Race 1
1 Colin Edwards, USA, Honda
2 Pierfrancesco Chili, Ita, Suzuki
3 Neil Hodgson, GB, Ducati
4 Noriyuki Haga, Jpn, Yamaha
5 Chris Walker, GB, Suzuki
6 James Haydon, GB, Ducati
7 Akira Yanagawa, Jpn, Kawasaki
8 Troy Corser, Aus, Aprilia
9 Aaron Slight, NZ, Honda
10 John Reynolds, GB, Ducati
11 Gregorio Lavilla, Spn, Kawasaki
12 Steve Hislop, GB, Yamaha
13 Robert Ulm, Aut, Ducati
14 Andy Meklau, Aut, Ducati
15 Ben Bostrom, USA, Ducati

Race 2
1 Neil Hodgson, GB, Ducati
2 Chris Walker, GB, Suzuki
3 Pierfrancesco Chili, Ita, Suzuki
4 Noriyuki Haga, Jpn, Yamaha
5 Akira Yanagawa, Jpn, Kawasaki
6 James Haydon, GB, Ducati
7 Aaron Slight, NZ, Honda
8 Ben Bostrom, USA, Ducati
9 Andy Meklau, Aut, Ducati
10 Haruchika Aoki, Jpn, Ducati
11 Alessandro Antonello, Ita, Aprilia
12 John Crawford, GB, Ducati
13 Katsuaki Fujiwara, Jpn, Suzuki
14 Vitto Guareschi, Ita, Yamaha
15 Alessandro Gramigni, Ita, Yamaha

Standings – 1 Edwards 124; 2 Haga 105;
3 Chili 99; 4 Corser 80; 5 Lavilla 60;
6 Izutsu 50

Round 5 – Italy
Monza, 21 May
Race 1
1 Pierfrancesco Chili, Ita, Suzuki
2 Colin Edwards, USA, Honda
3 Akira Yanagawa, Jpn, Kawasaki
4 Troy Bayliss, Aus, Ducati
5 Aaron Slight, NZ, Honda
6 Gregorio Lavilla, Spn, Kawasaki
7 Ben Bostrom, USA, Ducati
8 Troy Corser, Aus, Aprilia
9 Alessandro Antonello, Ita, Aprilia
10 Robert Ulm, Aut, Ducati
11 Katsuaki Fujiwara, Jpn, Suzuki
12 Vitto Guareschi, Ita, Yamaha
13 Mauro Sanchini, Ita, Ducati
14 Giovanni Bussei, Ita, Kawasaki
15 Markus Barth, Ger, Yamaha

Race 2
1 Colin Edwards, USA, Honda
2 Pierfrancesco Chili, Ita, Suzuki
3 Akira Yanagawa, Jpn, Kawasaki
4 Troy Bayliss, Aus, Ducati
5 Noriyuki Haga, Jpn, Yamaha
6 Troy Corser, Aus, Aprilia

7 Aaron Slight, NZ, Honda
8 Andy Meklau, Aut, Ducati
9 Katsuaki Fujiwara, Jpn, Suzuki
10 Ben Bostrom, USA, Ducati
11 Alessandro Antonello, Ita, Aprilia
12 Markus Barth, Ger, Yamaha
13 Jurgen Oelschlaeger, Ger, Yamaha
14 Lance Isaacs, RSA, Ducati
15 Paolo Blora, Ita, Ducati

Standings – 1 Edwards 169; 2 Chili 144;
3 Haga 116; 4 Corser 98; 5 Yanagawa 79;
6 Lavilla 70

Round 6 – Germany
Hockenheim, 4 June
Race 1
1 Troy Bayliss, Aus, Ducati
2 Akira Yanagawa, Jpn, Kawasaki
3 Noriyuki Haga, Jpn, Yamaha
4 Colin Edwards, USA, Honda
5 Aaron Slight, NZ, Honda
6 Andy Meklau, Aut, Ducati
7 Troy Corser, Aus, Aprilia
8 Robert Ulm, Aut, Ducati
9 Alessandro Antonello, Ita, Aprilia
10 Ben Bostrom, USA, Ducati
11 Simon Crafar, NZ, Kawasaki
12 James Haydon, GB, Ducati
13 Juan Borja, Spn, Ducati
14 Steve Plater, GB, Kawasaki
15 Markus Barth, Ger, Yamaha

Race 2
1 Noriyuki Haga, Jpn, Yamaha
2 Colin Edwards, USA, Honda
3 Pierfrancesco Chili, Ita, Suzuki
4 Troy Bayliss, Aus, Ducati
5 Aaron Slight, NZ, Honda
6 Troy Corser, Aus, Aprilia
7 Alessandro Antonello, Ita, Aprilia
8 Andy Meklau, Aut, Ducati
9 Robert Ulm, Aut, Ducati
10 Katsuaki Fujiwara, Jpn, Suzuki
11 Ben Bostrom, USA, Ducati
12 Juan Borja, Spn, Ducati
13 Vitto Guareschi, Ita, Yamaha
14 Simon Crafar, NZ, Kawasaki
15 Markus Barth, Ger, Yamaha

Standings – 1 Edwards 202; 2 Chili 160;
3 Haga 157; 4 Corser 117; 5 Yanagawa 99;
6 Lavilla 70

Round 7 – San Marino
Misano, 18 June
Race 1
1 Troy Corser, Aus, Aprilia
2 Troy Bayliss, Aus, Ducati
3 Katsuaki Fujiwara, Jpn, Suzuki
4 Juan Borja, Spn, Ducati
5 Akira Yanagawa, Jpn, Kawasaki
6 Ben Bostrom, USA, Ducati
7 Noriyuki Haga, Jpn, Yamaha
8 Peter Goddard, Aus, Aprilia
9 Haruchika Aoki, Jpn, Ducati
10 Alessandro Antonello, Ita, Aprilia
11 Andy Meklau, Aut, Ducati
12 Alessandro Gramigni, Ita, Yamaha
13 Lucio Pedercini, Ita, Ducati
14 Frederic Protat, Fra, Ducati
15 Lance Isaacs, RSA, Ducati

Race 2
1 Troy Corser, Aus, Aprilia
2 Troy Bayliss, Aus, Ducati
3 Ben Bostrom, USA, Ducati
4 Katsuaki Fujiwara, Jpn, Suzuki
5 Juan Borja, Spa, Ducati
6 Akira Yanagawa, Jpn, Kawasaki
7 Alessandro Antonello, Ita, Aprilia
8 Peter Goddard, Aus, Kawasaki
9 Aaron Slight, NZ, Honda
10 Colin Edwards, USA, Honda
11 Haruchika Aoki, Jpn, Ducati
12 Giovanni Bussei, Ita, Kawasaki
13 Andy Meklau, Aut, Ducati
14 Lucio Pedercini, Ita, Ducati
15 Alessandro Gramigni, Ita, Yamaha

Standings – 1 Edwards 208; 2 Corser 167;
3 Haga 166; 4 Chili 160; 5 Yanagawa 120;
6 Bayliss 104

Round 8 – Spain
Valencia, 25 June
Race 1
1. Troy Corser, Aus, Aprilia
2. Ben Bostrom, USA, Ducati
3. Noriyuki Haga, Jpn, Yamaha
4. Troy Bayliss, Aus, Ducati
5. Colin Edwards, USA, Honda
6. Peter Goddard, Aus, Kawasaki
7. Aaron Slight, NZ, Honda
8. Katsuaki Fujiwara, Jpn, Suzuki
9. Alessandro Antonello, Ita, Aprilia
10. Akira Yanagawa, Jpn, Kawasaki
11. Andy Meklau, Aut, Ducati
12. Vitto Guareschi, Ita, Yamaha
13. Mauro Sanchini, Ita, Ducati
14. Paolo Blora, Ita, Ducati
15. Markus Barth, Ger, Yamaha

Race 2
1. Noriyuki Haga, Jpn, Yamaha
2. Ben Bostrom, USA, Ducati
3. Troy Bayliss, Aus, Ducati
4. Colin Edwards, USA, Honda
5. Troy Corser, Aus, Aprilia
6. Peter Goddard, Aus, Kawasaki
7. Aaron Slight, NZ, Honda
8. Juan Borja, Spa, Ducati
9. Pierfrancesco Chili, Ita, Suzuki
10. Katsuaki Fujiwara, Jpn, Suzuki
11. Haruchika Aoki, Jpn, Ducati
12. Akira Yanagawa, Jpn, Kawasaki
13. Vitto Guareschi, Ita, Yamaha
14. Alessandro Gramigni, Ita, Yamaha
15. Mauro Sanchini, Ita, Ducati

Standings – 1 Edwards 232; 2 Haga 207;
3 Corser 203; 4 Chili 167; 5 Bayliss 133;
6 Yanagawa 130

Round 9 – USA
Laguna Seca, 9 July
Race 1
1. Noriyuki Haga, Jpn, Yamaha
2. Colin Edwards, USA, Honda
3. Troy Corser, Aus, Aprilia
4. Ben Bostrom, USA, Ducati
5. Pierfrancesco Chili, Ita, Suzuki
6. Akira Yanagawa, Jpn, Kawasaki
7. Katsuaki Fujiwara, Jpn, Suzuki
8. Aaron Slight, NZ, Honda
9. Juan Borja, Spa, Ducati
10. Giovanni Bussei, Ita, Kawasaki
11. Haruchika Aoki, Jpn, Ducati
12. Andy Meklau, Aut, Ducati
13. Lucio Pedercini, Ita, Ducati
14. Mauro Sanchini, Ita, Ducati
15. Igor Jerman, Slo, Kawasaki

Race 2
1. Troy Corser, Aus, Aprilia
2. Noriyuki Haga, Jpn, Yamaha
3. Ben Bostrom, USA, Ducati
4. Colin Edwards, USA, Honda
5. Akira Yanagawa, Jpn, Kawasaki
6. Pierfrancesco Chili, Ita, Suzuki
7. Troy Bayliss, Aus, Ducati
8. Katsuaki Fujiwara, Jpn, Suzuki
9. Aaron Slight, NZ, Honda
10. Peter Goddard, Aus, Kawasaki
11. Giovanni Bussei, Ita, Kawasaki
12. Lance Isaacs, RSA, Ducati
13. Larry Pegram, USA, Ducati
14. Robert Ulm, Aut, Ducati
15. Lucio Pedercini, Ita, Ducati

Standings – 1 Edwards 265; 2 Haga 252;
3 Corser 244; 4 Chili 188; 5 Bostrom 152;
6 Yanagawa 151

Round 10 – Europe 1
Brands Hatch, 6 August
Race 1
1. Troy Bayliss, Aus, Ducati
2. Neil Hodgson, GB, Ducati
3. Chris Walker, GB, Suzuki
4. John Reynolds, GB, Ducati
5. Noriyuki Haga, Jpn, Yamaha
6. Troy Corser, Aus, Aprilia
7. Aaron Slight, NZ, Honda
8. Pierfrancesco Chili, Ita, Suzuki
9. Akira Yanagawa, Jpn, Kawasaki
10. Colin Edwards, USA, Honda

11. Juan Borja, Spa, Ducati
12. Gregorio Lavilla, Spa, Kawasaki
13. Andy Meklau, Aut, Ducati
14. Alessandro Antonello, Ita, Aprilia
15. Ben Bostrom, USA, Ducati

Race 2
1. Neil Hodgson, GB, Ducati
2. Troy Bayliss, Aus, Ducati
3. Pierfrancesco Chili, Ita, Suzuki
4. Noriyuki Haga, Jpn, Yamaha
5. Akira Yanagawa, Jpn, Kawasaki
6. Colin Edwards, USA, Honda
7. Chris Walker, GB, Suzuki
8. Gregorio Lavilla, Spn, Kawasaki
9. Andy Meklau, Aut, Ducati
10. Katsuaki Fujiwara, Jpn, Suzuki
11. Alessandro Gramigni, Ita, Yamaha
12. Vitto Guareschi, Ita, Yamaha
13. Markus Barth, Ger, Yamaha
14. Marco Borciani, Ita, Ducati
15. Lance Isaacs, RSA, Ducati

Standings – 1 Edwards 281; 2 Haga 276;
3 Corser 254; 4 Chili 212; 5 Bayliss 187;
6 Yanagawa 169

Round 11 – Holland
Assen, 3 September
Race 1
1. Colin Edwards, USA, Honda
2. Juan Borja, Spn, Ducati
3. Noriyuki Haga, Jpn, Yamaha
4. Troy Corser, Aus, Aprilia
5. Aaron Slight, NZ, Honda
6. Akira Yanagawa, Jpn, Kawasaki
7. Doriano Romboni, Ita, Ducati
8. Giovanni Bussei, Ita, Kawasaki
9. Jurgen Oelschlaeger, Ger, Yamaha
10. Katsuaki Fujiwara, Jpn, Suzuki
11. Lucio Pedercini, Ita, Ducati
12. Robert Ulm, Aut, Ducati
13. Igor Jerman, Slo, Kawasaki
14. Alessandro Gramigni, Ita, Yamaha
15. Vitto Guareschi, Ita, Yamaha

Race 2
1. Noriyuki Haga, Jpn, Yamaha
2. Akira Yanagawa, Jpn, Kawasaki
3. Juan Borja, Spn, Ducati
4. Aaron Slight, NZ, Honda
5. Colin Edwards, USA, Honda
6. Alessandro Gramigni, Ita, Yamaha
7. Troy Corser, Aus, Aprilia
8. Katsuaki Fujiwara, Jpn, Suzuki
9. Andy Meklau, Aut, Ducati
10. Robert Ulm, Aut, Ducati
11. Doriano Romboni, Ita, Ducati
12. Jurgen Oelschlaeger, Ger, Yamaha
13. Lucio Pedercini, Ita, Ducati
14. Lance Isaacs, RSA, Ducati
15. Gerald Muteau, Fra, Honda

Standings – 1 Edwards & Haga 317;
3 Corser 276; 4 Chili 212; 5 Yanagawa 199;
6 Bayliss 187

Round 12 – Germany
Oschersleben, 10 September
Race 1
1. Colin Edwards, USA, Honda
2. Gregorio Lavilla, Spn, Kawasaki
3. Troy Bayliss, Aus, Ducati
4. Akira Yanagawa, Jpn, Kawasaki
5. Aaron Slight, NZ, Honda
6. Pierfrancesco Chili, Ita, Suzuki
7. Troy Corser, Aus, Aprilia
8. Alessandro Antonello, Ita, Aprilia
9. Noriyuki Haga, Jpn, Yamaha
10. Ben Bostrom, USA, Ducati
11. Alessandro Gramigni, Ita, Yamaha
12. Wataru Yoshikawa, Jpn, Yamaha
13. Robert Ulm, Aut, Ducati
14. Katsuaki Fujiwara, Jpn, Suzuki
15. Markus Barth, Ger, Yamaha

Race 2
1. Colin Edwards, USA, Honda
2. Troy Bayliss, Aus, Ducati
3. Akira Yanagawa, Jpn, Kawasaki
4. Gregorio Lavilla, Spn, Kawasaki
5. Noriyuki Haga, Jpn, Yamaha
6. Pierfrancesco Chili, Ita, Suzuki

7. Ben Bostrom, USA, Ducati
8. Katsuaki Fujiwara, Jpn, Suzuki
9. Wataru Yoshikawa, Jpn, Yamaha
10. Robert Ulm, Aut, Ducati
11. Alessandro Gramigni, Ita, Yamaha
12. Andy Meklau, Aut, Ducati
13. Markus Barth, Ger, Yamaha
14. Lance Isaacs, RSA, Ducati
15. Marco Borciani, Ita, Ducati

Standings – 1 Edwards 367; 2 Haga 335;
3 Corser 285; 4 Chili 232; 5 Yanagawa 228;
6 Bayliss 223

Round 13 – Europe 2
Brands Hatch, 15 October
Race 1
1. John Reynolds, GB, Ducati
2. Troy Bayliss, Aus, Ducati
3. Chris Walker, GB, Suzuki
4. Neil Hodgson, GB, Ducati
5. Juan Borja, Spa, Ducati
6. Akira Yanagawa, Jpn, Kawasaki
7. Troy Corser, Aus, Aprilia
8. Colin Edwards, USA, Honda
9. Gregorio Lavilla, Spn, Kawasaki
10. Pierfrancesco Chili, Ita, Suzuki
11. Katsuaki Fujiwara, Jpn, Suzuki
12. Vitto Guareschi, Ita, Yamaha
13. Aaron Slight, NZ, Honda
14. Steve Plater, GB, Kawasaki
15. Markus Barth, Ger, Yamaha

Race 2
1. Colin Edwards, USA, Honda
2. Pierfrancesco Chili, Ita, Suzuki
3. Troy Corser, Aus, Aprilia
4. John Reynolds, GB, Ducati
5. Gregorio Lavilla, Spn, Kawasaki
6. Chris Walker, GB, Suzuki
7. Akira Yanagawa, Jpn, Kawasaki
8. Aaron Slight, NZ, Honda
9. Katsuaki Fujiwara, Jpn, Suzuki
10. Ben Bostrom, USA, Ducati
11. Alessandro Gramigni, Ita, Yamaha
12. Vitto Guareschi, Ita, Yamaha
13. Steve Plater, GB, Kawasaki
14. Juan Borja, Spa, Ducati
15. Robert Ulm, Aut, Ducati

FINAL STANDINGS – 1 Edwards 400;
2 Haga 335; 3 Corser 310; 4 Chili 258;
5 Yanagawa 247; 6 Bayliss 243

2001 season

Round 1 – Spain
Valencia, 11 March
Race 1
1. Troy Corser, Aus, Aprilia
2. Troy Bayliss, Aus, Ducati
3. Ben Bostrom, USA, Ducati
4. Regis Laconi, Fra, Aprilia
5. Gregorio Lavilla, Spa, Kawasaki
6. Colin Edwards, USA, Honda
7. Pierfrancesco Chili, Ita, Suzuki
8. Akira Yanagawa, Jap, Kawasaki
9. Hitoyasu Izutsu, Jap, Kawasaki
10. Stephane Chambon, Fra, Suzuki
11. Steve Martin, Aus, Ducati
12. Lucio Pedercini, Ita, Ducati
13. Marco Borciani, Ita, Ducati
14. Juan Borja, Spa, Ducati
15. Javier Rodriguez, Spa, Honda

Race 2
1. Troy Corser, Aus, Aprilia
2. Troy Bayliss, Aus, Ducati
3. Gregorio Lavilla, Spa, Kawasaki
4. Colin Edwards, USA, Honda
5. Neil Hodgson, GB, Ducati
6. Akira Yanagawa, Jap, Kawasaki
7. Pierfrancesco Chili, Ita, Suzuki
8. Ruben Xaus, Spa, Ducati
9. James Toseland, GB, Ducati
10. Stephane Chambon, Fra, Suzuki
11. Marco Borciani, Ita, Ducati
12. Robert Ulm, Aut, Ducati
13. Broc Parkes, Aus, Ducati
14. Juan Borja, Spa, Ducati
15. Lucio Pedercini, Ita, Ducati

Standings – 1 Corser 50; 2 Bayliss 40;
3 Lavilla 27; 4 Edwards 23;
5 Chili & Yanagawa 18

Round 2 – South Africa
Kyalami, 1 April
Race 1
1. Colin Edwards, USA, Honda
2. Troy Bayliss, Aus, Ducati
3. Troy Corser, Aus, Aprilia
4. Ben Bostrom, USA, Ducati
5. Akira Yanagawa, Jap, Kawasaki
6. Pierfrancesco Chili, Ita, Suzuki
7. Gregorio Lavilla, Spa, Kawasaki
8. Regis Laconi, Fra, Aprilia
9. Ruben Xaus, Spa, Ducati
10. Stephane Chambon, Fra, Suzuki
11. Giovanni Bussei, Ita, Ducati
12. Broc Parkes, Aus, Ducati
13. Robert Ulm, Aut, Ducati
14. James Toseland, GB, Ducati
15. Marco Borciani, Ita, Ducati

Race 2
1. Ben Bostrom, USA, Ducati
2. Troy Bayliss, Aus, Ducati
3. Troy Corser, Aus, Aprilia
4. Neil Hodgson, GB, Ducati
5. Ruben Xaus, Spa, Ducati
6. Regis Laconi, Fra, Aprilia
7. Gregorio Lavilla, Spa, Kawasaki
8. Pierfrancesco Chili, Ita, Suzuki
9. Giovanni Bussei, Ita, Ducati
10. Stephane Chambon, Fra, Suzuki
11. Broc Parkes, Aus, Ducati
12. Robert Ulm, Aut, Ducati
13. Michele Malatesta, Ita, Kawasaki
14. Lucio Pedercini, Ita, Ducati
15. Bertrand Stey, Fra, Honda

Standings – 1 Corser 82; 2 Bayliss 80;
3 Bostrom 54; 4 Edwards 48; 5 Lavilla 45;
6 Chili 36

Round 3 – Australia
Phillip Island, 22 April
Race 1
1. Colin Edwards, USA, Honda
2. Tadayuki Okada, Jap, Honda
3. Troy Bayliss, Aus, Ducati
4. Akira Yanagawa, Jap, Kawasaki
5. Broc Parkes, Aus, Ducati
6. Troy Corser, Aus, Aprilia
7. Pierfrancesco Chili, Ita, Suzuki
8. Stephane Chambon, Fra, Suzuki
9. Robert Ulm, Aut, Ducati
10. Martin Craggill, Aus, Ducati

11. Neil Hodgson, GB, Ducati
12. Steve Martin, Aus, Ducati
13. Alistair Maxwell, Aus, Kawasaki
14. James Toseland, GB, Ducati
15. Jiri Mrkvka, CZ, Ducati

Race 2

Cancelled due to bad weather

Standings – 1 Bayliss 96; 2 Corser 92;
3 Edwards 73; 4 Bostrom 54;
5 Chili & Lavilla 45

Round 4 – Japan
Sugo, 29 April
Race 1
1. Makoto Tamada, Jap, Honda
2. Troy Corser, Aus, Aprilia
3. Hitoyasu Izutsu, Jap, Kawasaki
4. Shinichi Itoh, Jap, Honda
5. Akira Ryo, Jap, Suzuki
6. Gregorio Lavilla, Spa, Kawasaki
7. Neil Hodgson, GB, Ducati
8. Pierfrancesco Chili, Ita, Suzuki
9. Ben Bostrom, USA, Ducati
10. Wataru Yoshikawa, Jap, Yamaha
11. James Toseland, GB, Ducati
12. Colin Edwards, USA, Honda
13. Troy Bayliss, Aus, Ducati
14. Regis Laconi, Fra, Aprilia
15. Stephane Chambon, Fra, Suzuki

Race 2
1. Makato Tamada, Jap, Honda
2. Hitoyasu Izutsu, Jap, Kawasaki
3. Tamaki Serizawa, Jap, Kawasaki
4. Ben Bostrom, USA, Ducati
5. Neil Hodgson, GB, Ducati
6. Troy Corser, Aus, Aprilia
7. Akira Ryo, Jap, Suzuki
8. Pierfrancesco Chili, Ita, Suzuki
9. Shinichi Itoh, Jap, Honda
10. Yukio Kagayama, Jap, Suzuki
11. Akira Yanagawa, Jap, Kawasaki
12. Tadayuki Okada, Jap, Honda
13. Colin Edwards, USA, Honda
14. Regis Laconi, Fra, Aprilia
15. Troy Bayliss, Aus, Ducati

Standings – 1 Corser 122; 2 Bayliss 100;
3 Edwards 80; 4 Bostrom 74; 5 Chili 61;
6 Lavilla 55

Round 5 – Italy
Monza, 13 May
Race 1
1. Troy Bayliss, Aus, Ducati
2. Colin Edwards, USA, Honda
3. Akira Yanagawa, Jap, Kawasaki
4. Gregorio Lavilla, Spa, Kawasaki
5. Regis Laconi, Fra, Aprilia
6. Stephane Chambon, Fra, Suzuki
7. Lucio Pedercini, Ita, Ducati
8. Giovanni Bussei, Ita, Ducati
9. Mauro Sanchini, Ita, Ducati
10. Marco Borciani, Ita, Ducati
11. Bertrand Stey, Fra, Honda
12. Alessandro Gramigni, Ita, Yamaha
13. Juan Borja, Spa, Ducati
14. Pierfrancesco Chili, Ita, Suzuki
15. Ludovic Holon, Fra, Kawasaki

Race 2
1. Troy Bayliss, Aus, Ducati
2. Colin Edwards, USA, Honda
3. Akira Yanagawa, Jap, Kawasaki
4. Tadayuki Okada, Jap, Honda
5. Pierfrancesco Chili, Ita, Suzuki
6. Ruben Xaus, Spa, Ducati
7. Neil Hodgson, GB, Ducati
8. Regis Laconi, Fra, Aprilia
9. Stephane Chambon, Fra, Suzuki
10. Alessandro Gramigni, Ita, Yamaha
11. Giovanni Bussei, Ita, Ducati
12. Robert Ulm, Aut, Ducati
13. Lucio Pedercini, Ita, Ducati
14. Steve Martin, Aus, Ducati
15. Mauro Sanchini, Ita, Ducati

Standings – 1 Bayliss 150; 2 Corser 122;
3 Edwards 120; 4 Yanagawa 79;
5 Bostrom & Chili 74

Round 6 – Great Britain
Donington Park, 27 May
Race 1
1. Neil Hodgson, GB, Ducati
2. Pierfrancesco Chili, Ita, Suzuki
3. Steve Hislop, GB, Ducati
4. Tadayuki Okada, Jap, Honda
5. Colin Edwards, USA, Honda
6. Ben Bostrom, USA, Ducati
7. Ruben Xaus, Spa, Ducati
8. James Toseland, GB, Ducati
9. Stephane Chambon, Fra, Suzuki
10. Gregorio Lavilla, Spa, Kawasaki
11. Troy Corser, Aus, Aprilia
12. Regis Laconi, Fra, Aprilia
13. Troy Bayliss, Aus, Ducati
14. Akira Yanagawa, Jap, Kawasaki
15. Martin Craggill, Aus, Ducati

Race 2
1. Pierfrancesco Chili, Ita, Suzuki
2. Neil Hodgson, GB, Ducati
3. Troy Corser, Aus, Aprilia
4. Ben Bostrom, USA, Ducati
5. John Reynolds, GB, Ducati
6. Colin Edwards, USA, Honda
7. Tadayuki Okada, Jap, Honda
8. Akira Yanagawa, Jap, Kawasaki
9. Troy Bayliss, Aus, Ducati
10. Ruben Xaus, Spa, Ducati
11. Regis Laconi, Fra, Aprilia
12. Stephane Chambon, Fra, Suzuki
13. Gregorio Lavilla, Spa, Kawasaki
14. Broc Parkes, Aus, Ducati
15. Giovanni Bussei, Ita, Ducati

Standings – 1 Bayliss 160; 2 Corser 143;
3 Edwards 141; 4 Chili 119; 5 Hodgson 103;
6 Bostrom 97

Round 7 – Germany
Lausitzring, 10 June
Race 1
1. Colin Edwards, USA, Honda
2. Troy Bayliss, Aus, Ducati
3. Tadayuki Okada, Jap, Honda
4. Pierfrancesco Chili, Ita, Suzuki
5. Troy Corser, Aus, Aprilia
6. Gregorio Lavilla, Spa, Kawasaki
7. Regis Laconi, Fra, Aprilia
8. Neil Hodgson, GB, Ducati
9. Hitoyasu Izutsu, Jap, Kawasaki
10. Stephane Chambon, Fra, Suzuki
11. Ben Bostrom, USA, Ducati
12. Akira Yanagawa, Jap, Kawasaki
13. Martin Craggill, Aus, Ducati
14. Broc Parkes, Aus, Ducati
15. Steve Martin, Aus, Ducati

Race 2
1. Troy Bayliss, Aus, Ducati
2. Neil Hodgson, GB, Ducati
3. Colin Edwards, USA, Honda
4. Hitoyasu Izutsu, Jap, Kawasaki
5. Pierfrancesco Chili, Ita, Suzuki
6. Ruben Xaus, Spa, Ducati
7. Troy Corser, Aus, Aprilia
8. Stephane Chambon, Fra, Suzuki
9. Tadayuki Okada, Jap, Honda
10. Akira Yanagawa, Jap, Kawasaki
11. Robert Ulm, Aut, Ducati
12. Mauro Sanchini, Ita, Ducati
13. Regis Laconi, Fra, Aprilia
14. Steve Martin, Aus, Ducati
15. Bertrand Stey, Fra, Honda

Standings – 1 Bayliss 205; 2 Edwards 182;
3 Corser 163; 4 Chili 143; 5 Hodgson 131;
6 Bostrom 102

Round 8 – San Marino
Misano, 24 June
Race 1
1. Troy Bayliss, Aus, Ducati
2. Ben Bostrom, USA, Ducati
3. Colin Edwards, USA, Honda
4. Gregorio Lavilla, Spa, Kawasaki
5. Akira Yanagawa, Jap, Kawasaki
6. Neil Hodgson, GB, Ducati
7. Troy Corser, Aus, Aprilia
8. Alessandro Antonello, Ita, Aprilia
9. Tadayuki Okada, Jap, Honda
10. Ruben Xaus, Spa, Ducati

11 James Toseland, GB, Ducati
12 Pierfrancesco Chili, Ita, Suzuki
13 Steve Martin, Aus, Ducati
14 Stephane Chambon, Fra, Suzuki
15 Alessandro Gramigni, Ita, Yamaha

Race 2
1 Ben Bostrom, USA, Ducati
2 Troy Bayliss, Aus, Ducati
3 Gregorio Lavilla, Spa, Kawasaki
4 Alessandro Antonello, Ita, Aprilia
5 Tadayuki Okada, Jap, Honda
6 Ruben Xaus, Spa, Ducati
7 Broc Parkes, Aus, Ducati
8 James Toseland, GB, Ducati
9 Troy Corser, Aus, Aprilia
10 Pierfrancesco Chili, Ita, Suzuki
11 Colin Edwards, USA, Honda
12 Alessandro Gramigni, Ita, Yamaha
13 Stephane Chambon, Fra, Suzuki
14 Giovanni Bussei, Ita, Ducati
15 Mauro Sanchini, Ita, Ducati

Standings – 1 Bayliss 250; 2 Edwards 203;
3 Corser 179; 4 Chili 153; 5 Bostrom 147;
6 Hodgson 141

Round 9 – USA
Laguna Seca, 8 July
Race 1
1 Ben Bostrom, USA, Ducati
2 Neil Hodgson, GB, Ducati
3 Troy Corser, Aus, Aprilia
4 Troy Bayliss, Aus, Ducati
5 Eric Bostrom, USA, Kawasaki
6 Colin Edwards, USA, Honda
7 Ruben Xaus, Spa, Ducati
8 Tadayuki Okada, Jap, Honda
9 Doug Chandler, USA, Kawasaki
10 James Toseland, GB, Ducati
11 Regis Laconi, Fra, Aprilia
12 Gregorio Lavilla, Spa, Kawasaki
13 Broc Parkes, Aus, Ducati
14 Steve Martin, Aus, Ducati
15 Giovanni Bussei, Ita, Ducati

Race 2
1 Ben Bostrom, USA, Ducati
2 Troy Corser, Aus, Aprilia
3 Neil Hodgson, GB, Ducati
4 Troy Bayliss, Aus, Ducati
5 Eric Bostrom, USA, Kawasaki
6 Colin Edwards, USA, Honda
7 James Toseland, GB, Ducati
8 Akira Yanagawa, Jap, Kawasaki
9 Regis Laconi, Fra, Aprilia
10 Ruben Xaus, Spa, Ducati
11 Tadayuki Okada, Jap, Honda
12 Stephane Chambon, Fra, Suzuki
13 Steve Martin, Aus, Ducati
14 Broc Parkes, Aus, Ducati
15 Peter Goddard, Aus, Benelli

Standings – 1 Bayliss 276; 2 Edwards 223;
3 Corser 215; 4 Bostrom 197; 5 Hodgson 177;
6 Chili 153

Round 10 – Europe
Brands Hatch, 29 July
Race 1
1 Ben Bostrom, USA, Ducati
2 Neil Hodgson, GB, Ducati
3 Colin Edwards, USA, Honda
4 Pierfrancesco Chili, Ita, Suzuki
5 Troy Bayliss, Aus, Ducati
6 Ruben Xaus, Spa, Ducati
7 Stephane Chambon, Fra, Suzuki
8 Troy Corser, Aus, Aprilia
9 Sean Emmett, GB, Ducati
10 Akira Yanagawa, Jap, Kawasaki
11 James Toseland, GB, Ducati
12 Tadayuki Okada, Jap, Honda
13 Peter Goddard, Aus, Benelli
14 Steve Martin, Aus, Ducati
15 Marco Borciani, Ita, Ducati

Race 2
1 Ben Bostrom, USA, Ducati
2 Neil Hodgson, GB, Ducati
3 Troy Bayliss, Aus, Ducati
4 Pierfrancesco Chili, Ita, Suzuki
5 Colin Edwards, USA, Honda
6 James Toseland, GB, Ducati

7 John Reynolds, GB, Ducati
8 Akira Yanagawa, Jap, Kawasaki
9 Stephane Chambon, Fra, Suzuki
10 Sean Emmett, GB, Ducati
11 Regis Laconi, Fra Aprilia
12 Ruben Xaus, Spa, Ducati
13 Troy Corser, Aus, Aprilia
14 Gregorio Lavilla, Spa, Kawasaki
15 Tadayuki Okada, GB, Honda

Standings – 1 Bayliss 303; 2 Edwards 250;
3 Bostrom 247; 4 Corser 226; 5 Hodgson 217;
6 Chili 179

Round 11 – Germany
Oschersleben, 2 September
Race 1
1 Colin Edwards, USA, Honda
2 Ruben Xaus, Spa, Ducati
3 Ben Bostrom, USA, Ducati
4 Akira Yanagawa, Jap, Kawasaki
5 Tadayuki Okada, Jap, Honda
6 Pierfrancesco Chili, Ita, Suzuki
7 Neil Hodgson, GB, Ducati
8 Regis Laconi, Fra, Aprilia
9 Troy Corser, Aus, Aprilia
10 James Toseland, GB, Ducati
11 Gregorio Lavilla, Spa, Kawasaki
12 Stephane Chambon, Fra, Suzuki
13 Juan Borja, Spa, Ducati
14 Giovanni Bussei, Ita, Ducati
15 Bertrand Stey, Fra, Honda

Race 2
1 Ruben Xaus, Spa, Ducati
2 Colin Edwards, USA, Honda
3 Troy Bayliss, Aus, Ducati
4 Ben Bostrom, USA, Ducati
5 Regis Laconi, Fra, Aprilia
6 Pierfrancesco Chili, Ita, Suzuki
7 Gregorio Lavilla, Spa, Kawasaki
8 Tadayuki Okada, Jap, Honda
9 Akira Yanagawa, Jap, Kawasaki
10 Neil Hodgson, GB, Ducati
11 Troy Corser, Aus, Aprilia
12 James Toseland, GB, Ducati
13 Stephane Chambon, Fra, Suzuki
14 Steve Martin, Aus, Ducati
15 Robert Ulm, Aut, Ducati

Standings – 1 Bayliss 319; 2 Edwards 295;
3 Bostrom 276; 4 Corser 238; 5 Hodgson 232;
6 Chili 199

Round 12 – Holland
Assen, 9 September
Race 1
1 Troy Bayliss, Aus, Ducati
2 Ruben Xaus, Spa, Ducati
3 Colin Edwards, USA, Honda
4 Pierfrancesco Chili, Ita, Suzuki
5 Neil Hodgson, GB, Ducati
6 Troy Corser, Aus, Aprilia
7 Tadayuki Okada, Jap, Honda
8 Akira Yanagawa, Jap, Kawasaki
9 Regis Laconi, Fra, Aprilia
10 James Toseland, GB, Ducati
11 Ben Bostrom, USA, Ducati
12 Gregorio Lavilla, Spa, Kawasaki
13 Stephane Chambon, Fra, Suzuki
14 Juan Borja, Spa, Ducati
15 Lucio Pedercini, Ita, Ducati

Race 2
1 Troy Bayliss, Aus, Ducati
2 Ruben Xaus, Spa, Ducati
3 Troy Corser, Aus, Aprilia
4 Pierfrancesco Chili, Ita, Suzuki
5 Neil Hodgson, GB, Ducati
6 Akira Yanagawa, Jap, Kawasaki
7 Regis Laconi, Fra, Aprilia
8 James Toseland, GB, Ducati
9 Gregorio Lavilla, Spa, Kawasaki
10 Colin Edwards, USA, Honda
11 Ben Bostrom, USA, Ducati
12 Stephane Chambon, Fra, Suzuki
13 Tadayuki Okada, Jap, Honda
14 Giovanni Bussei, Ita, Ducati
15 Lucio Pedercini, Ita, Ducati

Standings – 1 Bayliss 369; 2 Edwards 317;
3 Bostrom 286; 4 Corser 264; 5 Hodgson 254;
6 Chili 225

Round 13 – Imola
Autodromo Enzo & Dino Ferrari, 30 September
Race 1
1 Ruben Xaus, Spa, Ducati
2 Troy Corser, Aus, Aprilia
3 Colin Edwards, USA, Honda
4 Ben Bostrom, USA, Ducati
5 Tadayuki Okada, Jap, Honda
6 Steve Martin, Aus, Ducati
7 Gregorio Lavilla, Spa, Kawasaki
8 Stephane Chambon, Fra, Suzuki
9 Lucio Pedercini, Ita, Ducati
10 Neil Hodgson, GB, Ducati
11 Giovanni Bussei, Ita, Ducati
12 Martin Craggill, Aus, Ducati
13 Mauro Sanchini, Ita, Ducati
14 Paolo Blora, Ita, Ducati
15 Alessandro Gramigni, Ita, Yamaha

Race 2
1 Regis Laconi, Fra, Aprilia
2 Ruben Xaus, Spa, Ducati
3 Tadayuki Okada, Jap, Honda
4 Ben Bostrom, USA, Ducati
5 Steve Martin, Aus, Ducati
6 Gregorio Lavilla, Spa, Kawasaki
7 Neil Hodgson, GB, Ducati
8 Broc Parkes, Aus, Ducati
9 Pierfrancesco Chili, Ita, Suzuki
10 Giovanni Bussei, Ita, Ducati
11 Alessandro Gramigni, Ita, Yamaha
12 Lucio Pedercini, Ita, Ducati
13 Peter Goddard, Aus, Benelli
14 Martin Craggill, Aus, Ducati
15 Marco Borciani, Ita, Ducati

FINAL STANDINGS – 1 Bayliss 369;
2 Edwards 333; 3 Bostrom 312; 4 Corser 284;
5 Hodgson 269; 6 Xaus 236

2002 season

Round 1 – Spain
Valencia, 10 March
Race 1
1   Troy Bayliss, Aus, Ducati
2   Noriyuki Haga, Jap, Aprilia
3   Ben Bostrom, USA, Ducati
4   Colin Edwards, USA, Honda
5   Ruben Xaus, Spa, Ducati
6   Neil Hodgson, GB, Ducati
7   Hitoyasu Izutsu, Jap, Kawasaki
8   Gregorio Lavilla, Spa, Suzuki
9   Pierfrancesco Chili, Ita, Ducati
10   Chris Walker, GB, Kawasaki
11   Juan Borja, Spa, Ducati
12   James Toseland, GB, Ducati
13   Alesandro Antonello, Ita, Ducati
14   Lucio Pedercini, Ita, Ducati
15   Broc Parkes, Aus, Ducati

Race 2
1   Troy Bayliss, Aus, Ducati
2   Noriyuki Haga, Jap, Aprilia
3   Colin Edwards, USA, Honda
4   Ben Bostrom, USA, Ducati
5   Neil Hodgson, GB, Ducati
6   Hitoyasu Izutsu, Jap, Kawasaki
7   Chris Walker, GB, Kawasaki
8   Juan Borja, Spa, Ducati
9   Steve Martin, Aus, Ducati
10   James Toseland, GB, Ducati
11   Lucio Pedercini, Ita, Ducati
12   Marco Borciani, Ita, Ducati
13   Ivan Clementi, Ita, Kawasaki
14   Serafino Foti, Ita, Ducati
15   Mauro Sanchini, Ita, Kawasaki

Standings – 1 Bayliss 50; 2 Haga 40;
3 Bostrom & Edwards 29; 5 Hodgson 21;
6 Izutsu 19

Round 2 – Australia
Phillip Island, 24 March
Race 1
1   Troy Bayliss, Aus, Ducati
2   Colin Edwards, USA, Honda
3   Ruben Xaus, Spa, Ducati
4   Ben Bostrom, USA, Ducati
5   Neil Hodgson, GB, Ducati
6   Hitoyasu Izutsu, Jap, Kawasaki
7   Gregorio Lavilla, Spa, Suzuki
8   James Toseland, GB, Ducati
9   Chris Walker, GB, Kawasaki
10   Lucio Pedercini, Ita, Ducati
11   Marco Borciani, Ita, Ducati
12   Juan Borja, Spa, Ducati
13   Steve Martin, Aus, Ducati
14   Alesandro Antonello, Ita, Ducati
15   Mauro Sanchini, Ita, Kawasaki

Race 2
1   Troy Bayliss, Aus, Ducati
2   Colin Edwards, USA, Honda
3   Ruben Xaus, Spa, Ducati
4   Neil Hodgson, GB, Ducati
5   Ben Bostrom, USA, Ducati
6   Noriyuki Haga, Jap, Aprilia
7   James Toseland, GB, Ducati
8   Gregorio Lavilla, Spa, Suzuki
9   Chris Walker, GB, Kawasaki
10   Juan Borja, Spa, Ducati
11   Alesandro Antonello, Ita, Ducati
12   Mauro Sanchini, Ita, Kawasaki
13   Broc Parkes, Aus, Ducati
14   Mark Heckles, GB, Honda
15   Ivan Clementi, Ita, Kawasaki

Standings – 1 Bayliss 100; 2 Edwards 69;
3 Bostrom 53; 4 Haga 50; 5 Hodgson 45;
6 Xaus 43

Round 3 – South Africa
Kyalami, 7 April
Race 1
1   Troy Bayliss, Aus, Ducati
2   Colin Edwards, USA, Honda
3   Ruben Xaus, Spa, Ducati
4   Ben Bostrom, USA, Ducati
5   Neil Hodgson, GB, Ducati
6   James Toseland, GB, Ducati
7   Hitoyasu Izutsu, Jap, Kawasaki
8   Chris Walker, GB, Kawasaki
9   Juan Borja, Spa, Ducati
10   Marco Borciani, Ita, Ducati
11   Broc Parkes, Aus, Ducati
12   Serafino Foti, Ita, Ducati
13   Mauro Sanchini, Ita, Kawasaki
14   Bertrand Stey, Fra, Honda

Race 2
1   Troy Bayliss, Aus, Ducati
2   Ruben Xaus, Spa, Ducati
3   Colin Edwards, USA, Honda
4   Neil Hodgson, GB, Ducati
5   Ben Bostrom, USA, Ducati
6   Noriyuki Haga, Jap, Aprilia
7   Hitoyasu Izutsu, Jap, Kawasaki
8   James Toseland, GB, Ducati
9   Chris Walker, GB, Kawasaki
10   Juan Borja, Spa, Ducati
11   Gregorio Lavilla, Spa, Suzuki
12   Lucio Pedercini, Ita, Ducati
13   Marco Borciani, Ita, Ducati
14   Broc Parkes, Aus, Ducati
15   Serafino Foti, Ita, Ducati

Standings – 1 Bayliss 150; 2 Edwards 105;
3 Xaus 79; 4 Bostrom 77; 5 Hodgson 69;
6 Haga 60

Round 4 – Japan
Sugo, 21 April
Race 1
1   Colin Edwards, USA, Honda
2   Makoto Tamada, Jap, Honda
3   Noriyuki Haga, Jap, Aprilia
4   Neil Hodgson, GB, Ducati
5   Troy Bayliss, Aus, Ducati
6   Akira Yanagawa, Jap, Kawasaki
7   Ben Bostrom, USA, Ducati
8   Wataru Yoshikawa, Jap, Yamaha
9   James Toseland, GB, Ducati
10   Takeshi Tsujimura, Jap, Yamaha
11   Chris Walker, GB, Kawasaki
12   Gregorio Lavilla, Spa, Suzuki
13   Eric Bostrom, USA, Kawasaki
14   Juan Borja, Spa, Ducati
15   Yuichi Takeda, Jap, Honda

Race 2
1   Makoto Tamada, Jap, Honda
2   Colin Edwards, USA, Honda
3   Neil Hodgson, GB, Ducati
4   Troy Bayliss, Aus, Ducati
5   Noriyuki Haga, Jap, Aprilia
6   Akira Yanagawa, Jap, Kawasaki
7   Ben Bostrom, USA, Ducati
8   Wataru Yoshikawa, Jap, Yamaha
9   Ruben Xaus, Spa, Ducati
10   Takeshi Tsujimura, Jap, Yamaha
11   James Toseland, GB, Ducati
12   Gregorio Lavilla, Spa, Suzuki
13   Chris Walker, GB, Kawasaki
14   Eric Bostrom, USA, Kawasaki
15   Juan Borja, Spa, Ducati

Standings – 1 Bayliss 174; 2 Edwards 150;
3 Hodgson 98; 4 Bostrom 95; 5 Haga 87;
6 Xaus 86

Round 5 – Italy
Monza, 12 May
Race 1
1   Troy Bayliss, Aus, Ducati
2   Neil Hodgson, GB, Ducati
3   Colin Edwards, USA, Honda
4   Pierfrancesco Chili, Ita, Ducati
5   James Toseland, GB, Ducati
6   Ruben Xaus, Spa, Ducati
7   Gregorio Lavilla, Spa, Suzuki
8   Alesandro Antonello, Ita, Ducati
9   Eric Bostrom, USA, Kawasaki
10   Steve Martin, Aus, Ducati
11   Juan Borja, Spa, Ducati
12   Mauro Sanchini, Ita, Kawasaki
13   Alesandro Valia, Ita, Ducati
14   Peter Goddard, Aus, Benelli
15   Mark Heckles, GB, Honda

Race 2
1   Troy Bayliss, Aus, Ducati
2   Colin Edwards, USA, Honda
3   Noriyuki Haga, Jap, Aprilia
4   Neil Hodgson, GB, Ducati
5   Gregorio Lavilla, Spa, Suzuki
6   Lucio Pedercini, Ita, Ducati
7   Eric Bostrom, USA, Kawasaki
8   Broc Parkes, Aus, Ducati
9   Ben Bostrom, USA, Ducati
10   Chris Walker, GB, Kawasaki
11   Steve Martin, Aus, Ducati
12   Serafino Foti, Ita, Ducati
13   Mauro Sanchini, Ita, Kawasaki
14   Ivan Clementi, Ita, Kawasaki
15   Alesandro Valia, Ita, Ducati

Standings – 1 Bayliss 224; 2 Edwards 186;
3 Hodgson 131; 4 Haga 103; 5 Bostrom 102;
6 Xaus 96

Round 6 – Great Britain
Silverstone, 26 May
Race 1
1   Colin Edwards, USA, Honda
2   Noriyuki Haga, Jap, Aprilia
3   Neil Hodgson, GB, Ducati
4   Pierfrancesco Chili, Ita, Ducati
5   Troy Bayliss, Aus, Ducati
6   Mark Heckles, GB, Honda
7   Ben Bostrom, USA, Ducati
8   Ruben Xaus, Spa, Ducati
9   Shane Byrne, GB, Ducati
10   James Toseland, GB, Ducati
11   Eric Bostrom, USA, Kawasaki
12   Michael Rutter, GB, Ducati
13   Peter Goddard, Aus, Benelli
14   Chris Walker, GB, Kawasaki
15   Mauro Sanchini, Ita, Ducati

Race 2
1   Troy Bayliss, Aus, Ducati
2   Colin Edwards, USA, Honda
3   Ruben Xaus, Spa, Ducati
4   Chris Walker, GB, Kawasaki
5   Shane Byrne, GB, Ducati
6   Neil Hodgson, GB, Ducati
7   Juan Borja, Spa, Ducati
8   Ben Bostrom, USA, Ducati
9   James Toseland, GB, Ducati
10   Noriyuki Haga, Jap, Aprilia
11   Pierfrancesco Chili, Ita, Ducati
12   Broc Parkes, Aus, Ducati
13   Alesandro Antonello, Ita, Ducati
14   Gregorio Lavilla, Spa, Suzuki
15   Peter Goddard, Aus, Benelli

Standings – 1 Bayliss 260; 2 Edwards 231;
3 Hodgson 157; 4 Haga 129; 5 Xaus 120;
6 Bostrom 119

Round 7 – Germany
Lausitzring, 9 June
Race 1
1   Troy Bayliss, Aus, Ducati
2   Colin Edwards, USA, Honda
3   Ruben Xaus, Spa, Ducati
4   Noriyuki Haga, Jap, Aprilia
5   Ben Bostrom, USA, Ducati
6   Pierfrancesco Chili, Ita, Ducati
7   James Toseland, GB, Ducati
8   Gregorio Lavilla, Spa, Suzuki
9   Steve Martin, Aus, Ducati
10   Lucio Pedercini, Ita, Ducati
11   Broc Parkes, Aus, Ducati
12   Marco Borciani, Ita, Ducati
13   Alesandro Antonello, Ita, Ducati
14   Mauro Sanchini, Ita, Ducati
15   Andy Hofmann, Ger, Kawasaki

Race 2
1   Troy Bayliss, Aus, Ducati
2   Colin Edwards, USA, Honda
3   Ruben Xaus, Spa, Ducati
4   Ben Bostrom, USA, Ducati
5   Noriyuki Haga, Jap, Aprilia
6   Pierfrancesco Chili, Ita, Ducati
7   James Toseland, GB, Ducati
8   Neil Hodgson, GB, Ducati
9   Chris Walker, GB, Kawasaki
10   Lucio Pedercini, Ita, Ducati
11   Steve Martin, Aus, Ducati
12   Marco Borciani, Ita, Ducati
13   Andy Hofmann, Ger, Kawasaki
14   Mauro Sanchini, Ita, Ducati
15   Peter Goddard, Aus, Benelli

Standings – 1 Bayliss 310; 2 Edwards 271;
3 Hodgson 165; 4 Haga 153; 5 Xaus 152;
6 Bostrom 143

Round 8 – San Marino
Misano, 23 June
Race 1
1 Troy Bayliss, Aus, Ducati
2 Colin Edwards, USA, Honda
3 Neil Hodgson, GB, Ducati
4 Noriyuki Haga, Jap, Aprilia
5 Ben Bostrom, USA, Ducati
6 Pierfrancesco Chili, Ita, Ducati
7 Chris Walker, GB, Kawasaki
8 James Toseland, GB, Ducati
9 Lucio Pedercini, Ita, Ducati
10 Gregorio Lavilla, Spa, Suzuki
11 Marco Borciani, Ita, Ducati
12 Mauro Sanchini, Ita, Kawasaki
13 Steve Martin, Aus, Ducati
14 Serafino Foti, Ita, Ducati
15 Peter Goddard, Aus, Benelli

Race 2
1 Troy Bayliss, Aus, Ducati
2 Colin Edwards, USA, Honda
3 Noriyuki Haga, Jap, Aprilia
4 Neil Hodgson, GB, Ducati
5 Ben Bostrom, USA, Ducati
6 Gregorio Lavilla, Spa, Suzuki
7 Pierfrancesco Chili, Ita, Ducati
8 Chris Walker, GB, Kawasaki
9 Lucio Pedercini, Ita, Ducati
10 Marco Borciani, Ita, Ducati
11 Mauro Sanchini, Ita, Kawasaki
12 Steve Martin, Aus, Ducati
13 Michele Malatesta, Ita, Ducati
14 Broc Parkes, Aus, Ducati
15 Bertrand Stey, Fra, Honda

Standings – 1 Bayliss 360; 2 Edwards 311;
3 Hodgson 194; 4 Haga 182; 5 Bostrom 165;
6 Xaus 152

Round 9 – USA
Laguna Seca, 14 July
Race 1
1 Troy Bayliss, Aus, Ducati
2 Ruben Xaus, Spa, Ducati
3 Colin Edwards, USA, Honda
4 Nicky Hayden, USA, Honda
5 Neil Hodgson, GB, Ducati
6 Eric Bostrom, USA, Kawasaki
7 Aaron Yates, USA, Suzuki
8 Ben Bostrom, USA, Ducati
9 James Toseland, GB, Ducati
10 Mat Mladin, Aus, Suzuki
11 Chris Walker, GB, Kawasaki
12 Pierfrancesco Chili, Ita, Ducati
13 Doug Chandler, USA, Ducati
14 Steve Martin, Aus, Ducati
15 Broc Parkes, Aus, Ducati

Race 2
1 Colin Edwards, USA, Honda
2 Troy Bayliss, Aus, Ducati
3 Neil Hodgson, GB, Ducati
4 Eric Bostrom, USA, Kawasaki
5 Ben Bostrom, USA, Ducati
6 James Toseland, GB, Ducati
7 Pierfrancesco Chili, Ita, Ducati
8 Aaron Yates, USA, Suzuki
9 Doug Chandler, USA, Ducati
10 Chris Walker, GB, Kawasaki
11 Steve Martin, Aus, Ducati
12 Broc Parkes, Aus, Ducati
13 Nicky Hayden, USA, Honda
14 Peter Goddard, Aus, Benelli
15 Mauro Sanchini, Ita, Kawasaki

Standings – 1 Bayliss 405; 2 Edwards 352;
3 Hodgson 221; 4 Bostrom 184; 5 Haga 182;
6 Xaus 172

Round 10 – Europe
Brands Hatch, 28 July
Race 1
1 Colin Edwards, USA, Honda
2 Neil Hodgson, GB, Ducati
3 Troy Bayliss, Aus, Ducati
4 Noriyuki Haga, Jap, Aprilia
5 Ruben Xaus, Spa, Ducati
6 Chris Walker, GB, Kawasaki
7 Ben Bostrom, USA, Ducati
8 Pierfrancesco Chili, Ita, Ducati
9 James Toseland, GB, Ducati
10 Shane Byrne, GB, Ducati

11 Juan Borja, Spa, Ducati
12 Alesandro Antonello, Ita, Ducati
13 Hitoyasu Izutsu, Jap, Kawasaki
14 Dean Ellison, GB, Ducati
15 Gregorio Lavilla, Spa, Suzuki

Race 2
1 Colin Edwards, USA, Honda
2 Troy Bayliss, Aus, Ducati
3 Neil Hodgson, GB, Ducati
4 Ben Bostrom, USA, Ducati
5 Noriyuki Haga, Jap, Aprilia
6 Ruben Xaus, Spa, Ducati
7 Pierfrancesco Chili, Ita, Ducati
8 Chris Walker, GB, Kawasaki
9 Michael Rutter, GB, Ducati
10 Shane Byrne, GB, Ducati
11 Juan Borja, Spa, Ducati
12 Gregorio Lavilla, Spa, Suzuki
13 Alesandro Antonello, Ita, Ducati
14 Glen Richards, GB, Kawasaki
15 Marco Borciani, Ita, Ducati

Standings – 1 Bayliss 441; 2 Edwards 402;
3 Hodgson 257; 4 Bostrom & Haga 206;
6 Xaus 193

Round 11 – Germany
Oschersleben, 1 September
Race 1
1 Colin Edwards, USA, Honda
2 Troy Bayliss, Aus, Ducati
3 Neil Hodgson, GB, Ducati
4 Ben Bostrom, USA, Ducati
5 Pierfrancesco Chili, Ita, Ducati
6 James Toseland, GB, Ducati
7 Noriyuki Haga, Jap, Aprilia
8 Gregorio Lavilla, Spa, Suzuki
9 Chris Walker, GB, Kawasaki
10 Broc Parkes, Aus, Ducati
11 Hitoyasu Izutsu, Jap, Kawasaki
12 Peter Goddard, Aus, Benelli
13 Lucio Pedercini, Ita, Ducati
14 Mark Heckles, GB, Honda
15 Mauro Sanchini, Ita, Kawasaki

Race 2
1 Colin Edwards, USA, Honda
2 Troy Bayliss, Aus, Ducati
3 Neil Hodgson, GB, Ducati
4 Noriyuki Haga, Jap, Aprilia
5 Ruben Xaus, Spa, Ducati
6 Ben Bostrom, USA, Ducati
7 Pierfrancesco Chili, Ita, Ducati
8 James Toseland, GB, Ducati
9 Gregorio Lavilla, Spa, Suzuki
10 Broc Parkes, Aus, Ducati
11 Marco Borciani, Ita, Ducati
12 Lucio Pedercini, Ita, Ducati
13 Ivan Clementi, Ita, Kawasaki
14 Mauro Sanchini, Ita, Kawasaki
15 Chris Walker, GB, Kawasaki

Standings – 1 Bayliss 481; 2 Edwards 452;
3 Hodgson 289; 4 Bostrom 229; 5 Haga 228;
6 Xaus 204

Round 12 – Holland
Assen, 8 September
Race 1
1 Colin Edwards, USA, Honda
2 Troy Bayliss, Aus, Ducati
3 Noriyuki Haga, Jap, Aprilia
4 Ruben Xaus, Spa, Ducati
5 Pierfrancesco Chili, Ita, Ducati
6 James Toseland, GB, Ducati
7 Gregorio Lavilla, Spa, Suzuki
8 Ben Bostrom, USA, Ducati
9 Broc Parkes, Aus, Ducati
10 Juan Borja, Spa, Ducati
11 Marco Borciani, Ita, Ducati
12 Peter Goddard, Aus, Benelli
13 Mauro Sanchini, Ita, Kawasaki
14 Serafino Foti, Ita, Ducati
15 Jeronimo Vidal, Spa, Honda

Race 2
1 Colin Edwards, USA, Honda
2 Pierfrancesco Chili, Ita, Ducati
3 James Toseland, GB, Ducati
4 Neil Hodgson, GB, Ducati
5 Ben Bostrom, USA, Ducati
6 Noriyuki Haga, Jap, Aprilia

7 Chris Walker, GB, Kawasaki
8 Broc Parkes, Aus, Ducati
9 Marco Borciani, Ita, Ducati
10 Lucio Pedercini, Ita, Ducati
11 Peter Goddard, Aus, Benelli
12 Mauro Sanchini, Ita, Kawasaki
13 Alessandro Antonello, Ita, Ducati
14 Ivan Clementi, Ita, Kawasaki
15 Mark Heckles, GB, Honda

Standings – 1 Edwards 502; 2 Bayliss 501;
3 Hodgson 302; 4 Haga 254; 5 Bostrom 248;
6 Xaus 217

Round 13 – Imola
Autodromo Enzo & Dino Ferrari, 29 September
Race 1
1 Colin Edwards, USA, Honda
2 Troy Bayliss, Aus, Ducati
3 Ruben Xaus, Spa, Ducati
4 Neil Hodgson, GB, Ducati
5 Noriyuki Haga, Jap, Aprilia
6 James Toseland, GB, Ducati
7 Pierfrancesco Chili, Ita, Ducati
8 Gregorio Lavilla, Spa, Suzuki
9 Broc Parkes, Aus, Ducati
10 Ben Bostrom, USA, Ducati
11 Chris Walker, GB, Kawasaki
12 Alessandro Antonello, Ita, Ducati
13 Steve Martin, Aus, Ducati
14 Lucio Pedercini, Ita, Ducati
15 Hitoyasu Izutsu, Jpn, Kawasaki

Race 2
1 Colin Edwards, USA, Honda
2 Troy Bayliss, Aus, Ducati
3 Ruben Xaus, Spa, Ducati
4 Noriyuki Haga, Jap, Aprilia
5 Neil Hodgson, GB, Ducati
6 James Toseland, GB, Ducati
7 Gregorio Lavilla, Spa, Suzuki
8 Broc Parkes, Aus, Ducati
9 Ben Bostrom, USA, Ducati
10 Hitoyasu Izutsu, Jpn, Kawasaki
11 Juan Borja, Spa, Ducati
12 Chris Walker, GB, Kawasaki
13 Lucio Pedercini, Ita, Ducati
14 Steve Martin, Aus, Ducati
15 Mauro Sanchini, Ita, Ducati

FINAL STANDINGS – 1 Edwards 552;
2 Bayliss 541; 3 Hodgson 326; 4 Haga 278;
5 B Bostrom 261; 6 Xaus 249

Superbike statistics

1990	David Sadowski	Yamaha
1991	Miguel DuHamel	Honda
1992	Scott Russell	Kawasaki
1993	Eddie Lawson	Yamaha
1994	Scott Russell	Kawasaki
1995	Scott Russell	Kawasaki
1996	Miguel DuHamel	Honda
1997	Scott Russell	Yamaha
1998	Scott Russell	Yamaha
1999	Miguel DuHamel	Honda
2000	Mat Mladin	Suzuki
2001	Mat Mladin	Suzuki
2002	Nicky Hayden	Honda

*Superbike became the Daytona 200 Mile formula in 1985

American Superbike Champions

1976	Reg Pridmore	BMW
1977	Reg Pridmore	Kawasaki
1978	Reg Pridmore	Kawasaki
1979	Wes Cooley	Suzuki
1980	Wes Cooley	Suzuki
1981	Eddie Lawson	Kawasaki
1982	Eddie Lawson	Kawasaki
1983	Wayne Rainey	Kawasaki
1984	Fred Merkel	Honda
1985	Fred Merkel	Honda
1986	Fred Merkel	Honda
1987	Wayne Rainey	Honda
1988	Bubba Shobert	Honda
1989	Jamie James	Suzuki
1990	Doug Chandler	Kawasaki
1991	Thomas Stevens	Yamaha
1992	Scott Russell	Kawasaki
1993	Doug Polen	Ducati
1994	Troy Corser	Ducati
1995	Miguel DuHamel	Honda
1996	Doug Chandler	Kawasaki
1997	Doug Chandler	Kawasaki
1998	Ben Bostrom	Honda
1999	Mat Mladin	Suzuki
2000	Mat Mladin	Suzuki
2001	Mat Mladin	Suzuki
2002	Nicky Hayden	Honda

German Pro-Superbike Champions

1991	Udo Mark	Yamaha
1992	Edwin Weibel	Ducati
1993	Edwin Weibel	Ducati
1994	Udo Mark	Ducati
1995	Jochen Schmid	Kawasaki
1996	Christer Lindholm	Ducati
1997	Christer Lindholm	Yamaha
1998	Andy Meklau	Ducati
1999	Christer Lindholm	Yamaha

Australian Superbike Champions

1989	Malcolm Campbell	Honda
1990	Malcolm Campbell	Honda
1991	Aaron Slight	Kawasaki
1992	Mat Mladin	Kawasaki
1993	Troy Corser	Honda
1994	Anthony Gobert	Honda
1995	Kirk McCarthy	Honda
1996	Peter Goddard	Suzuki
1997	Martin Craggill	Kawasaki
1998	Martin Craggill	Kawasaki
1999	Steve Martin	Ducati
2000	Shawn Giles	Suzuki
2001†	Shawn Giles	Suzuki

†non FIM regulations (1,000cc limit)

British Superbike Champions

1995	Steve Hislop	Kawasaki
1996	Niall Mackenzie	Yamaha
1997	Niall Mackenzie	Yamaha
1998	Niall Mackenzie	Yamaha
1999	Troy Bayliss	Ducati
2000	Neil Hodgson	Ducati
2001	John Reynolds	Ducati
2002†	Steve Hislop	Ducati

†non FIM regulations (1,000cc limit)

Japanese Superbike Champions

1994	Wataru Yoshikawa	Yamaha
1995	Takuma Aoki	Honda
1996	Takuma Aoki	Honda
1997	Noriyuki Haga	Yamaha
1998	Wataru Yoshikawa	Yamaha
1999	Shinichi Itoh	Honda
2000	Hitoyasu Izutzu	Kawasaki
2001	Akira Ryo	Suzuki

World Superbike Manufacturers' Championship

1988	Honda	1996	Ducati
1989	Honda	1997	Honda
1990	Honda	1998	Ducati
1991	Ducati	1999	Ducati
1992	Ducati	2000	Ducati
1993	Ducati	2001	Ducati
1994	Ducati	2002	Ducati
1995	Ducati		

Daytona Superbike Race Winners

1976	Steve McLaughlin	BMW
1977	Cook Neilson	Ducati
1978	Steve McLaughlin	Suzuki
1979	Ron Pierce	Suzuki
1980	Graeme Crosby	Suzuki
	Freddie Spencer	Honda
1981	Wes Cooley	Suzuki
	Freddie Spencer	Honda
1982	Freddie Spencer	Honda
	Mike Baldwin	Honda
1983	Freddie Spencer	Honda
	Fred Merkel	Honda
1984	Freddie Spencer	Honda
	Fred Merkel	Honda
1985*	Freddie Spencer	Honda
	Fred Merkel	Honda
1986	Eddie Lawson	Yamaha
1987	Wayne Rainey	Honda
1988	Kevin Schwantz	Suzuki
1989	John Ashmead	Honda